MY YEAR 2011:
NO ONE'S HOME

SELECTED BOOKS BY THE AUTHOR

My Year 2011:

No One's Home

READINGS
EVENTS
MEMORIES

by
Douglas Messerli

GREEN INTEGER
KØBENHAVN & LOS ANGELES
2018

GREEN INTEGER
Edited by Per Bregne
København / Los Angeles
(323) 937-3783 / www.greeninteger.com

Distributed in the United States by
Consortium Book Sales & Distribution / Ingram Books
(800) 283-3572 / www.cbsd.com

First Green Integer Edition 2018
Copyright ©2018 by Douglas Messerli
Essays in this volume have previously appeared in *American Cultural Treasures, Art Là-bas, EXPORINGfictions, Green Integer Blog, Jacket 2, Los Angeles Review of Books, N^th^ Position, USTheater, Opera, and Performance, Rain Taxi, World Cinema Review,* and in the books *Contemporary Fictions* (College Park, Maryland: Sun & Moon Press, 1983) and *From the Sea of Discovery to the Sea of Communication* (Seoul/Jukjeon: Dankook University, 2010).

Back cover copy ©2018 by Green Integer

Design: Per Bregne
Typography: Pablo Capra
Cover photographs (clockwise, from top left):
David Antin, Ivo Michiels, Jaimy Gordon, Ko Un

LIBRARY OF CONGRESS CATALOGING-IN-PUBLICATION DATA
Douglas Messerli [1947]
My Year 2011: No One's Home
ISBN: 978-1-55713-442-4
p. cm – Green Integer 266
I. Title II. Series

Green Integer books are published for Douglas Messerli
Printed in Canada

Table of Contents

There's No Place Like Home: An Introduction

I FIRST ENCOUNTERED my 2011 connecting theme in a story by the German fiction writer Alois Hotschnig in March of 2010, but I couldn't have imagined just how appropriate it would be. During that year I traveled to Iowa, New York, Netherlands, Belgium, France, and Korea—proving that, at least, I was seldom home. And in so many different ways that theme kept returning in the works I saw and read.

In the musical *Women on the Verge of a Nervous Breakdown*, Almodóvar's heroine burned her bed and left the house, not to return until nearly everyone else in the work had visited it. The characters of Williams' *Camino Real* seemed trapped, far from their homes, in a strange surreal village. The mother and father of Beckett's *Endgame* had been moved into barrels, presumably by the nervous Hamm. And my own mother had been moved out of her beloved home into an assisted living

9

facility—a future I foresaw, as well, for both Howard and myself.

In Bernard-Marie Koltès' *In the Solitude of Cotton Fields*, men roamed the streets, as did the figures of Willem Elsschot's *Will-o'-the Wisp*. J. Pierrepont Finch of *How to Succeed in Business Without Really Trying* appeared to have permanently moved into various offices of the World Wide Wicket Company, and, ultimately, into its executive suite; while the children of Mabou Mines' version of *Peter Pan* appeared to be lost in space. A teacher and his student suddenly wandered off into the countryside in Hugo Claus' great novel *Wonder*; Ory moved into a nunnery in Rossini's *Le Comte Ory*; and Nixon flew off to China in the opera by John Adams. The young Hugo in Martin Scorsese's film found home in Paris' Gare Montparnasse; Johnny "Rooster Byron" of Jez Butterworth's *Jerusalem* lived as an outcast in a rotting trailer; and Mattie of *True Grit* took off into the wilderness for revenge.

Sonny Wortzik of *Dog Day Afternoon* holed up in a bank; and tennis player Guy Haines got into trouble with a stranger on a train. Tom Jones leaped from bed to bed; while "birthers" such as Donald Trump argued that even the US President was not legally permitted to sleep in the temporary bed he claimed. Wotan destroyed the home of the gods; while Mark Zuckerberg took all of our faces into internet space.

To represent my visit to Flanders, without actually thinking of its appropriateness, I chose the metaphor of a visit from town to town, achieved in aching pain. Perhaps only Susan Walker of *Miracle on 34th Street* actually found a "home," but even that seemed more like a vast sales pitch to me, or, if nothing else, a kind of miracle that shouldn't really have existed except for her determination to believe that she might get a home for Christmas, awarded her by Santa Claus.

In such a transitional time, understandably, everyone seemed on the move, and even staying home—as in the case of Washington, D.C. journalist and social entertainer Viola Drath—could have dangerous consequences. Perhaps it was simply better to follow the crowd, getting up and going out.

As always, the deaths of several major figures—writer and director Arthur Laurents, novelist Reynolds Price, and filmmakers Sidney Lumet, Michael Cacoyannis, and Raúl Ruiz—led me to reassess their work.

Fortunately, I had a pleasant Los Angeles condominium to return to and a supportive companion in Howard Fox, who welcomed me back. Good friends and new acquaintances, as always, offered me support for my activities and appreciation for my writing, including Ana-María Abraham, David Antin, Eleanor Antin, Brother Anthony, Thérèse Bachand, Charles Bernstein, Edward Bernstein, Sherry Bernstein, Paul

Bogaert, Lee Breuer, Diane Butterman, Hyon Chough, Antonio Colinas, Dankook University, Barbara Epler, The Flemish Literature Fund, Thomas Frick, Rebecca Goodman, Jaimy Gordon, Peter Goulds, Hae Yisoo, Jerzy Illg, Kim Soo-Bok, Ko Un, Tom La Farge, Lee Shang-wha, Lee Si-young, Stacey Levine, Tess Lewis, Eric Lorberer, Deborah Meadows, David Messerli, Jill Messerli, Matthew Messerli, Ivo Michiels, Thomas Möhlmann, Martin Nakell, Asbjørn Øverås, Marjorie Perloff, Dennis Phillips, Joe Ross, Katia Sainson, Jill Schoolman, Peter Sellars, Rob Singer, Soo Min, Béla Tarr, Pat Thieben, David Van Reybrouck, Tom Van de Voorde, Wendy Walker, Laura Wilber, and Jenny Witte.

Howard also offered comments and corrections on many of these pieces. And editor, typesetter, and friend Pablo Capra helped me to whip this material into publishable form, as well as making the volume look so beautiful.

My thanks and love to all of them!

A Glimpse into the Future

MARIANNE HAUSER **ME & MY MOM** (LOS ANGELES: SUN & MOON PRESS, 1993)
MY TRIP TO IOWA TOOK PLACE FROM SEPTEMBER 1, 2010 (WHEN I FLEW FROM LOS ANGELES THROUGH DALLAS-FORT WORTH TO CEDAR RAPIDS) TO SEPTEMBER 4, 2010 (FLYING HOME THROUGH CHICAGO)

ON MY WAY to visit my mother—just turned 85 and residing in an assisted living home, Bickford Cottage, in my hometown of Marion, Iowa—I subliminally grabbed a copy of Marianne Hauser's gentle satire of an aging mother and a mother-daughter relationship, *Me & My Mom*, published by my Sun & Moon Press in 1993. I should add that I planned to teach this book the following Tuesday in my Otis College M.F.A. course on American Satire.

The big issue of this book is the daughter's own social and psychological problems, created in part by her mother's obsessive focus on a dead son (a child, who, evidently, because of numerous birth defects, died in the womb), and the result, more importantly, of her own lack of sensibility and intelligence. The two must now switch roles, the daughter becoming the mother, her mom the overlooked child.

Tucked away at the Bide-a-Wee nursing home, the mother—whom one might describe as an intelligent and sensitive romantic—is bitter to have lost her home, her cats, and, most of all, her personal freedom. She spends much of her time apart from the other nursing-home inmates, having learned from her first few months of internment not to cause a ruckus. Indeed, as the daughter describes it, she has slipped off into a private world except for occasional linguistic outbursts that betray her simmering anger.

The daughter, the source of income for her out-of-work, alcoholic husband and her young child, continues to confront her mother in short visits it is clear she resents having to make. The two argue and console one another with their memories, alternating between anger and simple love.

What is immediately apparent in Hauser's version of a painful relationship, played out in a hundred ways in millions of lives, is the lack of sensibility in the daughter—and by extension, in the younger generation. The world may have become more "realistic" in the daughter's often coarse and unimaginative perceptions, but it has lost the wonderment and beauty inherent in the older woman's memories, one of the richest of which is a breakfast of Eggs Benedict, perfectly cooked, at the beautiful Majestic Grand with a handsome architect, of whom the mother remembers little else. The Majestic Grand has long since become a building inhabited by homeless people, and shortly after its mention in the fiction, it collapses, killing several of its inhabitants. Yet it stands for something that can never be replaced. If the mother cannot remember the name of the man, the meal becomes a motif throughout the book of a world that has disappeared. Throughout Hauser's short fiction, New York and the remnants of past life are fading, being destroyed and forgotten. A new, less glorious landscape is built up in its absence.

The daughter is without a clue how to rediscover the beauty of that world, and finally, with husband and son, and a new child in her womb, she retreats to an equally rundown country life, which promises an even more dilapidated vision of reality. At least the daughter no longer has to confront her mother. She gradually becomes unable even to write her a note. The old woman has been abandoned, like most of her generation, to her own disappearing memories. And since even the names of presidents as recent as Jimmy Carter are unknown (in what I would argue is a slightly unbelievable premise), evidently, to the daughter and, by extension, to her generation, we can only imagine a world that is being eaten away from both ends; so that by work's completion, we have only those momentary encounters between the two. When even those confrontations disappear perhaps history ends. A new birth is about to occur, but for what purpose? What meaning might that child discover in a world that no longer holds any significance?

My own mother, Lorna, I reassured myself, was happy in her assisted-living residence, consisting of two rooms and a bathroom. We had attempted to return her to her large suburban house a couple of years after an accident that sent her hurtling down the basement stairs, with her right hand permanently damaged. And she seemed eager to return, to give her former life another chance. I particularly had fought hard for that, insisting that we could hire a nurse to stop in for a few hours in order to help her bathe, and that we could provide her with food through deliveries from "Meals on Wheels." On Thanksgiving in 2007, I returned to fix the big meal in her empty house, inviting the whole family to gather round that table once more, partially in the attempt to draw my mother home.

Soon after she returned to the house on Concord Drive, but after one night in the place she had so loved, she called my brother to return her to Bickford Cottage. "I'm lonely," she wailed. There was no one there to talk to. She hated her Meals on Wheels, and feared most of all, I presume, the endless silence of the place. Most of her neighbors, although friendly, were younger couples with families. Many of her friends had died or were themselves now in assisted-living homes. Soon after, my brother sold her home.

Visiting Lorna the day after her 85th birthday, I met her so-called friends. What I wasn't completely prepared for was the rudeness with which they often treated one another. Like Hauser's central character, my mother has remained slightly aloof, a "lady," as the nurses call her, who most of the residents love because of her slightly magisterial behavior. Yet as we shuffled down the hall to lunch, a three-pronged, decorative cane at her side, my mother pointed to the woman ahead and spoke in a voice she might once have used only at a football game. "You see the woman with the scraggly hair? That's our nurse."

Another woman was "The one I told you about! Rose, meet my son." A few feet away my mother continued, "She comes to the table and reads the newspaper every day. Doesn't say a word!"

I presume the nurses have all grown accustomed to this elderly "honesty," and that many of her friends are so deaf they can't hear what she says "just out of speaking distance," but the behavior, nonetheless, took me

aback.

My mother, how-
ever, was not the only
seemingly insensitive
being in the place. The
woman who usually
sat next to my moth-
er, Ann, spent the whole lunch telling me that both her
former husbands had been secretly—unknown to her
at least—gay, that she herself had had a nervous breakdown and "gone in for shock therapy," and that her
daughter was in AA...confessions, I presume, brought
on by my casually mentioning my "companion." Perhaps my mother had previously told her I was gay, and
she had regaled my mother with these same tales many
times, for my somewhat proper mother didn't blink an
eye. Lorna later reported that before Ann's shock therapy, Ann had attempted to come to dinner "dressed in
her birthday suit." Rose, the woman who my mother
told me read the newspaper throughout the meal, sat
at this lunch at another table, but soon came forward
to tell Ann to shut up so that my mother and I might
talk to one another. Ann didn't miss a beat, moving on
to tell me about all of her "artist friends." "That's why I
never suspected my husbands," she declared. "I had so
many artist friends."

Back in my mother's room I observed that Ann

certainly did have a lot to say. "But at least she talks," my mother snapped back.

What I was also not entirely prepared for was the number of times my mother repeated each piece of information. During our weekly telephone conversations she often repeated news up to three times in each conversation. What I hadn't imagined is that, if one spent more time with her, that repetition would increase to six, seven times...occurring endlessly, depending upon how long one had time to speak with her. Reminding her that she had said it before helped not a bit; for she stubbornly repeated every last sentence, refusing to even acknowledge my attempted interruption. At first I simply chalked it up to the fact that she didn't have a great deal of information to impart, and that she repeated things simply to fill up the conversational space. But I soon realized that it was simply a kind of dementia; she could not help repeating herself.

The future was equally open to reiteration. When I mentioned that my brother David and sister-in-law Jill would be visiting just before dinner, she asked me numerous times if I knew whether they might stop by. My sister Pat, who I told her was visiting for lunch the following day, elicited my mother's continued resentment, since she *never* visited. "Why won't she come by?"

"She plans to tomorrow, Mom."

"She never visits."

After spending breakfast and lunch with her and touring her around town to visit the various houses in which we had lived (there are five, she imagines others), I took a short two hours off, returning to the hotel before I stopped back at Bickford Cottage to see David and Jill. They laughingly reported that upon calling her, they asked if I had been there all day. "No, he wasn't," she snorted. Jill corrected, "Has he visited today?" "Oh yes, he was here all morning." Logistically, she was correct: I was not there *all day*.

"Is Pat going to visit?" my mother plaintively asked.

"Tomorrow," I laughed.

"Time for dinner!" my mother spoke up.

"All right," you go ahead, I answered.

"You see that woman with the scraggly hair over there? She's the nurse," she proudly pointed.

"Did you meet my son?" she accosted the kindly, "scraggly"-haired girl.

Later David, Jill, and I met near the cars to briefly confer about the future. "How many years can we afford to keep her here?" I finally asked.

"About four years," Jill confided.

"Oh dear, it would be quite devastating if she had to move," I sighed. "But perhaps, like Howard's father, when the time comes, she won't even know it's happening." I cringed at the thought.

"That's, sadly to say, what we're hoping for," my

brother said.

Yes, we too were now plotting for the past to be gone. Now in our 60s, the three of us realized that we might soon be sitting in similar situations. Dave and Jill, at least, had their children, three loving boys, to turn to. To whom would Howard and I entrust our forgetfulness, to share a past that no longer mattered to anyone?

The next day my sister arrived, the charming two-year-old twins, her grand-children, in tow. They were delighted to see their great-grandmother and to meet a new relative. One of them, Savannah, insisted that I return home with them, crawling into my arms and refusing to let go. Soon after, my nephew Matt's wife arrived with their new baby, Eva. I held Eva for a long while, the child falling asleep on my lap. My mother held her for a half hour. The young girls where urged into the front room, where they entertained many of the residents by reciting their numbers and alphabet, dancing across the hearth as they spoke. At once it again became apparent to me that my mother was not all like the poor woman in Hauser's book.

That evening, at dinner with my mother at Bickford, Ann, the woman who had told me her life story the day before, spoke more quietly, reporting that my mother didn't truly have a great many people to talk to at the Cottage. "She's—well how can I say this?—so much better educated and more intelligent than many of our residents. She's a true lady amidst these rustic folk."

Cap (whose real name was Casper, oddly enough, my mother's maiden name), a former farmer to whom I spoke, couldn't remember where he had farmed or to what crops he had devoted his life.* When I tried to speak to some of the other "ladies," most complacently smiled, one of them giggled. Another woman intermittently hovered over our table to tell me that I reminded her of someone she knew from Grand Rapids who worked at *The Journey* (presumably a religious publication). "I've never been in Grand Rapids," I apologized.

Finally, I came to realize that, despite these occasional family visits, my mother was not very different at all from the mother in Hauser's poignant book. She too, although seemingly most open and friendly, was somehow aloof, sitting apart from the other Cottage residents.

Would I too, when the time came, be an old man,

reading in the corner in an attempt to escape the fellow lunatics wandering the halls? Yes. I was sure of that. But what if my eyes were no longer strong enough to see the words upon the page, my hands unable to type out the sentences of my personal commentaries? And who would be coming to see me? And when? My mother had generations of family. I would have none.

When I said goodbye that evening, she cried. But the tears where those of joy, not loneliness or fear. She was not being "abandoned" as was the romantic survivor of Hauser's satire—and, as my glimpse of the future revealed, I might someday be. "I'll call when I get home. And I'll be back to visit as soon as I can," I softly spoke as I bent down to hug her. "I know," she answered, wiping away the tears. Yet her knowledge sounded somehow distant, inurned to some other reality she might have imagined. Like Hauser's agèd mother she was preparing herself for disappointment.

Did my mother ever have Eggs Benedict? I order them rather often, but at breakfast with my brother the next morning I confused the poached eggs I wanted—not on the menu—with an omelet. "Do you want cheese with 'em?" asked the waiter. "Oh, no," I blithely complained.

*Cap did, however, tell me a story with startling detail. One day his wife came home, he reported, and suggested that there was a nearby farmhouse for sale that she'd love to see. So that evening he took her out to see the house. She was delighted with everything about it. "It's perfect," she proclaimed. And before he knew it, they had bought the new farm and were moving in. "Only later did she tell me that she'd long had her eye on that place, and she'd seen the inside dozens of times throughout the years." "She knew what she wanted, and how to get it," I joked. "She sure did!" was his response. "We lived in that house the rest of our lives."

CEDAR RAPIDS, IOWA, SEPTEMBER 2, 2010;
REVISED SEPTEMBER 4, 2010
Reprinted from *Green Integer Blog* (September 2010).

Remembrance of Things Past

APICHATPONG WEERASETHAKUL (WRITER AND
DIRECTOR), **UNCLE BOONMEE WHO CAN RECALL HIS
PAST LIVES (LUNG BUNMI RALUEK CHAT)** / 2010

IT'S ALWAYS DIFFICULT to characterize a film by Thai
director Apichatpong Weerasethakul, because each
film is so original and clearly stands outside of the
Western filmmaking traditions, while still embracing
certain of its tropes.

Weerasethakul creates extraordinarily quiet films,
in which characters sit for long periods of time without speaking, or wherein the director presents long
scenes, often filmed in nighttime, jungle locations, in
which the viewer can barely see the images of animals
or ghosts, let alone comprehend their significance. *Uncle Boonmee Who Can Recall His Past Lives* bears close
relationships with Weerasethakul's *Tropical Malady*,
filmed in Northeastern Thailand, the Isan region, bor-
dering Laos.

This film, in fact, was part of a series of art installations, documentaries, and films in 2009 devoted to that region of Thailand, which suffered the violent 1965 Thai army crackdown on Communist sympathizers, which killed thousands. Like *Tropical Malady* where we witness the capture and destruction of a tiger-man, in the new film the director links this region to strange ghosts and human-like animals that were also destroyed in the army's "rehabilitation" of the region.

Although the political ramifications of that period create a sub-theme of *Uncle Boonmee*, the film primarily is a long series of meditations on larger issues, including love and loss, the past and the present, actions and their moral ramifications, and, most notably, issues of life and death.

Boonmee, suffering from kidney failure, is dying in his country farm, which raises bees for their honey and tamarinds (useful also in the makeup of the bees' honey). Sensing that he is soon to die, Boonmee (Thanapat Saisaymar) invites his wife's sister, Auntie Jen (Jenjira Pongpas), to come stay with him, she, in turn, bringing along Thong (Sakda Kaew-buadee) to help cook

for her brother-in-law within his limited diet. Already gathered at the farm are numerous immigrant workers, hired by Boonmee, including his Laos-born head worker Jai (Samud Kugasang) who helps with Boonmee's constant dialysis needs. If this is an odd gathering—the outspoken and somewhat bigoted Jen (the Laotians are smelly, she proclaims), the open-minded and loving Jai, the dying Boonmee, and the equally faithful and loving Thong—it soon is joined by an even odder couple, the ghost of Boonmee's long-dead wife Huay (Natthakarn Aphaiwonk), as beautiful and young as upon the day she died, and Boonmee's long-missing son, Boonson (Geerasak Kulhong), who, having become infatuated with a monkey ghost, has himself become one of the furry, red-eyed creatures.

The latter two suddenly show up at a family dinner, and are greeted by all with, after a bit of wonderment, amazing acceptance, leading to a slightly surreal discussion of what their lives are now like, and how they have come to be there. It is Boonmee, of course, in his death throes that has drawn them, and according to Bongsong, dozens of other spirits and monsters. But their appearance, although based on Thai science-fiction figures Weerasethakul encountered as a child, frightens less than it produces a sense of awe, as we realize that in this place and in the director's universe the dead and alive, the past and the present, and animal and human

are all interlinked.
A later story about a
plain-looking prin-
cess who sees herself
in the water as a beau-
tiful young woman,
a vision created, ap-
parently, by a loving
catfish, ends with her
giving up her jewels and dresses for intercourse with
the randy fish in order that she might turn into the vision itself, the woman with white skin. Other visions
include Boonmee's who believes that he, in another
life, was born in a cave and that his present death relates to the karma caused by his collaboration with the
Thai army which not only killed communists but all the
"outsider" beings that existed in this isolated territory.

In a Weerasethakul work, all things interrelate,
even if we cannot comprehend the links he suggests.
And this work is also about the transformations of art,
particularly film, as the director explores various cinematic styles: documentary mixed with epic fantasy,
silent-film-like acting with realist psychological scenes.
Weerasethakul's own trademark experimentalism, consisting of what he himself describes as "my kind of film
when you see long takes of animals and people driving,"
alternates with scenes reminding one of Thai comic

books and older Thai television shows. If this sounds "arty," well, as far as I'm concerned, given the artless film presentations of American cinema, good for it! Weerasethakul's films demand attention, but in their dark and daring beauty enchant the viewer in the process. There are never easy answers in this director's works, but the questions they pose make his works matter in a way that few contemporary films achieve.

Boonmee's strange death is followed up by a Buddhist ceremony and an aftermath in which Jen and her daughter sit in a hotel room counting up the contributions of money sent in memory of Boonmee. Into this cold and inhospitable room, where Jen and her daughter appear somewhat mercenary, enters a Buddhist monk, clearly unhappy with his future role in life and unable to sleep in the isolated and desolate temple in which he lives. In a strange interaction that reminds one a bit of Cary Grant entering a lover's room, the monk asks if he might take a shower in their bathroom (Grant takes showers in women's rooms in both *North by Northwest* and *Charade*). Changing his clothes to that of a modern Thai boy, the monk invites Jen to dinner. She (at least one aspect of her) agrees, and later we observe her at a nearby restaurant where the two begin to talk. Another part of her stays, she and the monk sitting at the end of the bed watching a television show while her daughter falls asleep. Either way, it is clearly, for the lonely Jen and dissatisfied young monk, the beginning of something new, suggesting a potential to start over again. One can only wonder, of course, if this is Uncle Boonmee come back to begin yet a new life.

LOS ANGELES, SEPTEMBER 14, 2011
Reprinted from *World Cinema Review* (September 2011).

A Sentimental Life

TERRENCE MALICK (WRITER AND DIRECTOR) **THE TREE OF LIFE** / 2011

> "There are two ways through life: the way of nature, and the way of Grace. You have to choose which one you'll follow."
> —Mrs. O'Brien in *The Tree of Life*

WINNER OF THE 2011 Cannes Film Festival's Palme d'Or and recipient of substantial critical praise to date, the movie I saw this past weekend was one of the most portentously pretentious paeans to American piety that I have ever witnessed. While one might certainly call Malick's *The Tree of Life* ambitious, the work was stretched so thin that its three parts almost snapped their sinews, leaving behind a tattered tale of the American dream of the 1950s.

Poor Jack O'Brien (Sean Penn), an extremely wealthy architect in (what I presume is) contemporary

 Houston, is in a funk, a real depression, conveyed from the moment he dresses for the office to when he drearily performs the tasks of his business day and prepares himself for his return home.

Companies are greedy, he quietly tells a cohort. The world is in a mess. Quite obviously, given the sleek high-rise his company inhabits, he has been nicely rewarded for his greed. But we already know through the first hurried scenes of the film that at the heart of his emotional problems is family life, most particularly the death at 19 of his younger brother, R.L., who appears to have died in the Vietnam War. Malick's premise is that Jack has never completely come to terms with his brother's death, nor, so we later discern, with his own relationship to his father and mother.

Raised as a devout Christian (Roman Catholic), Jack is still unable to understand how a beloved creator can also destroy, how a caring parent can hurt their children. The film begins with a quote from Job, and God's torments of Job are repeated as a theme throughout. Jack's first cries (presented in voice-over) parallel those of numerous literary children, most notably the child in James Agee's poem "Knoxville, Summer of 1915," who puzzles that none of the beloved family around him can tell him "who I am." And how, moreover, can one ever come to comprehend one's own life without being able to reconcile a loving God with a destructive one? These are not stupid questions to be waved away, although they certainly have been voiced countless times. There are, of course, no answers for true believers. As priests and ministers have repeated over and over (and so do friends in this movie), "God acts in mysterious ways."

In order to explore this dilemma, Malick apparently feels he must take us back to the Creation, and spends a long portion of his film on images from lush microbiological pictures, *National Geographic*-like spreads of oceans, Icelandic and Hawaiian volcanoes, marine life and other animals, and, finally, through his visual effects supervisor, Dan Glass, animations of dinosaurs, both preying upon others and in the throes of death. The publicity department described these scenes as not being narratively linked to the other parts of the film, and certainly there is some truth to that; but, in fact, it is clear that Jack must ponder these images— at least in his imagination—in order to comprehend the links of living beings. At least, this is what Malick seems to intimate. Unfortunately, the images he tosses out, while quite beautiful, in this cinematic context almost become kitsch, as Malick takes all those stunning scientific and geographic images and frames them as if to say, here is my art. Do we really need to see frame

after frame of whirling waters, fiery volcanoes, swirls of various early invertebrates and plants, and unconvincing animations of ancient animals to comprehend that everything in life is interrelated, that there is, to use Malick's transparent symbol, a tree of life?

At least now the brooding Jack can focus on family itself, as the director turns his attention to Mr. and Mrs. O'Brien (the beautiful couple Brad Pitt and Jessica Chastain) of Waco, Texas, beginning with their early years as a couple and growing a family of what eventually become three boys, Jack, R.L, and Steve. As in his other films, Malick works less through narratively conventional scenes than through a series of fast-moving images. As film critic Dave Kehr (in his 2011 collection of reviews, *When Movies Mattered*) describes Malick's *Days of Heaven*, so too might we characterize the direc-

> Throughout the film, the director seems remarkably stingy with his visual creations. A brief glimpse is all we are given of a particular composition, and then Malick is off to something else, rarely granting us the leisure to contemplate and assimalate the images he puts before us. If this movie is a coffee table book, someone is turning the pages too fast. For all the languor of the plot, *Days of Heaven* plays like a taut, driven film, relentless in its rhythm, hurrying the viewer along from image to image, scene to scene, tableau to tableau. The dialogue scenes, few and far between, are terse, clipped. Exchanges seldom last longer than three or four lines, as Malick insists on cutting away just as the characters seem ready to reveal themselves.

For Kehr this creates a dynamic pattern or rhythm that makes for a graceful, moving film. And we must grant that Malick's approach is perhaps the best one for an exploration of childhood. For all we are left with as adults and, perhaps, all we can assimilate from childhood, is a series of glimpses of moments recalled or slightly perceived.

In one scene in particular, I recognize the appropriateness of Malick's technique. An elderly man suddenly falls to the ground, suffering what seems to be a seizure, while in the foreground the mother draws her children to her, moving in the other direction, as if to protect them from what is probably the death of their grand-  father. If we blinked we could miss the entire scene, but obviously Jack has subliminally witnessed it in a split-second, reminding us of another young child of cinema, Frankie Addams from Carson McCullers' *A Member of the Wedding*, and her quick glimpse of boys sexually intertwined in an alley.

The trouble is that in shooting this glowingly-lit world of the 1950s, the camera becomes mannered, lingering endlessly on the strawberry-haired mother and the serious-minded music-loving father. The boys are all action, racing through the streets with sticks, cans, and other play toys with which boys have done battle since the beginning of time. In the fairly well-to-do neighborhood in which the O'Briens live, lights come on with a golden aura, children are called inside, and meals are served with formal pleasure. It is a flow of Norman Rockwell scenes that, at times, is so saccharine that I was afraid my teeth might rot. And, of course, there are trees (one tree in particular) that the camera,

obviously flat upon the ground, looks longingly up at again and again and again.

I can assure you that in the 1950s small-town life *was* a sort of idyll. I lived, in many respects, with the same family as did Jack, with only superficial differences—a reversal of the characters of my parents, less participation in typical male behavior—during that same period. But I don't think I would want to impose that daily blandness upon anyone else. These may have been the magical "days of heaven," but gradually, as I grew older, they transformed into the days of hell.

Just as in that earlier film, Malick associates the shadowy figures of *The Tree of Life* with different natural elements. Mrs. O'Brien—a woman who believes less in nature than in grace, representative in the film of (who'd have guessed?) love ("Unless you love, your life will flash by," she tells her son)—is associated with water, as she sprays that element over the yard again and again, gracefully washing her feet in the pulse of the hose.

Mr. O'Brien—a would-be musical artist, disappointed with his job, but determined to make the best of it—is tied to the earth, warning his son to make something of his life, continually insisting that he learn the simplest of gardening skills so that he might redeem their Eden. The impossibility of that redemption is what begins to transform him into a stern taskmaster, as simultaneously he turns his son against him and nature itself, the force he has chosen to obey.

That transformation, finally, is the most satisfying element of Malick's prose song to everyday American life. As one might not have perceived back then, the tensions between Jack's parents, his secret witness of death and intimations of evil, ultimately begin to show up in psychological manifestations that include violence, breaking and entering, petty robbery, and even thoughts of patricide. He's on his way to becoming what we would have called a "bad kid." Disobedience clearly is the only way he can begin to define himself. In short, he associates himself with the element of fire, forging eventually the world of steel and glass he later inhabits.

In this rebellion he even comes to torture his beloved younger and more passive brother, a child who, like his father, is musically inclined, but gentler, lighter in manner, almost airborne, returned to them in the film's earliest scenes as a body borne by an airplane.

A temporary resolution comes in the form of the humbling of the ambitious father, as he loses his job,

and they must move to another town or house. Father and son draw closer in the crisis, while his mother slides into silence. But the guilt of that childhood rebellion remains. Self-hate is inevitable, and we finally come to suspect it is what Jack describes as his lifelong inner wrestling with his mother and father that has brought this successful man to such a terminus.

The last scenes in Malick's film, while inevitable I suppose, are the emptiest, revealing just how vacuous is the director's vision. Exhausted by his memories, Jack plays out various Jungian tropes along with visions of an afterlife. In a desert landscape, he follows figures of his mother, father, and brothers until he reaches a doorframe through which, with some hesitation, he passes, only to discover himself now walking on a beach where the dead stroll in small groupings, greeting and holding one another with tenderness and love. To me it resembles something like a Mormon vision of the afterlife, a world into which I would never want to be reborn. But to Malick, clearly, it is a grand resolution to the questions Jack has posed: Who am I? Who is our creator? What is the purpose of life?

The film closes with an image of a bridge, connecting, quite obviously, Jack's past and present, while symbolizing his trip home to his possibly redeemed relationship.

Thinking back to my dismissals of the Coen brothers' approach to some of the same questions in their 2009 film *A Serious Man*, I now feel a little guilty; at least they had a sense of adolescent humor about it all. Malick is dead serious, and clearly doesn't give a damn about those of us who don't share his angst and ready-made solutions.

I am certain that those who desperately seek out this kind of spiritual reconfirmation, will love this film. If nothing else, one has to admire Malick for considering these issues and for presenting them in a way that Hollywood producers might not have allowed. Yet, it seems to me that he might have been better served by an old-fashioned studio head shouting out, "Cut the crap!"

LOS ANGELES, MAY 30, 2011
Reprinted from *World Cinema Review* (June 2011).

The Perfect Kiss

WILLIAM ARCHIBALD AND TRUMAN CAPOTE
(SCREENPLAY, BASED ON *THE TURN OF THE SCREW* BY
HENRY JAMES), JOHN MORTIMER (ADDITIONAL SCENES
AND DIALOGUE), JACK CLAYTON (DIRECTOR) **THE IN-
NOCENTS** / 1961

AFTER SEEING the Los Angeles Opera production of
Benjamin Britten's *The Turn of the Screw*, I determined
to revisit Jack Clayton's 1961 film, *The Innocents*, based
on the same James novella. Although I saw it the year
of its release, I had not seen it since, forgetting almost
all of its details.

The plot remains the same as in the opera, with a
new Governess, Miss Giddens (Deborah Kerr), coming
to care for Miles (Martin Stephens) and Flora (Pamela
Franklin) in Bly Hall, but the effect is far different from
the Britten piece, and significantly more focused on
the psychological (more even than James, who was certainly a psychologically-focused author). Although it is

often spoken of as a variation of a horror story—being named by Britain's *The Guardian* as one of the 25 best horror films of all time—I wouldn't describe it as having any real horror, and, perhaps, not even ghosts.

It is apparent from the beginning that the young governess (Kerr, a not-so-young 40 at the filming), the daughter of a minister, is completely inexperienced with regard to worldly matters. Indeed, except for the fact that Kerr is always so capably in command, we might suggest the character is still a kind of child. And, for that reason, it might have been better to cast an ingénue in the role instead of the gifted Kerr. Nonetheless, Kerr works hard—and somewhat successfully—to convince us of her innocence. If nothing else, we realize that she has no clue of how to deal with children, and is far less sexually aware than they are.

Of course, Miss Giddens has led a thoroughly protected life, while the children grew up under the influences of Miss Jessel (Clytie Jessop) and Peter Quint (Peter Wyngarde), who, at least according to the housekeeper, Mrs. Grosse, became sexually involved, performing their sexual acts openly, perhaps even where the children might see them. Quint, moreover, was a close companion to Miles, as Miss Jessel was to Flora.

Yet Clayton's film strangely resists any of the suggestion that pilots Britten's interpretation that Miles and Flora might have been the subject of sexual abuse.

Here, the ghosts of the past were apparently only bad influences upon the children, not perpetuators of horrors. In fact, Archibald's and Capote's screenplay strongly plays down the idea that there really are "ghosts." Every sighting of these figures is made by the Governess alone, while the children and Mrs. Grosse claim to not be able to see anything. Unlike the haunting ululations of Britten's Quint, these ghosts never speak.

It is quite apparent in this version, accordingly, that much of the surrounding "horror" of Bly belongs to the imagination of Miss Giddens, which narrows the possibilities of James' original significantly. By so clearly suggesting that it is all the product of a slightly hysterical woman, Clayton loses much of the richness and, most certainly, the true darkness of James' version. Cinematographer Freddie Francis does his best to hint at the "blackness" of the place by filming brightly lit objects against totally darkened backgrounds, and positioning objects at long distances from each other. Yet, in the end, these often seem like gestures towards something that we cannot truly believe is there.

What the film does offer in place of the suggestion of child abuse is the children's eroticism, expressed in their constant whispers and strange outbursts—amid absolutely perfect behavior—of obscene language and violent acts, and, in Miles' case, a flirtatiousness that suggests experiences far beyond his years. The most notable of these is the long kiss upon the lips he gives Miss Giddens, and her inability to reject it demonstrates that it may be her first kiss, a kind of "perfect" kiss since it cannot be reciprocated, only enjoyed. There need not be nor *cannot* be any emotional commitment on her part, the perfect way for a potential old maid to enjoy that in which she is too frightened to participate.

Nonetheless, Miss Giddens has, at least mentally, committed herself to Miles, and she is clearly jealous of the dominating past that Peter Quint and Miss Jessel represent (even if they are specters of her own imagination). Her only way to free the children of that past is to cast out the demons, psychologically speaking, by having her charges admit they are communing with the dead.

Flora goes into an absolute fit, spewing out obscenities, according to Mrs. Grosse, of which it should be impossible for her to have knowledge. Miss Giddens packs off Mrs. Grosse and Flora to Flora's uncle, despite his command to leave him out of any family situation. Suddenly she is left alone with the focus of her misguided love, Miles.

If she can only get him to say Quint's name, she muses—as if the saying of the name were a magic elixir that would free him from all former influences. Symbolically speaking, that would mean that he would have no past—in short, it would mean his death, which, as he speaks out Peter Quint's name, comes to pass. She, at first relieved, goes to him upon his faint before discovering that his heart has stopped. Now there are no longer any consequences, and she can kiss him upon the lips as he had her. The abuser, so Clayton suggests, exists not in the past but in the present, trapped in innocence.

LOS ANGELES, APRIL 17, 2011
Reprinted from *World Cinema Review* (April 2011).

The Piper's Son

MYFANWY PIPER (TEXT, BASED ON A NOVELLA BY HENRY JAMES), BENJAMIN BRITTEN (COMPOSER) **THE TURN OF THE SCREW** / LOS ANGELES, LOS ANGELES OPERA / THE PRODUCTION I SAW WAS A MATINEE PERFORMANCE ON MARCH 20, 2011

AS I SUGGEST ABOVE, Britten's powerful opera, *The Turn of the Screw*, is quite different from both the film version and, even at times, from James' original. In James' novella and Jack Clayton's *The Innocents*, for example, the ghosts may or may not be manifestations of the governess' imagination; or, at least, we can never be certain. But, while in the Britten version the phantoms may still be in the mind of Miss Giddens (Patricia Racette, who is given no name in the opera), they are, on stage, very corporeal, singing and moaning, with the children appearing to see them or hear them and responding to their commands. The specters clearly, in the Britten work, have an influence on their charges even beyond death. And Britten strongly suggests that the greatest part of that influence has to do with sexuality, not only between the for-mer valet Peter Quint (William Burden) and former govern-

ess Miss Jessel, but between Quint and the young boy Miles (credibly sung and performed by 12-year-old Mi-chael Kepler Meo) and between Miss Jessel and Flora (Ashley Emerson).

Consequently, Britten's carefully structured two acts of eight scenes explore not just the psychology of its characters, but their metaphysical encounters with good and evil. The question of innocence, so central to the film version, is embraced, accordingly, within the larger question of the battle between these forces.

It is clear from the very first scene, when the Gov-erness, charged with all responsibilities concerning the two children, expresses her anxieties, that she will never be up to the task. She is too young and untried to take on the battle with the unsavory forces of history repre-sented by Miles and Flora's short past. In this society of the *fin de siècle* (which is, one must recall, the period in which this "ghost story" was written), forces are moving in two opposing directions; with Victorian conventions still in full force, the unspoken dominating over the open and honest presentation of sexuality, the era also saw a rise of unconventional behavior represented by and in literary figures created by Wilde, Huysmans, Schnitzler, Zola, Shaw, etc.

The children's seemingly perfect behavior creates a sense for the two women, Governess and Housekeeper, that everything is as it should be, while we witness, through Britten's cunning music and Myfanwy Piper's text, that something is terribly wrong. From the first moment of their obedient bows and curtseys, we suspect there is something amiss, our first real clue being the news of Miles' dismissal from school. In Britten's work the reasons for that dismissal are even vaguer than in James and the film, but the fact that he will never be allowed to return hints at the gravity of the situation, and Britten allows our imaginations to take us where we want.

Mrs. Grosse, who cannot quite say what she has seen except to suggest that it was terrible and not to her liking, also hints at something more evil, perhaps, than what the reality was. And, in that sense, like the busybody housekeeper in *Wuthering Heights*, she helps to create the hysterical atmosphere which defeats any logical solutions the Governess might have come to.

But then, there are those visitations, and Quint's banshee-like cries for Miles in Britten's Act I, Scene 8—cries to which Miles does respond—seem to make it quite apparent that the relationship he had with Miles was more than a simple case of bad influence. His ululations come from a deeper place than a simple relationship between a young master and servant. And so too does Miss Jessel's sad soliloquy in Act II, Scene 3, in which she bemoans her loss of love with both Quint and Flora, indicating something far more serious than a Governess-pupil encounter.

Even greater revelations, however, come in the form of how the children play. While it may at first seem totally innocent, the children's haunting song "Tom, Tom, the Piper's Son," with, in the Los Angeles production, Miles astride his sister holding a whip, is more disturbing, I feel, than even the presence of the ghosts. We recognize almost immediately that there is something sadomasochistic about the game, and that it obviously is connected to something sexual of which children should have no knowledge. Moreover, the subject of that song, Tom, the son of the piper, has been naughty, is beaten, and "howls through the streets." There is also the suggestion in the word piper that Miles must eventually "pay the piper," that he must eventually face the consequences of his acts, and, along with that, there is the underlying story of the Pied Piper of Hamelin, who, when the city refused to pay for his services of removing rats, turned the children into rats.

Similarly, Britten's hidden joke of Miles' Latin lessons, wherein Miles sings Latin words that all pun on sexual body parts,

> amnis, axis, caulis, collis,
> clunis, crinis, fascis, follis,
> fustis, ignis, orbis, ensis,
> panis, piscis, postis, mensis,
> torris, unguis and canalis,
> vectis, vermis, and natalis
> sanguis, pelvis, cucumis,
> lapis, cassis, manis, glis.

while the Governess, apparently not terribly knowledgeable in Latin, smilingly listens, points to a world far more evil than the one the Governess has ever imagined.

Miles' strange "Malo" song, with its references to "malo," a variation of bad or evil, "naughty boy," and an "apple tree," reveals that Miles, himself, recognizes the

condition of his world, and expresses his fears for his own condition that he is bad because he has eaten of the tree.

If James only hints at these possibilities, Britten projects them, plays with them, and through them makes a case for why the situation must come to the close as it does in all versions. In the battle between good and evil—even if we can describe the Governess as representing *good*—she is no match. Her absurd belief that by speaking something you can exorcise it (not entirely different, of course, from Freud's methods) does not deal with the possibility that evil can swallow up the truth and spit it out. The many unsaid things about life at Bly House may have silenced any truth forever.

Although Miles may recognize Peter Quint as the Devil with his last words, the Devil has stolen the boy from the living as surely as if he was an obscene lover. The Governess, in her battle to "win over" Miles, to transform him, does not know enough to love him as the boy he is.

Finally, it is evident that the composer may have been drawn to these concerns because of his own inclinations, particularly his love of young boys, sensitively revealed in John Bridcut's *Britten's Children*. Although Britten lived for years with his singer-partner Peter Pears, he also became close friends and a father-like figure for dozens of 12- to 14-year-old boys, showering them with gifts and letters. Many of these boys came from children's choruses, and for some of them he wrote roles in his operas. Only one boy, 13-year-old Harry Morris, accused him of sexual molestation, claiming that Britten entered his bedroom in Cornwall where the composer had taken the boy on a sailing trip; charges were never filed.

Britten chose the young singer David Hemmings (later a noted actor) for the role of Miles and, according to friends, was obviously obsessed with the boy, an adoration which Hemmings, strikingly handsome at 12, readily accepted. But Hemmings later insisted that Britten made no sexual advances. It is apparent, nonetheless, that Britten very well knew what Quint might have felt for Miles, and understood the ramifications of such involvements. And, to my way of thinking, it is why Britten was so focused on those aspects of James' tale.

LOS ANGELES, APRIL 20, 2011
Reprinted from *Green Integer Blog* (April 2011).

The day before we attended Britten's The Turn of the Screw, *Howard and I, along with our cleaning woman and friend Ana-María Abraham, saw a production by the Los Angeles Opera, with various young orchestras and choirs, of Benjamin Britten's setting of the Chester Miracle Play,* Noye's Fludd. *The groups included members of the Los Angeles Opera Orchestra, the Hamilton High School Academy of Music Orchestra, the Colburn School String Orchestra, the choir of St. John Etudes Church and School, members of the Cathedral of Our Lady of the Angels Choir, the Colburn School Children's Choir, Pueri Cantores San Gabriel Valley Children's Choir, the Padre Serra Parish Choir, the Jubilate Catholic Korean Choir, the St. Mel Parish Choir, and the Musical Youth of California Children's Choir. Eli Villanueva directed, with opera singers Richard Paul Fink performing Noye, and Kate Lindsey performing Mrs. Noye, along with Richard K. Price singing the voice of God.*

Like past productions at the Cathedral of Our Lady of Angels, the production was a joyful one, which included participation in three songs from the congregation, along with lovely costumes—particularly with the entry of dozens of pairs of animals performed by teens and young chil-

dren—and the joyful music of the entire work, conducted by the beloved LA Opera conductor James Conlon.

Perhaps the most fun of this piece involves the stubborn refusal of Mrs. Noye to join her husband, as she remains on land surrounded by her gossip friends until finally Noye and his sons drag her onto the ark and to salvation!

It was a perfect afternoon for all those who attended, which we followed with an excellent dinner at Los Angeles' famed Pacific Dining Car.

LOS ANGELES, APRIL 20, 2011

The Locked Window

JULIE ARCHER AND LEE BREUER (CO-CREATORS, BASED ON THE NOVEL *PETER AND WENDY* BY J. M. BARRIE) **PETER AND WENDY**, PRESENTED BY MABOU MINES AT THE NEW VICTORY THEATER, NEW YORK / THE PRODUCTION I ATTENDED WAS ON MAY 6, 2011

ON MAY 6 I had tickets to see Tom Stoppard's play *Arcadia*, but when I heard of the short return of Mabou Mines' *Peter and Wendy* to The New Victory Theater (running from May 6-22), I could not resist the opportunity to see the play, and joyfully changed my plans.

In a strange way, although these British-based works are entirely different, there is an odd connection between the two in that they both episodically, often without coherent connections between changes of characters and place, present a kind of Arcadian world in which things are seemingly simpler—although the characters in both are faced with complexities that they might not wish to face.

In *Peter and Wendy* those complexities have to do with their childhood vision of reality. But unlike the earlier play and novel, *Peter Pan*, Barrie's 1911 *Peter and Wendy* presents a less sweet and simple vision of things. It is not simply that Peter, Wendy, her brothers and the other Lost Boys who make up Peter's band perceive things as children might, but that they sometimes all too readily have perceived the traumatic and threatening issues of the adults and the society that surrounds them. In this version, Peter is not just a child who refuses to grow up but, in his kind of wise puppet guise, is a "puppet" to his own childish insistence and the longings that go with that. Like a stubborn and undeterred brat, as spoken by the marvelous narrator Karen Kandel, he is, although always fairly charming, at times also a selfish bully of contradictory forces.

While *The New York Times* critic saw these marvelous puppets as too sweet, I saw them quite differently, as forces representing an adamant refusal to join in the Victorian society around them, and, in that sense, not at all innocent boys and girls living in a time outside of reality, but slightly terrifying rebels against the transformation of Victorian society into a gentler and more civil society.

Peter may offer these timeless children adventure, but those adventures, the battles with the absurd Hook and his gang, are not unlike the ridiculous wars fought

throughout the century. Wendy may be part and party to the fun, but she is wooed away from her home less as an equal adventurer than as a mother to all the boys, a mother who in her nurturing and care for her "children" has little room to truly discover herself, more indentured than adventured.

Even Hook, in this version, is less of a free adventurer than he is caught up in the societal whirl, a man who wants to become a figure of style, a class-inspired man of aspirations. The wonderful Croc is a fearful villain less because of his potential to feast on Peter Pan's boys, than because he is unable to free himself from a kind of infatuation with his own tail/tale.

All of this darkness is reinforced by the Celtic songs composed by Johnny Cunningham and performed by Aidan Brennan, Tola Custy, Steph Geremia, Alan Kelly, Laoise Kelly, Siobhan Miller, and Jay Peck; these songs are not your children-friendly hymns, such as "I'm Flying," "I Gotta Crow," and "I Won't Grow Up," but rather tap into the real roots of J. M. Barrie's darker Scottish heritage.

The marvelous puppetry of Basil Twist and Lute Breuer, accompanied by a whole ensemble of marvelous players, supported this slightly fractured fairytale-feeling about the whole event.

It is notable that, when Wendy reports that she and her brothers want to return home, Peter considerably chastises them and, for a few minutes, closes the open windows of their home, barring them from returning while hinting that their parents have not been anxiously awaiting them. In those minutes it becomes apparent that *this* Peter, unlike the earlier Peter Pan, is not only mischievous but envious and even revengeful.

When Wendy returns to the Darlings' house, the first thing she does is pick up all the "toys," the tokens of the children's imagination—including the toy soldiers, the lost boys, the stuffed Nana—pouring them back into the chest to keep them out of reach of insidious influences.

A pall overcomes the entire work as we realize that Pan, Tinkerbell, and their opponents are now out there, all alone in space. There is no love, not even, any longer, a sense of adventure! Of course Pan will return to steal away future generations, but in his eternal, darkened childish vision, he will never find the fulfillment of home

and hearth.

I cried. I wish I'd had a child along with me to observe and share his or her experiences of this profound version of Barrie's enduring myth.

LOS ANGELES, JUNE 22, 2011
Reprinted from *US Theater, Opera, and Performance* (June 2011).

At a party after in a nearby club I had the opportunity to meet with and talk to the famous designer and puppeteer Basil Twist, whose Arias with a Twist *I had seen and reviewed in Los Angeles in 2009 (see* My Year 2010*). I think I also met there Lute Breuer, Ruth Maleczech, and Lee's talented son.*

Having already published Lee's remarkable drama-fiction La Divina Caricatura, *and having published* B. Beaver Animation *in my and Mac Wellman's drama anthology* From the Other Side of the Century II, *we were already good friends.*

Lee suggested Mabou Mines might be interested in presenting one of my plays, but nothing ever came of it.

Having so enjoyed the Mabou Mines version of the classic, I determined to revisit the musical I so fondly recalled from youth, in the days when television occasionally still looked to real theater for re-stimulation—or, at least, an occasional family fix. It took almost three years before another Peter Pan *showed up, and, alas, he came too late. What magic may have been in the original had long ago died, and poor Tinkerbell could simply not be brought back to life.*

Walkin' the Plank

IRENE MECCHI (TELEPLAY, BASED ON THE PLAY BY J. M. BARRIE), CAROLYN LEIGH, BETTY COMDEN AND ADOLPH GREEN (LYRICS, WITH ADDITIONAL LYRICS BY AMANDA GREEN), MOOSE CHARLAP AND JULE STYNE (MUSIC) **PETER PAN LIVE!** / ON N.B.C. (THE NATIONAL BROADCASTING COMPANY), DECEMBER 4, 2014

LAST NIGHT I sat through the entire three hours of slickly-conceived advertisements punctuated with brief scenes from the ongoing and ongoing musical *Peter Pan* flashed in between. It's cruel, I suspect, to attempt to piece together a review of a television musical, hiding out in the morass of Christmas jingles rung out to encourage its audience to ring-up a big profit for the impresarios of this fragile fairy tale, but it's what I pay myself to do!

From what I can remember, arising out of that fog of blurry commercial daydreams was a very pleasant group of young men and women—pretending to be at least two decades younger than the dates on their drivers' licenses—eagerly trying to engage any audience they might have imagined as having tuned in. I can't believe that many children actually lasted it out until 11:00. And I gather from the media reports that a great number of this work's supposed observers fell away as the hours ticked along with Captain Hook's vengeful croc.

Alas, if even *I* couldn't believe, I suspect poor Tinkerbell truly did not survive. It's hard to get a TV cam to clap along, let alone to believe in the goings-on it is so faithfully recording. Let me begin by simply asserting the actors in Neverland (and even those back home nursing Nana) are obviously talented folk, with nice personalities, good looks, and very pleasant voices. The

 former school boys
and Indian bucks
could even dance—
quite marvelously at
moments!

Allison Williams
has a very lovely voice which pertly warbled out Pan's
standards, "I Won't Grow Up" and "I Gotta Crow."
And Taylor Louderman as Wendy sweetly sang her
brothers and all the lost boys to sleep. I'm sure that, if
she is already a mother, she is a very nice one, or if she
isn't a mother, she someday will become what the character so passionately longed to be.

Everyone flew off quite expertly, without a single
one of their body ropes twisting up!

For all that, I could not even have imagined a more
pallid production of a musical that depends almost entirely on its characters' physical presence. *Pan* was never
a very great example of the Broadway musical, but Mary
Martin, who, back in the black-and-white days, seemed
able to convince everyone of anything she wanted to,
certainly crowed out tunes with such a committed
tunefulness that you might certainly be convinced that
she could climb every mountain (in case you've forgotten, as the star of the stage version of *The Sound of
Music*, she beat Julie Andrews to the top!). None of the
actors in this lackluster misadventure seemed to be able

to even convince themselves that they could accomplish anything but to show up back in Wendy's nursery, hoping to be adopted in the end.

I kept praying for an over-the-top, campy, slightly naughty rendition of the near-pedophilic Captain (with "a hook on each boy and a boy on each hook") by Christopher Walken. Sadly he was unable to show up for his performance. The ghost of the actor who appeared seemed to be doing just that, "walkin'" through what should have been at least a quick shuffle, or, at best, a wry-little tap—even if he couldn't quite get it up to tango or turn in a proper tarantella. As Mary McNamara put it, his performance might have been camp, "if camp weren't soooo exhausting." As it was, the usually enchanting actor appeared to be on barbiturates—despite the fact that his pirate friends did everything they could to help him to revive. Christian Borle (as Smee) should get an award just for reminding Walken, from time to time, that he was supposed to be onstage. Even the crucial third-act battle between Pan and boys against the pirates seemed to be the actions of stumbling somnambulists. Hook predictably falls even while attempting to walk the plank.

Is it any wonder that everyone but Peter Pan is desperate to go home again?

At home, at least, sits the beautiful Kelli O'Hara, beautifully singing her heart out—a real Broadway star praying that the kids might soon come home so she can blow out the lights and kiss us all goodnight!

LOS ANGELES, DECEMBER 6, 2014
Reprinted from *US Theater, Opera, and Performance* (December 2014).

Bond of Age

IF BARRIE'S *PETER PAN* can be described as the refusal of youth to become old, the two short plays I saw
this past Sunday—although still very much centered
on the issues of young and old—might be said to hint
at strange bonds between the two. One might almost
be tempted to take that further and suggest a kind of
"bondage." After all, if Wendy and her brothers had not
been surrounded by loving, if sometimes disapproving,
adults, there would have been no need to seek another
world. Indeed, in Barrie's works, the desire for new adventures is not at all like Dickens' world, peopled with
tortured children and waifs who must escape simply to
survive. In Barrie's child-like fables, the figures reach
out to other worlds simply for solace and psychological

needs. As in our own youth-obsessed culture, Barrie's adults and children simply prefer to stay young.

It is that relationship between the young and the old that is the focus of these two slightly sentimental, but still entertaining short plays. In *Rosalind*, a middle-aged woman (Mrs. Page) sits in a country home which she has rented with her slightly older landlady (Dame Quickly). Mrs. Page greedily eating bon-bons or nuts while they gossip. The conversation mostly centers on Mrs. Page's satisfaction about being middle-aged, her feeling that it is wonderful to be aging and much more enjoyable than the activities of her actor-daughter who, at the moment is in Monte Carlo. The somewhat disheveled, graying Mrs. Page is obviously proud of her daughter Beatrice—she has her photograph prominently displayed—but she is not at all distressed that she seldom gets the opportunity to see her, and, she later admits, has never seen the girl upon stage.

Into this quaint tea-time setting stumbles a young man, Charles Roche, seeking, improbably, a short respite from the rain before his train returns to the city. At first he is refused by the landlady, as Mrs. Page pretends to sleep, but gradually he wiggles his way to the warm hearth, intending to read and leave the tenant to herself. But all that changes when he spots Beatrice's photograph! The actress is at the center of his attentions, and, we soon discover, he has met her and dined with her. He is unable to comprehend, accordingly, why her photograph should appear on the mantel of the "far from London" setting. Gradually he awakens the sleeping Mrs. Page, and, little by little, discovers that the woman he has just met is the actress' mother.

So obsessed with Beatrice is Charles that he feels equally strong attachments to her mother, and opens his heart to her, telling the older woman how much he is in love with her daughter. Surprisingly Mrs. Page puts these sentiments and the trinkets that go with them (a photograph he keeps in his wallet across from the picture of his sister) into perspective, even mocking them. And in a quick dismissal of his emotions, Mrs. Page rips up the cherished photograph.

He is horrified, shocked by her behavior, but gradually discovers, through her knowledge of him and growing revelations, that the middle-aged woman before him and his beloved Beatrice are one and the same. Beatrice, it appears, is not at all in Monte Carlo, but has escaped as Mrs. Page to be able to discover herself at her true age instead of as the eternally young figure she must play upon the stage.

Charles is disheartened. How could such a beauty have been transformed into the woman standing before his eyes? Yet, as she reveals her—and every young star's—dilemma, he gallantly offers her marriage in order to protect her in her old age! The gesture may be gallant but, of course, it is ridiculous! It is also, perhaps, somewhat obscene. It is quite impossible that the young, handsome boy come out of the rain could sit for the rest of his life gossiping with his aging wife.

Barrie, fortunately, has another surprise up his sleeve, as Beatrice/Mrs. Page is called back to London to play Rosalind in Shakespeare's *As You Like It*. Suddenly the actress is in a flurry, running to pack, to change clothes, and to accompany her potential "lover" back to the city. Her entry after dressing says it all: she is now young again, not a real human being plagued with age, but a creature of the stage, a made-up simulacrum of a young beauty for all her audiences to love. In a sense, Mrs. Page has become her own Peter Pan, a reimagining of her own being.

The second of these solidly staged plays, *The Old Lady Shows Her Medals*, is simpler in plot, but far more complex emotionally than the first play. After bearing through a recitation of four charwomans' recountings of their sons, all at war (acted, unfortunately, as we have come to expect from small companies, with a babble of unfocused English accents), the play turns to the central character, Mrs. Dowey (excellently performed by Penny Safranek), whose son, so the vicar reports, has just returned for a leave from the front. His arrival is almost breathtaking, as a brawny, kilted man from the "Black Watch" enters Mrs. Dowey's

basement hovel, while the other women are sent scurrying off.

The actor playing Kenneth Dowey (Joe McGovern) has the Scottish brogue down rather well, and is stunningly handsome enough that, despite his overly self-confident sense of being, his presence almost does take away the breath. Certainly, his appearance seems to have startled his mother. Rightfully so, for as we soon discover, although they share last names, they are no relation to one another. Mrs. Dowey has "stolen" his name and address from the local paper. Having no son or even previous husband, she has felt so alien from the "war effort," and so excluded from her friends, all of whom have boys in the service, that she has "made him up," so to speak, sending him cakes and other treats under a different name, and following his wartime adventures through the papers. The stack of letters she has shown her friends that he has written her are all blank.

At first the soldier is justifiably angry with the lying woman, but gradually, as he discovers the extent to which she had deceived everyone, including himself, and her explanations for her acts, he grows more tolerant. He, we soon discover, is himself an orphan, and her desperate interest in his being suits his high impression of himself. When she offers him a bed and clean sheets he cannot resist.

A few nights later we discover, they have dined out each evening, he buying her an astrakhan, she serving as a doting and somewhat gay confidant for a lonely man in the city. By the end of the play, Kenneth kneels before her, as if about to propose, and does so: will she accept the role of his mother? It is a beautifully conceived, if sentimental, gesture. But it is also so revealing of the author's strange entanglements with youth and age. As in *Rosalind*, youth bows to age always, although it understands itself as the superior. But it is just youth's own shining being that so attracts the old to it. There is a whiff here almost of "pedophilia," and given Barrie's own relationship with his mother—for whom he often played his preferred dead brother—and his deep (and apparently detrimental) involvement with the boys of the Davies family, there is certainly much more to be said about this "bond between the ages."

As Kenneth tearfully leaves, however, we are awarded the delightful sight of the old woman opening the package of trinkets, a hat, medals, etc., which he has awarded her. And we feel, despite her lies and, now, perhaps his self-deceptions, this bonding of the two has been nearly inevitable, and is surely a good thing.

LOS ANGELES, AUGUST 31, 2011
Reprinted from *US Theater, Opera, and Performance* (August 2011).

The Last Friend

AARON SORKIN (SCREENPLAY, BASED ON A BOOK
BY BEN MEZRICH), DAVID FINCHER (DIRECTOR) **THE
SOCIAL NETWORK** / 2010

AARON SORKIN'S AND DAVID FINCHER'S *The Social
Network* might be described as one of the most interesting films with a hollow center that I've ever seen. To put it another way, it is a beautiful film about, as the rookie lawyer Marylin Delpy describes the film's "hero" Mark Zuckerberg, a man "trying so hard" to be an asshole. From the very beginning scene, Zuckerberg (played by the talented near-lookalike Jesse Eisenberg) reveals his inability to engage in sensitive communication.

From his early dismissal of his date Erika Albright's (Rooney Mara) education (Zuckerberg is a student at Harvard)—

ERICA ALBRIGHT: Why do you keep saying I don't
   need to study?

MARK ZUCKERBERG: You go to B.U....

—to his later promise to take her to places where she might otherwise never be able to go, he proves that he is as close to being what Delpy has suggested. Erica's farewell sums him up:

> ERICA ALBRIGHT: You are probably going to be a very successful computer person. But you're going to go through life thinking that girls don't like you because you're a nerd. And I want you to know, from the bottom of my heart, that that won't be true. It'll be because you're an asshole.

Certainly there have been numerous works of literature and film with foolish or totally incompetent heroes. This "hero" is the opposite, becoming fabulously wealthy as the creator of Facebook, a social networking tool that is immensely popular. But as Betty White recently joked on *Saturday Night Live*, thanking Facebook users for helping to put her on the show, "Now that I know what it is, it sounds like a huge waste of time." Frankly, it is, even though I use it daily to announce to my thousand or more "friends" (a large number of whom I've never met) what I've posted on my cultural blogs and to wish happy birthday to acquain-

tances whose birthdays I might otherwise have overlooked. Basically, however, it still seems to me to be a network for those for whom it was originally intended, people looking for a place for quick, speed-date-like conversations: the young and lonely.

For all that, we come not only to sympathize with this "asshole," but—given the alternatives of what the film portrays as the Harvard rich, handsome, and elitist snobs represented by the Winklevoss twins (both played by Armie Hammer, grandson of Armand) and their friend Divya Naryenda—we cannot help but root for Zuckerberg in their legal suits against him. Their claim that they created the idea of Facebook in their HarvardConnection (later ConnectU) may have resulted in a huge settlement from Zuckerberg, but in the larger perspective of things does seem, as Zuckerberg claims in this film, absurdly unfair: "A guy who makes a nice chair doesn't owe money to everyone who has ever built a chair."

Sorkin presents this reprehensible hero, moreover, as enormously smart and—like all great American entrepreneurs—extremely hardworking and creative. Zuckerberg is a social underdog who through his enter-

prise wins, the epitome of what all Americans understand as being at the heart of the American Dream.

The film extends that by introducing yet another loser-winner, Sean Parker (a smart aleck portrayed by singer Justin Timberlake), the man who created Napster and, later, Plaxo. Parker is presented as a now nearly paranoid being who has already been nailed to the cross of his own creations, destroyed for having created something ahead of its time. Perhaps only Zuckerberg's friend Eduardo Saverin (Andrew Garfield) cannot comprehend why the younger computer genius would be immediately attracted to such a figure. The two are a natural pair, and Parker, playing on Zuckerberg's incompetent social skills—he himself being well known for his involvement with drugs, women, and liquor—provides him a kind of father-figure who encourages both Zuckerberg's creativity and his social inadequacy. Far more than any abuse of the Winklevosses, whom Zuckerberg cleverly refers to as the Winklevii, we cannot so easily forgive his betrayal of Saverin, who, after all, as Chief Financial Officer funded Facebook in its infancy, and, although he did little to advance it, worked hard, if unsuccessfully, to raise money for its development.

Saverin, a smart but clueless young businessman, who was finally ousted from the company and, perhaps more importantly, removed from any rational influence he might have provided his friend, has little choice but to sue Zuckerberg also. As he puts it quite clearly, "I was your only friend."

In the end, accordingly, we have to wonder what each of us wants more, friendships or financial success. The irony here, of course, is obvious. What Zuckerberg created was based precisely on the attempt to create a social network, a series of interchanges with friends. And, accordingly, we must also ask ourselves, did Facebook ever achieve that? Certainly for some individuals, and there are thousands who are addicted to communicating on this network, it probably does provide precisely that, an outlet that allows people to keep in close communication with others. But one also has to ask what kind of communication that represents, given its limitations of the number of words one can send, and its distancing of true-life communication, replacing, as it does, words on a screen for real human interchange.

Fincher and Sorkin do not even attempt to ask,

much less to answer those questions. But they do suggest the moral consequences for what Zuckerberg achieved. The several lawsuits against him result in the payment of millions of dollars—although for a billionaire that amount probably, as lawyer Delpy aptly describes it, is merely "a speeding ticket," ultimately of little consequence. In today's *The New York Times* we are told Facebook is now worth some 50 billion dollars.

Yet at the end of the film, the writer and director present our "hero," dysfunctional as ever, pathetically asking his ex-girlfriend, Erika, to become his Facebook "friend." Sitting like Michael Corleone in the dark of *The Godfather II*, Zuckerberg keeps refreshing his browser, impatiently awaiting her reply. We suspect she will probably never answer. Or, if she does, that it will have little significance. A friend on a network, after all, is not necessarily a friend in real life. And an asshole may think forever that he lost everyone because of his genius.

LOS ANGELES, JANUARY 2, 2011
Reprinted from *World Cinema Review* (January 2011).

The Company Way

ABE BURROWS, JACK WEINSTOCK, AND WILLIE GIL-
BERT (BOOK, BASED ON THE BOOK BY SHEPHERD MEAD),
FRANK LOESSER (MUSIC AND LYRICS) **HOW TO SUCCEED
IN BUSINESS WITHOUT REALLY TRYING** / NEW YORK,
AL HIRSCHFELD THEATER, 2011 / THE PERFORMANCE I
ATTENDED WAS A MATINEE ON MAY 7, 2011

I WILL ADMIT to a certain sentimental attachment to
the American musical theater, although I feel, given the
quality of the musicals I care for, there is no reason for
apology. Most of my friends who cannot comprehend
my love of this genre have perhaps never seen a musical comedy before 1970. The handful of good musicals
since that time have been so few (most of them composed by Stephen Sondheim) that one might almost say
that the form has died out. Today, except for revivals,
musical comedy is for audiences who like songs consisting of three memorable notes, repeated through chorus
upon chorus of driveling lyrics sung at very high deci-

bels. But then, we do, from time to time, have wonderful revivals of the older works of this genre that remind us of what the musical theater was all about.

How to Succeed in Business without Really Trying, the 1961 New York Drama Critics and Pulitzer Prize-winning gem by Frank Loesser, was not, I am afraid, one of the "wonderful revivals." I do not mean to suggest that it was not worth attending, for, at moments, this version was absolutely delightful, but overall it simply couldn't live up to the standards of the original and the movie version.

I have never before sat in an audience with so many first-time theatergoers, mostly teenage girls and their slightly stunned families in tow. The girl next to me was celebrating her 16th birthday and "just had see" Daniel Radcliffe, this revival's star attraction, "in the flesh." In some senses the freshness of the fans was a treat. And Radcliffe, a trouper already at age 22, was not about to disappoint them.

Radcliffe, who I suspect has by this time quite settled into his performance, was better by far than the critics led audiences to believe. Although, as *The*

New York Times suggested, he is not a natural "song and dance man" (I am not quite sure what that means, and when I think of such figures I can only conjure up Robert Preston and Robert Morse, the original J. Pierrepont Finch, neither of them great singers or even able dancers!), he can belt out a tuneful song and, with the help of the able chorus, jump, leap, and hoof it across the stage quite ably. Once in a while you can still see him grimace a bit, as if muttering deep within, "I'm gonna be great!" And, at moments, he is! If nothing else you have to recognize that Radcliffe is giving his all, which unfortunately, if you have seen Robert Morse in the role—I saw only the movie version, but listened to the original cast recording so many hundreds of times in my youth that the old wax stereo recording is all scratches and scrapes—is just not enough.

Oddly, given the fact that he has now been nominated for a Tony for a supporting role (while Radcliffe was ignored), John Larroquette seemed far less engaged in the piece, speeding through his lines at times as if he were trying to catch a plane, and other times performing on cruise control. When Larroquette "woke up" once or twice in his role as J. B. Biggley, as he did in "Grand Old Ivy," he was quite charming, with both he and Radcliffe performing brilliantly. Unfortunately, director/choreographer Rob Ashford could not leave a good thing alone, bringing a whole chorus of foot-

ball players to dance along, wiping away one the few enchanting character encounters.

Most of the other cast members are quite excellent, particularly Ellen Harvey as Biggley's executive secretary, Miss Jones, Mary Faber as Smitty, and, although a little young for the role, Rose Hemingway (at 27 she seems more a neophyte than Radcliffe). Christopher Hanke makes the nasty Bud Frump almost likeable. And, although her humor switched on and off at times, Tammy Blanchard is basically a hilarious Hedy LaRue.

Perhaps the most serious problem about this revival is that, despite its obvious satirical intentions, the work seems extraordinarily outdated and unnecessarily coy today. For those who have never seen the musical,

I'll briefly relay the plot: window-washer J. Pierrepont Finch enters the executive suites of the World Wide Wicket Corporation in search of a job, armed with a little book that promises immediate success, *How to Succeed in Business without Really Trying*. Within minutes he has literally bumped into the president of the company, J. B. Biggley, encountered a woman, Rosemary Pilkington, who falls in love with him at first sight, and captured a job in the mailing room by transforming the unpleasant encounter with Biggley into what the employment head interprets as a friendship.

Finch is highly likeable, even charming, but he is without a single moral principle in his desire to rise up the corporate ladder, and within hours, so it seems, he shifts into the positions of a junior executive, advertising manager, and, even after a disastrous failure, is elected Chairman of the Board, all before you can say, ROSEMARY, the woman with whom, along the way, he has reluctantly fallen in love.

Biggley's nincompoop nephew, Budd Frump, tries his best throughout to trip up Finch, as the other executives, terrified by Ponty's swift rise in the company and fearing the discovery of their own ineptitudes, plot to destroy him; yet Finch (as he reminds everyone, F-I-N-C-H) miraculously survives each battle, primarily because he is so self-centered that he fails to see the restless men on the prowl.

The most famous song of the musical is Finch's love song to himself, "I Believe in You," sung into a mirror of the men's room as he shaves:

FINCH:
Now there you are;
Yes, there's that face,
That face that somehow I trust.
It may embarrass you to hear me say it,
But say it I must, say it I must:
You have the cool, clear
Eyes of a seeker of wisdom and truth;
Yet there's that upturned chin
And that grin of impetuous youth.
Oh, I believe in you.
I believe in you.

Women in this male-dominated world are all sec-retaries, who, the males are reminded, should not be treated like toys—but nonetheless are. In today's world, it is clear that the efficient and trustworthy Miss Jones, the smart Smitty, and the quick-plotting Rosemary would be at the head of the World Wide Wicket Com-pany instead of out bowling or wickedly spinning webs to find husbands. But in 1961...well, those gender lines were at the musical's satirical heart. Today the plot ap-pears somewhat as a stale joke with little resonance.

For all that, I think the audience was willing to overlook the datedness of the piece if only the actors could come together and enjoy their own spoof. But time and again, it seemed Radcliffe was not the only one grimacing. Everybody seemed

to be playing it "the company way," refusing to get excited about anything. Two of the best dance numbers in directors Hugh Lambert and Bob Fosse's original, "Coffee Break" (such a difficult number that the movie dropped it) and the sprightly "A Secretary is Not a Toy," seemed lackluster in Ashford's staging, while at other times, as I mentioned, the director seemed to suck all the attention away from the actors through the introduction of gratuitous routines.

Finally, despite Radcliffe's pluck and elfin charm, I kept missing the puckish comedy of Robert Morse, the silly imperiousness of Rudy Vallee, and the jazz inflections of Michele Lee's voice.

One piece alone came to life and created for its few minutes the magic that might have stood as a beacon to these young performers. The last full number of the musical, "Brotherhood of Man," was so richly sung, punctuated by Ellen Harvey's coloratura soprano, and so thrillingly danced that it almost redeemed everything else. If only the cast had realized that "brotherhood" earlier in the show, *How to Succeed* might have gone straight to the top!

In the end, however, it didn't matter. The young girls and their families stood up in celebration and absolutely roared (I've never heard as loud of an applause) as Radcliffe bowed appreciatively to his fans.

LOS ANGELES, MAY 13, 2011
Reprinted from *US Theater, Opera, and Performance* (May 2011).

People Without Choices

J. C. CHANDOR (WRITER AND DIRECTOR) **MARGIN CALL** / 2011

AS THE CAMERA winds in and out of the population of the offices within the glass-lined halls of a downtown New York City office building, we are quickly swept up into a world that we immediately recognize as being both exhilarating (even the window views, when we get a glimpse, are vertiginously beautiful) and extremely claustrophobic (not only can everyone see each other, but the camera scans the row upon row of computers where the lowest of company employees must daily sit shoulder to shoulder as they convince their favorite customers to buy and sell). All in all, it is a most unpleasant world; yet everyone in view is well dressed and groomed and apparently eager to go about his or her daily business. And, so we soon learn—mostly through the inquiries of the youngest and most junior man on the company payroll, the brash self-centered Seth Bregman

(Penn Badgley)—they have good reason: they each make a lot of money, from hundreds of thousands to millions!  These are the Wall Street investment traders of whom we have read so much about in the past few years because of the myths surrounding them (dished up mostly in overwrought films) and the effects they have had upon our lives (related through the news).

Almost before we can completely assimilate the world in which he have suddenly discovered ourselves, several younger employees, including Bregman and his associate Peter Sullivan (Zachery Quinto) catch a glimpse of a small herd of hired henchmen about to fire a large percentage of their coworkers and mutter to their soon-to-be senior supervisor, Paul Bettany (Will Emerson), "They're going to do it right here, in front of everybody?" He suggests they simply hunker down, pretending that they don't exist, as the evil-minded squadron calls out individuals one by one to meet with them. We follow the firing of Head of Risk Management Eric Dale (Stanley Tucci) where we observe the impeccable scouring process: he has 49 hours to accept their benefit program and must immediately collect his personal belongings and leave the building; his computer access, and codes, and even his personal cell phone have been deactivated.

A long-time employee, Dale meets the situation with a kind of sad reassignment. Certainly, he's seen it all before, but he cannot resist mentioning that he is in the middle of important computer research. All activities will be taken up by the others who remain, he is told. Even though Bregman and Sullivan have been told beforehand of what was about to "go down," they are startled by the turn of events—particularly since Dale has taught them nearly everything they know— and attempt to apologize to their former colleague. At the last moment, as he is about to take the elevator down into a metaphorical non-existence, he hands Sullivan a USB drive, warning him to handle the data he finds there carefully.

By the time Dale and other company regulars have been axed we have already journeyed from a kind of documentary-like presentation of the back halls of companies like Lehman Brothers, which brought down the US economy in 2008, to a kind of would-be horror film in which the monsters are not as mythic as they are disturbed and troubled fellow human beings. As the other late-workers clean up their desks, Sullivan remains, obviously intrigued by Dale's warning. Opening up this new Pandora's Box, he discovers a series of imaginary projects of the volubility of his company's accounts

which quickly reveals that, in their combination of good and outright rotten securities (failed loans and other investments without any real money behind them), their trading has already resulted in possible losses far beyond the worth of the entire company. In short, if any of their trades had come up for question, the entire company would have immediately gone into a bankruptcy that would affect the world stock market. Indeed, they have in the past week reached days in which the bad securities have outweighed the good. By day's end, it is suddenly suggested, the entire financial world may collapse because of their activities.

Writer and first-time director J. C. Chandor has done such a remarkable job in these few scenes to set up the entire situation that, despite the terrifying encounters we know must occur throughout the rest of this story, we can now almost sit back and watch, with some comic relief, how this truth plays out as the evidence slowly makes its way up the corporate ladder, where each person of high rank knows less than the one before him. Sullivan calls back his junior partner, Bregman, who confirms his findings. Together the two call in the not very bright street-fighter Emerson, who demands they find the now missing Dale, and takes the information up to his supervisor, Sam Rodgers, Head of Sales and Trading (Kevin Spacey), perhaps the most likeable and conscience-stricken of all this film's characters. Rodgers, has been with the firm nearly longer than anyone except the company's CEO. We first meet him in tears as he suffers the loss of his dog from cancer, and he receives the information with all its due terror, recognizing that, despite whatever decision they make that night, it will change everything for everyone.

Jared Cohen, Head of Capital Markets (Simon Baker), a self-loving body-obsessed individual involved in wheeler-dealer international deals, recognizes the implications without really being able to understand the consequences. Chief of Risk Management Sarah Robertson (Demi Moore) has long recognized the consequences, and has even warned of the implications previously, but has refused to admit the reality of the situation actually taking place. Even the fact that she has warned against it will ultimately be held against her, as she finds herself, in the end, asked to play the company fall-guy. By slowing his film down and restating, each time in slightly different terms, what the problem is, difficult for those not in finance to understand, the director allows us to engage with each of these rather despicable figures. Yes, they are all greedy, and they would kill each other to keep their positions in the firm, but they are also all very human, very much like business-men and -women in every field of endeavor. Even if we do not want to quite admit it, they are visions of people somewhat like us, men and women trying to find and maintain the good life.

The sound of a helicopter announces the arrival of company CEO John Tuld (a reminder, obviously, of Lehman Brothers' head Richard Fuld), brilliantly acted by Jeremy Irons. Tuld knows little of what Sullivan has actually discovered, despite the fact that he has inten-tionally created the very circumstances in which this situation could occur, while denying that he has ever "cheated." His job, he insists, is not to know the details of company actions, but to imagine a future in which the company can continue to survive and financially exist. Although every individual introduced to us has already perceived the only choice with which the com-pany is faced, none of them has the effortless disdain of the human species that Tuld exudes. For him, every-thing can be reduced to an inverted truism, a kind of il-logical maxim that justifies his acts. Even destroying his own customer base by selling them bad products and, in that process, destroying his own company and the lives of thousands throughout the United States and abroad is preferable to losing the lionized position as the man at the top; besides, he knows that no matter how much money is lost, how many lives are destroyed,

the company is—as we later learned in reality—too big to be allowed to completely fail, that, like a phoenix, it will rise again. Besides, he will receive a whopping bonus for just having remained at the helm.

In one of the last scenes of this emotionally tense film, we return to the men and women (shackled a bit like the oarsmen in *Ben Hur* to the chains of a Roman warrior ship), who know they are losing everything, friendship, admiration, self-respect, and their own jobs, by selling out the bad company wares to the very customers who have previously lined their and the company's pockets. How do such individuals return home to look into the faces of their families that night? One can only ask.

The fired Dale is rounded up and told that the company will destroy his benefit package if he does not return to the company to serve as another head to be rolled out to trustees and government inspectors. For a moment, even the long-term denier Sam Rodgers, realizing that he does have a conscience, rushes up to confront Tuld, demanding to be let out. Tuld threatens to withhold all his benefits. What is an individual

to do without the
money to pay for his
new house? By film's
end even the former
rocket scientist, Sul-
livan, offered and ac-
cepting a promotion
in the company, has been corrupted.

This sad film ends with Sam, having returned to
the home in which he once lived and where his ex-wife
continues to reside, digging the yard in the dark. Earlier
he has told a colleague how he began life as an engineer,
building a bridge between two local cities that saved the
citizens of the region thousands of hours of automobile
time in their daily travels. Perhaps, he postulates, he
was meant to be a digger, a man who makes his mark
in the world by creating a deep nothing, a hole. At least
it would be something real, something you can see, he
muses. Into the hole he now digs he will put something,
his beloved dog, perhaps the only living "thing" he has
truly been able to love.

If Chandor's film does not openly offer an alternative, I'd argue it certainly does suggest one. Surely,
none of the money-loving creatures the film presents
truly believes in their object of desire. They, better
than anyone, realize just how meaningless money is as
an actual object: a piece of paper with painted figures

 upon it. It is only a kind of commodity, a symbol of something else that lures them on. Yet one by one, they proclaim—just like the Nazi soldiers and ordinary citizens after World War II—they had no choice but to do what they did. If my metaphor is seemingly exaggerated, I apologize. Yet these people—and all of the others of us—who insist upon choosing the lies and frauds of daily business over honesty and fairness, who swindle our friends in the very process of pretending to provide them with something necessary to their lives, might well proclaim the same thing: we have no choice; it's the way of business. But, of course, we do have choices, if only we are willing to forego, even temporarily, the reward of allegiance to that empty cause.

LOS ANGELES, NOVEMBER 5, 2011
Reprinted from *World Cinema Review* (November 2011).

Voice and Mind

THOMAS FRICK **THE IRON BOYS** (SANTA FE, NEW MEXICO: BURNING BOOKS, 2011)

THOMAS FRICK'S 2011 fiction, *The Iron Boys*, is full of rich characterizations and is densely plotted. By the book's completion, the reader has a strong sense of early 19th-century northern English communities, in which many individuals were involved in the Luddite Movement, destroying machines and mills in strong reaction against the Industrial Revolution. Not only were these individuals angered by the incessant noise of the new mills, run, in Frick's fiction, by George Cogent Meadows Richard Pilfer Withy, but they were disturbed by the economic shift from hand labor to machines, forcing some of them out of jobs and fair payment. The central characters of this book gather on street corners, in pubs, and in each other's homes, or take long walks together, permitting the author to present us with dialogues between all sorts of beings, from radical agitators

The
Iron Boys
Thomas Frick

like Pank, hard-working women such as Rose Stonewarden and Sarah Maldon, and poor, wandering, poverty-stricken children such as Milky, to homosexual intellects like Eddard Weedy, lovers such as Silvy, and brutal drunkards, one of whom—in the most vicious act of the book—kills and eats a puppy. The world Frick paints is nearly Dickensian in its depiction of people of enormous appetites and hard lives.

Yet for all its density of good, old-fashioned storytelling, the brilliance of *The Iron Boys* lies not in its secondary characters or plot, but in its focus on the voice of its narrator, Corbel Penner, an intelligent but uneducated local, who tangentially gets involved in a violent attack on Withy's lace-making mill. And concentrating on Penner, Frick's story, following the free-associations of the character's thinking and his personal language, turns what may at first seem like straightforward realism into a fairly radical and highly poetic text. While Frick gives us a good story that will end, we know from the beginning, in a highly dramatic attack and destruction of the mill, crippling our hero, what really matters in this book is the sound and movement of that figure's voice and mind.

How Frick—who was born and raised in Kentucky and Arkansas, before living in England, Michigan, New York City, Boston, Strasbourg, and, for the past several years, Los Angeles—was so able to create a credible North England dialect for his character is unimaginable. But then perhaps this character's voice, in its open eccentricity, is nothing like what it pretends to be. Who cares, when a fictional figure can speak so wondrously?

> Hangin over that year is the comet. Cant never forget that. It first appear in that cold spring. Biggest comet ever seen Weedy says. That should tell you something. Aint but a smudge in the sky at first. I make nothing of it but I don't see so good. Theys some talk in the square. Misfigewsured lambs an blight in the comin crop. Bad twins. The fortunes a Napoleon. One crystal night seem all close at once. I can see a blood red tail brushed out like feather malt. Wide an tall an just that spiky. Weedy says it were a Frenchman spot it first. Out a their froggy pride they drum up all the virtues a their comet wine.... What we did have that autumn is the fattest sweetest penny lucre melon you ever taste.

If, at first, this language seems a bit too close to a work in dialect, the reader soon comprehends this is a masterly made-up language. And along with the meandering mind of our hero, which determines the various directions the tale takes, the fiction becomes something closer to a long narrative poem. Even though the Burning Books format is small, and the work is only about 260 pages, it took me longer to read, at times, than the momentous novel I was encountering during the same period, *Remembrance of Things Past* by Proust.

Consequently, Frick's central figure, although he may be a kind of everyday man, is transformed into something very extraordinary, beginning the book by being able to comprehend the language of the birds, and ending up with a kind Homeric nobility in his late discovery that the boy from Child Town whom he has so long admired is his own son, the mother his former lover. And like Homer's heroes, throughout Penner sings—such as the song sung about the mentally retarded local, New Billy:

> O New Billy my charm a New Billy
> When shall I see my New Billy again
> When the fishes fly over the fountain
> Then I shall see my New Billy again
> When your fishes fly over the fountain
> Then you shall see your New Billy again.

Penner also has a sense of moral being that far outweighs most of the other figures in his world, growing disgusted with himself and others in the bar where, as the drunk skins and eats a puppy, he and others sit passively watching. The result of that outrage ends in him murdering the drunk soon after, which, obviously, represents his personal fall from grace. If the book begins with his being one with nature, as opposed to the mechanical world created by Withy and other capitalists, his and the Luddites' actions to do not result in any real change, as Withy simple builds a new and grander factory. Having lost the use of his legs, Penner himself is forced to rely on a kind of machine, a cart-like contraption fixed up for him so that he can travel about.

By novel's end, the birds no longer can be comprehended or, as Penner suggests, no longer even sing; however, the human voice of Frick's picaresque has sung such a memorable song that you might be tempted to wander its pages all over again.

LOS ANGELES, JULY 18, 2011
Reprinted from *EXPLORINGfictions* (January 2014).

Learning to Pretend

JEAN-BAPTISTE LÉONETTI (WRITER AND DIREC-
TOR) **CARRÉ BLANC (WHITE SQUARE)** / 2011

LÉONETTI'S first feature film, *Carré blanc*, is a rather
stylish but dramatically empty dystopian view of the
future. This director's future is more pernicious, in
some ways, than was Orwell's or Huxley's in that instead of an all-powerful central government controlling
behavior and thought, here—in what is perhaps a sign
of the times—large corporations are in control. Certainly the government is in collaboration, encouraging,
through large speakers night and day throughout the
city, its populace to produce babies (even girls of 12 are
encouraged to get artificial inseminations) and families
to play what is clearly the popular sport, croquet.

Léonetti shows us only two of these corporations—
perhaps part of the same "white square" industrial com-
bines but different in their roles. The first organization,
for which the mother of the "hero" works, is a meat-

processing plant. But the meat being processed is apparently human flesh, cut up and cured into sandwich meat for an eagerly awaiting public. After all, they have plenty of human corpses available. Large numbers of the population, we soon discover, jump from balconies in despair (many of the high-rises contain nets over areas of the parking lots, where it is suggested cars should not park). Others, we later perceive, are pummeled to death by gangs of executives, or tortured to death by executive evaluators, testing the loyalty and inventiveness of their employees.

Families are encouraged to have children, consequently, because it is a society that is losing much of its population to the violence and heartlessness imbued by the society itself. Who would want to bring a child into this dreadful world, only to see it emotionally and, ultimately, literally "chewed up"?

In the very first scene we observe the young Philippe's (Sami Bouajila) mother climbing a fence to escape the human meat plant wherein she works, her suicide quickly following. The young boy, furious with his mother for her cowardice, is taken into a facility for the numerous parentless children, where they are taught survival skills and how to violently torture one another for their failures. Early on Philippe attempts suicide by hanging himself, and is saved by a young girl, Marie, who later becomes his wife. But the scars

never leave, as he is punished by having to beat to death another child who has mistakenly agreed to get into one of the numerous black body bags. The society, the teacher explains, has no room for someone willing to enter such a space.

Philippe's mother has warned him that he will have to learn "how to pretend" in order to survive, a lesson which, we soon realize, he has learned only too well. For Philippe, we are shown, has grown into an adult who tortures the company's workers. When asked to stand flat against a wall and then back up, employees cannot comprehend what to do, as they dutifully attempt the impossible, obviously failing. Not one of them imagines that they might turn laterally against the wall and back up alongside it. Told to remain in the circle while they are beaten with heavy sticks, not one of them perceives that the cardboard circle might be moved away from the man and the workers intent on the punishment.

Obedience is required, but they seldom challenge the strictures enough that they might be saved. It reminds me of the laboratory experiments with students at the University of Wisconsin—an experiment in which I myself participated—where individuals were told that in another room there were participants trying to learn lessons; one had the choice, when they made mistakes, of electrically shocking them at three levels of power. Many participants chose the highest level of pain, particularly as the experiment continued. Contrarily, I usually chose the lowest so that they might not give up. But none of us asked why we were being told to send shocks to other human beings!

Meanwhile, Marie has left Philippe, in part, because he refuses to have a child and, primarily, because of the role he has taken on for himself, that of being another monster in a world of monsters determined to survive. Yet, Marie cannot entirely abandon him, and returns again and again, haunting his offices, trying to convince him of the errors of his life.

Like others in this society, Philippe is tortured by his own actions, but cannot cease the "pretense" that might allow him to survive.

But this is precisely where Léonetti's script is the

weakest, because we lose contact with the vague and sometimes vapid acts of a man who himself has suffered just such abuses. Of course, any psychologist might tell us that it is often the abused who go on to abuse others; violence begets violence; monsters come from a monstrous society.

The worst monsters of this work appear as roving bands of wannabe office execs, beating and killing a waiter who accidently drops a champagne tray at a party, and attempting to beat and kill Marie simply because she stares at them with a mixture of amazement and disgust. A company parking guard saves the day by threatening the group with a toy gun. And he, in turn, is seen as one of the most tortured beings of all, forced to smile at every company employee while trapped within a box from which he is released for only a few counted seconds, never permitted to actually speak.

Yet as the film moves towards these moral implications, it seems to lose its way, the story elliptically unfolding in time, unnecessarily crisscrossing between the characters' childhoods and their insufferable existence in the present. After Marie takes matters into her own hands, killing one of the murderers by running over him in a car, Philippe begins to awaken from his own self-induced trance. But she too has now become a kind of monster, and Philippe's recognition of his own monstrousness cannot redeem his acts. How will either of them survive in a world of this sort? Both survive suicide, he for the second time (the net has saved them from the fate of Philippe's mother). The legions of violent workers, however, will clearly not cease their hate. If the now wiser couple are even able to survive long enough to produce Marie's wished-for child, can they live to raise it up with an understanding of moral consequence?

Léonetti's film asks some fascinating questions, but makes no attempt to actually deal with them, the director's visions coming alive more in the scenes of torture and abuse than in the potential salvation of his heroes. Perhaps, the director hints, the monsters will destroy their own kind; when asked by the company director to punish the four murderers, Philippe presents them with a bottle of champagne sitting upon on a table. The winner will be the one who can first drink the entire bottle. The four rush forward, furiously and brutally battling with each other, before one crashes the bottle into one man's head. On the table there were also four straws, but none of them could imagine that they might have shared the substance. The other three soon after kill Jean-Luc, the most violent of their group. Yet there is little evidence that they will not soon turn again against the innocent and the weak, destroying those who might re- fuse to pretend.

LOS ANGELES, NOVEMBER 12, 2011
Reprinted from *World Cinema Review* (November 2011).

Casting Out the Self

RICHARD WAGNER **DIE WALKÜRE** / NEW YORK, THE
METROPOLITAN OPERA / THE PERFORMANCE I SAW WAS
THE *LIVE IN HD* BROADCAST ON MAY 14, 2011

ONE OF THE major questions of Wagner's great opera,
Die Walküre, is how it is possible to exile or renounce
oneself, and a great deal of the argumentative and
pleading discussion between Wotan and his warrior
daughter, Brünnhilde, is precisely about this issue. She
claims, rightfully, that in protecting Siegmund she has
only followed the *will* of Wotan, even if it is no longer
his stated command. She is, she argues, only a manifestation of his will, and has no other existence. On his
part, Wotan must suffer the strictures of his own laws,
particularly since he has himself ignored those laws in
search of power and love. Fricka, who insists on his destroying Siegmund in favor of Hunding, may seem unable to comprehend love or even to forgive, but she is
right: Wotan has disobeyed his own rules, and so too

have his offspring, the brother and sister lovers Siegmund and Sieglinde.

In this opera, Wotan painfully loses those whom he loves most, Siegmund and Brünnhilde, in order to obey his own proclamations. Suddenly the omnipotent god must be punished for his own sins. And, in that sense, he is, symbolically speaking, renouncing his own power; by casting out Brünnhilde from Valhalla, he is also assuring his own destruction and, ultimately, the fall of the gods. Brünnhilde, now human, becomes a Christ-like figure who shifts the center of reality from heaven and the underworld to earth itself.

It is for these very reasons, I would argue, that, although there is great music and drama in the other operas of the *Ring* cycle, *Die Walküre* is the most poignant, the easiest of all to hear and love.

Strangely, a similar "outcasting" almost happens with the god of this new Met production, director Robert Lepage, and most of the opera's characters. The final Met *Live in HD* broadcast of the season began 45 minutes late because of computer difficulties with the great, galumphing set of 24 rotating planks at the center of this production.

People patiently waited, both inside the opera house and at my movie theater, yet there was a sense that only grew as the production got underway that the wonderful performers—Deborah Voigt (Brünnhilde),

Eva-Maria Westbroek (Sieglinde), Stephanie Blythe (Fricka), Jonas Kaufmann (Siegmund), Bryn Terfel (Wotan), and Hans-Peter König (Hunding)—were now subject to the machine. Kaufmann was a stunning Siegmund, portraying a character with whom the audience could not help but be sympathetic, as he and the lonely wife of Hunding, Sieglinde, slowly fell in love. The planks, standing vertically to suggest a forest of trees, was quite effective, except that the image projected upon them also was reflected across the faces of the singers (primarily Hunding).

The great ride of the Valkyries was quite terrifying given the see-saw movements of Brünnhilde and her sisters, particularly after we had been told, during another intermission, that in some of the early produc-

tions dresses had been caught in the apparatus. I am afraid that I missed a few of the Valkyrie's cries simply worrying about the actors as they slid one by one down the planks to the floor.

At one stunning moment, as Brünnhilde was left by Wotan on her burning rock, the apparatus rose to the heavens, with a body-double Brünnhilde suspended upside down over the fire. One felt that the machine had finally done something, created a kind of cinematic effect, that would have been otherwise impossible. Yet, for the most part, the expensive contraption (estimated at costing over 40 million dollars), so heavy that the Met needed to reinforce the underpinnings of the stage itself, was more an intrusion than a delight. As some critics have suggested, it seems that the singing, excellent as it is in this production, was sacrificed to the art of staging.

It seems to me, moreover, that the kinds of effects achieved—far tamer than the recent Archim Freyer production in Los Angeles—might have been accomplished with more standard stage devices, light, scrims, etc.

Let us hope that in *Siegfried* and *Götterdämmerung* Lepage will find a way to justify the immense cost of his device without ousting Wagner's singers from the stage!

LOS ANGELES, MAY 27, 2011
Reprinted from *USTheater, Opera, and Performance* (May 2011).

Borders that Can't be Crossed

CHANTAL AKERMAN (WRITER AND DIRECTOR, BASED ON JOSEPH CONRAD'S *ALMAYER'S FOLLY*) **LA FOLIE ALMAYER (ALMAYER'S FOLLY)** / 2011

DIRECTOR CHANTAL AKERMAN takes Joseph Conrad's fiction, *Almayer's Folly*, and transforms it from a tale of colonial angst into a kind of feminist fable about how patriarchal forces conspire to destroy even the women (and, in this case, girls) they love.

Indeed her film of 2011 begins with a murder, as a former servant of Captain Lingard, Chen (Solida Chan), walks slowly into a dive where Daïn, a former small-time smuggler and now a karaoke-like performer (lip-synching the words to the tacky Dean Martin ballad "Sway"), is on stage with his girlfriend/wife Nina. Chen suddenly mounts the stage and kills Daïn. The backup girls swaying along with the lyrics all scatter, except one, who, almost as if drugged out of her mind, continues her pointless maneuvers until someone fi-

nally gets through to her, announcing that Daïn is now dead; she takes up the microphone and quietly and quite impressively sings, *a capella,* Mozart's *Ave Maria.*

We have no idea who she is, or what her relationship to the performer is. But by featuring her so immediately at the start of her film, Akerman makes clear that the remainder of the film will be her story, not that of the title character nor even the singers with whom she was performing.

The woman we first encountered is Nina (Aurora Marion), the daughter of Almayer (Stanislas Merhar) and his Malaysian wife. And in the very next scene we are introduced to her again, this time as a kind of wild child at play in the river with young boys. Soon after, she is called to come home by her mother, Zahira, the maltreated wife of Almayer; and immediately after, mother and child go on the run, trying to escape Almayer and his visiting guest, Captain Lingard (Marc Barbé), who has come to take Nina away to assure her of a proper European education.

In the novel we learn that Lingard is an entrepreneur and explorer who has used Almayer's belief in the existence of secret goldmines to his advantage, even insisting that Almayer marry the Malaysian Zahira until Lingard finds the mines and brings home great riches. Little of this, except for his role as marriage broker, is made clear in Akerman's film, and we are left to speculate upon what the relationship between the stronger Lingard and the weaker Almayer might really be; indeed the film seems to hint at a kind of homosexual kinship, particularly since the two Dutch males share handsome faces and lean bodies, and we quickly perceive that Almayer, in particular, is disgusted by the dark-eyed sensuality of his wife. For him, women are idealized as gentle, broad-faced beings, presumably individuals meant for daily hearing out the woes of their male companions.

At no point does Akerman make clear what is essential in Conrad's work, that Almayer has built his  "lavish" house on the Pantai River because of hearing that the British were soon to conquer the river, and that he intended to welcome them while serving as a lucrative trading post. Locals have come to describe the place as "Almayer's folly." The invasion never occurred, the goldmines were never discovered, and all Almayer now has is his daughter. Now, when he and Lingard track down Nina and Zahira, even she is taken from

him. The loss of her daughter drives Zahira mad.

Yet, as I mentioned earlier, this film is not about them, but about Nina, who as a girl of mixed-blood is tortured by her teachers and schoolmates, and who is reprimanded again and again for her demeanor, even the very way she walks. Although she excels in her studies, any normalcy, certainly any joy she might have, is expunged from her life until Lingard, who pays for her education, dies. Expelled from her school, Nina wanders the streets, taking in a world that she has been previously removed from, even eating the hot native dishes she has been denied. Finding a boat, she returns home, to the delight of both her father and mother. But she remains in a state of near catatonia, hating the man who, like Abraham, dared to sacrifice her on the altar of his European-based gods.

Like a zombie, the teenage girl now wanders the

jungles, encounter-
ing Daïn, who she
promises to meet in
the night. During a
typhoon-like storm,
he nearly drowns, but
she saves him (while
killing a companion who might have reported her to
Almayer), embracing him in a kind of imposed sexual
marriage. By the time Almayer discovers the couple, she
is passively committed to a man that even she knows
can never truly offer her anything she might seek. But
then, as we see in the very first scene of the film, her life
has already been stolen, and she is now little more than
an automaton used by others for their own purposes.

Devastated by the loss of his daughter, and recognizing that she will never find happiness, Almayer can
still not quite comprehend how he has destroyed her
through his belief in European cultural superiority. In
fact, although he cannot recognize it, in Akerman's film
it is he who is the savage.

In a *Cinemascope* review, critic Eva-Lynn Jagoe describes the final scenes quite brilliantly:

> What we witness in Akerman's final, extended shot
> is Almayer's tortured oscillation between opening
> and shutting, knowing and not knowing: we watch

him understand something, deny it, confront it again, shrug it off, not be able to control the spill of tears that has irrevocably exposed it to his consciousness. It is as if he is trying to create his own montage, and cannot make the film cut, jump to another scene. His folly of not knowing, of not opening the door to an understanding of his motivations and his manias, turns, at the moment of recognition, into a madness that condemns him to a harsh and unavoidable downfall. Thus he says, twice, "Tomorrow I would have forgotten my daughter." Not "I will have forgotten" but "I would have..."

What in Conrad's hands was an adventurous love tale—in his version Daïn was a Malayan prince—is in Akerman's imagination a tale of domination, the men, quite literally, sucking the life out of the formerly vibrant young girl, as well as her mother. The colonial world and other such patriarchal systems, Akerman suggests, create borders you cannot cross.

LOS ANGELES, NOVEMBER 5, 2011
Reprinted from *World Cinema Review* (November 2011).

SEVEN CITIES IN DUTCH

Antwerp—Walking

IN JUNE 2010 I was invited, along with publishers from several countries*, to Antwerp to explore Flemish literature and meet with publishers of Flemish writers. I have long enjoyed Flemish writing, and had already published Stijn Streuvels, Maurice Gilliams (on both Sun & Moon and Green Integer), Paul Snoek, and Hugo Claus, and had made commitments to publish Ivo Michelis and Paul van Ostaijen. Yet I had never been to Belgium or even to the more popular Amsterdam!

What I hadn't prepared for was that in the past couple of years I had begun to suffer from serious arthritis, and although I could walk for long

periods, after a few hours my knees gave way and both legs ached from the knees down. Yet the busy schedule the Flemish Literature Fund had  prepared involved, primarily, city walks.

I love walking, and in my younger days I walked European cities for hours at a time. I think I have walked the length and width of Paris several times, and I had just been to Paris to visit Joe Ross, Laura Wilber and their children (for whom I represent a kind of uncle) a few days before I arrived in Antwerp. In Paris I had also done a great deal of walking with the kids, including a long walk through Jardin du Luxembourg (where the children played happily in an enclosed playground), to the Marché Saint Quentin from their apartment on Boulevard de Magenta, and, by myself, a walk from Boulevard de Magenta to the Left Bank for an appointment with publishers at P.O.L, which unintentionally included a walk back. So by the time I reached Antwerp with my huge suitcase I described as being akin to traveling with a fat aunt, my legs were already in pain.

Yet the moment one reaches Antwerp by train, the architecture overwhelms everything else. Barbara Epler, head editor of New Directions, recognized the

 station so wonderfully described in W. B. Sebald's *The Emigrants*. Having not yet read that Sebald book, I, moving up the dark swath of the escalator, was hit in the eyes by the visage of a gold insigniaed and glass wall of stunning beauty as if I'd suddenly arrived in a great cathedral instead of a mere place of passage. And for a few minutes, the aches I had been feeling disappeared.

I quickly taxied to our lovely hotel, a former convent, called Elzenveld. There were the original chapel and sculptures in the courtyard below our windows, one of Gilliam's. I visited a bar across the street where I had good soup and a drink. That evening we were invited to a festive party at the offices of the Flemish Literature Fund. A representative from the Fund arrived at 6:00 to take us, via tram, to the offices, but the affair was primarily a cocktail event, which meant hours of standing. I simply had to sit, taking me somewhat away from the center of the conversation. I would stand for a while and sit again. Stand and sit.

The group decided that it would be preferable to walk back to the hotel, so I trudged along, knowing that I would suffer again the next day. I think it was then that I realized I was the eldest of the group, maybe only 5-6 years older than Asbjørn, but several years older than most of them. My seemingly decrepit condition truly angered me, for a few years before I'd have joyously walked from sunrise to sunset!

The next morning, after an early breakfast with Czech publisher Marek Seckar, there was a walking tour of the city, as we passed by the Grand Place and the Cathedral before arriving at and touring (standing even while the docent lectured) the Heritage Library Hendrik Conscience. The visit lasted longer than expected, so we did not get to see the Carolus Borromeus church on the way to the House of Literature.

The House of Literature (Letterenhuis) is an amazing place, a museum of literature, impossible to imagine in the US. There were books, informative panels of dozens of writers, films, letters, and other material on all the great Flemish authors since the beginning of the breakup of Belgium from the Netherlands in 1830. The tour occasioned a crash history in Flemish politics, literature, and the language, Dutch with some French-sounding words and other colloquial differences. The lecture helped me to better understand the prickly forces which are now threatening to split Belgium apart; and by pointing up the self-consciousness of Flemish writers, it helped to explain why I had been so taken with almost all the authors from Flanders I had read. In part, it is this sense of difference, so potent in an otherwise French-speaking country, that somewhat isolates the Flemish authors from even their Dutch neighbors. And, at the same time, the history of Flanders includes, to varying degrees, some Flemish citizens capitulating to or, at least, *associating with* the Nazis, making for a darker vision, so apparent in Hugo Claus' work.

Our next walk was to the WPG Publishers Group offices, where we had lunch and met with three presses, all of which I had previously dealt with: De Arbeiderspers, De Bezige Bij, and Querido. In my meetings, perhaps the only time we were permitted to sit, I updated them about my projects and discussed missing contractual items.

Following those meetings, we walked to a bar near the bay where Jewish immigrants had once arrived. From there, author Joseph Pearce, having written a book on his Jewish background, took us on a tour across the city to the Jewish quarter, where we entered a bookstore and he read from passages of the memoir-fiction.

Another short walk brought us to a brasserie near

the railroad station, where I ordered steak "bleau," as did Asbjørn, with my pommes frittes. I found the steak so rare that it was difficult to cut.

Finally, we walked the long way back again to Elzenveld, late in the night. I ached all over.

The next morning we walked again, this time at 8:30 in the morning, to the Antwerp Museum of Contemporary Art, where we were lectured to by the boek.be distributors—a truly uninspired event during which, for the first time in my life, I kept nodding off—followed by a roundtable discussion by Flemish critics Tom Van Imschoot, Jos Borré, and Matthijs de Ridder. In the afternoon the Fund had scheduled more publisher meetings with Amstel, Contact, Wereldbibliotheek, De Geus, and Podium. In short, spaces when we were allowed free time between meetings, I walked down to the galleries of the museum, which were displaying a vast array of Flemish contemporary art, some pieces of which appeared like imitations of other European work, other pieces of which were quite fascinating.

After some soup and quiche at Patine's, we were taken to a beautiful house, now rented out for art events, where we heard readings and saw films by writers Rodaan Al Galidi, Paul Bogaert, Rachida Lamrabet, Jeroen Olyslaegers, Koen Peeters, and Paul Verhaeghen, all published by one of the largest Flemish-Dutch publishers, Meulenhoff/Manteau. A lovely dinner fol-

lowed with, once more, a long trek back to Elzenveld

On June 3, we were slated to travel by bus to Brussels, the trip I describe below. But beforehand, we were slated again for a walking tour of Antwerp, this one with the gay author and charming raconteur Tom Lanoye. He took us first to the famed Theo eyeglass shop, sporting some of the most charming and outrageous eye glasses available, popular with celebrities throughout the world. I dared to ask for the prices, whereupon our group got a small sampling of the range of glasses available, from relatively low prices to eyewear that cost thousands of dollars.

We then visited, across the street, Boerentoren (the farmers' tower), the tallest building in Antwerp and first skyscraper on the European continent, from whose glass-walled top we could witness the entire landscape of the city. There Tom talked about his own writing and read us some of his work.

Tom later took us to a fashion designer several blocks away, in the fashion district, for a short visit before we caught our bus to the town of Mechlin and the city of Brussels.

By the end of these three Antwerp days, I had almost lost all feeling in my legs, and my feet were swollen and red. It seemed sad that a walking trip of a city like Antwerp was no longer a possibility for me. I was pleased, however, by what I had witnessed.

It was interesting to me that in the Elsschot novel I read upon my return to the US, the plot consisted mostly of scenes where the characters walked the streets of Antwerp, lost and searching for a woman they had previously met. Yet the easier transportation suggested by the train and its glorious station is the image you take with you as you leave.

---

*The other publishers were Asbjørn Øverås (from Aschehoug in Norway), Giovanna de Angelis (from Fazi in Italy), Seid and Sibila

Serdarvić (from Fraktura in Croatia), Marek Seckar (from Host in the Czech Republic), Christine Popp (from Luchterhand in Germany), Barbara Epler (from New Directions in the US), and Beata Stasińska (from W.A.B. in Poland).

AMSTERDAM, JUNE 5, 2010
LOS ANGELES, JUNE 10, 2010

Cartoon in a Mirror

WILLEM ELSSCHOT **WILL-O'-THE-WISP** IN *THREE NOVELS*, TRANSLATED FROM THE DUTCH BY A. BROTHERTON (LEYDEN, NETHERLANDS: A. W. SIJTHOFF / LONDON: HEINEMANN / NEW YORK: LONDON HOUSE & MAXWELL, 1965)

THE FLEMISH WRITER Willem Elsschot's last fiction, *Het Dwaalicht* (1946, translated into English as *Will-o'-the-Wisp*), is perhaps his best, if shortest, work. The story is so simple that it feels a bit more like a cartoon image than a narrative "plot." Three "blackies," as a grocery-store owner characterizes the three major characters, suddenly appear at her door, and when a customer—Elsschot's Chaplinesque hero, Laarmans, who appears in several of his fictions—exits the store, they approach him for help with directions, thrusting what becomes an almost sacred piece of cardboard into his hand. The card contains the name Maria Van Dam and an address, Kloosterstraat 15.

To elude further relations with the strangers, Laarmans attempts to quickly give them simple directions. But he finds it difficult in English, the only language he and the leader of the three, whom he has secretly named Ali Khan, share. Instead of going left or right, one street snakes into twists and turns, and he attempts to describe the route, accordingly, in grand gestures that only draw a crowd to the small gathering. A local tough attempts to lead them off to a sailor's brothel, but after Laarmans explains where the boy plans to take them, the visitors, sailors from the ship Delhi Castle, insist they want only to see Maria Van Dam, and head off vaguely along the path that Laarmans has provided.

Laarmans moves off to head home to his wife and family (we later discover that he has six children), but while waiting for his tram he encounters them once again; and this time he becomes determined to help them find the right address. Thus begins a voyage as surreal and comically meaningless as any tale by Beckett.

It is apparent from the outset that they will never

find the beautiful young woman whom the three men met that very morning when she visited their ship to mend bags. So taken are the three by this beauty that they award her almost everything they have, a scarf, a pot of ginger, and six packs of cigarettes. She, in turn, reciprocates with her name and address scrawled on the piece of cardboard they carry. But the search, spurred on by the slightly selfish and secretly bigoted kindnesses of Elsschot's Flemish fool, is everything, for the journey tells us much more about these four men than any possible resolution.

Despite the constant paternalism of Laarmans and his inner feelings that the "Indians" can comprehend little that his culture puts before them, it is the Flemish "leader," if you can call him that, who is utterly confused, so desperate in his own married and bourgeois life that he imagines even this tawdry encounter between three men and one woman to be an exciting adventure. It is he, not the three "foreigners," who imagines that the young girl might be underage, fourteen or even younger. Ali and his friends are quite shocked; no, the woman they seek is in her 20s. Laarmans justifies his imaginative slip as part and parcel of his general disdain of his own country's values and religion. He is the kind of small-minded burgher who refuses to see himself as a sexual prude. But the men who follow him are, we later discover, as moral as can be. They, so they later tell him, are not from India, but from Afghanistan, loyal Muslims who are totally immersed in their religion and cultural values, and who later chastise Laarmans for his drinking.

Yet, their very appearance in this world of blonds leads them into danger. The first address they visit sells birdcages, empty cages that lock away not only animals, but, symbolically, the sons and daughters of the Flemish merchants. Laarmans and his Afghani charges cannot help but wonder whether the old woman at the counter and her young brute of a son are hiding Maria in a back room.

The second of their visitations leads directly to the police station, a notorious place of lock-up obviously dangerous to these strangers, aware of the racial restrictions of the culture; they will not even enter. Laarmans takes over, prying information from the fat officer at the front desk. But even though they wait outside this gigantic cage, Ali is captured and brought inside to be charged for a nonexistent crime. Without Laarmans' identification of his friend, he would surely have been incarcerated.

Their final destination is also a kind of prison-like warren of rooms, a dilapidated hotel used partially, it is apparent, as a brothel. Here both customers and clients are locked away in tawdry little rooms where the bartender-owner warns that some of the hotel's registered denizens have been dead for years.

Through this strange night voyage, the three Afghani men behave with the greatest of grace and honor, while the Flemish citizens, even the obsequious Laarmans, dismiss, doubt, and threaten the holy trio on their search for their own Mary. These three strangely wise men do finally find, in the wretched hotel, their mother and child, but when they attempt to award her the flowers they have purchased for Maria, she merely snarls.

As they return to their ship, the exhausted Laarmans heads home, suddenly realizing the brutal irony that the object of their search likely was, after all, to be found in the brothel where the butcher's boy originally had intended to take them. Their dream, this likeable fool now comprehends, is far superior to the utterly and endlessly boring ties that bind him. The cartoon image with which the book seems to begin has been mirrored back onto the society which created it.

ANTWERP, JUNE 2, 2010
Reprinted from *EXPLORINGfictions* (July 2010).

I did not visit Mortsel, a small town not far from the Antwerp airport, on my trip to Northern Belgium. Had I known at the time that it was the birthplace of Ivo Michiels, I might have taken a taxi out to visit it. I have now visited it through the internet, and perceive it as the kind of village Michiels describes in his Alpha Cycle, *published by my Green Integer press. The events that occurred in that village in World War II, which I mention in a footnote to the piece below, make for a particularly poignant commentary on how Flanders (and all of Belgium) was affected during that war. But Antwerp and the surrounding region had been a gathering place of various warring sides for centuries. Last year I saw both* Lohengrin *and* Don Carlo, *operas in which the Antwerp region is presented as the center of battles.*

Mortsel—The Cry

IVO MICHIELS **BOOK ALPHA** AND **ORCHIS MILITARIS, THE ALPHA CYCLE: VOLUMES 1 AND 2** (LOS ANGELES: GREEN INTEGER, 2012)

BORN IN MORTSEL, BELGIUM to a Flemish family, Henri Ceuppens began writing, with the pseudonym

Ivo Michiels, in 1946 with the book of poetry *Begrendse verten*.  His second publication the following year, *Daar tegenover*, was also poetry, but the same year he wrote a novella, *Zo, ga dan*, which began a career of writing fiction, essays, and film. At the age of 88, the author has produced some 39 books, and won major literary awards in Belgium, including the Arkprijs van het Vrije Woord (1958), the Belgische Staatsprijs voor Verhalend Proze (1977), and the Prijs van de Vlaamse Gemeenschap (1993).

In 1963, Michiels wrote the first volume, *Het boek Alfa,* of his *De Alfa-Cyclus*, a series of 4½ books including *Orchis militaris* (1968), *Exit* (1972), *Samuel, o Samuel* (1973, the book he describes as no. 3½), and *Dixi(t)* (1981). Along with his other writings, these books strongly influenced several generations of younger Flemish writers, encouraging them to explore highly experimental forms, and to focus, as Michiels does, on more poetic tropes than fiction usually displays.

During World War II, Michiels served as a nurse in a hospital in Lübeck, Germany, an experience that plays a great part in *The Alpha Cycle*. The entire work is an outcry against violence, while the events of the fictions take us through the war and back through the pre-war-experiences of the narrative voices that reveal that the likely roots of the war existed in the culture previous to the outburst of destruction.*

In the same way that Beckett's writing is often described as a response to World War II, so are Michiels' works determined by the shattering war which tore apart Belgium, not only through the German invasions, but through the various pro-German, pro-Allied battles within various Flemish communities. Like Beckett, Michiels uses numerous poetic devices to tell his stories, most notably repetition, recapitulation, litanies, and antiphons. The time-sense of most of his fictions is indeterminate, as events bring to mind other experiences in the near-present and past, which, in turn, trigger yet other such memories. Readers who need a clear comprehension of who is speaking, and when and where he or she is located, will have a difficult time reading this author. But, in some respects, Michiels' simple and stark language makes for great clarity and power.

Upon the publication of *Orchis Militaris*, Samuel Beckett wrote that, stylistically, it was the best book he had read that year, 1968.

It is difficult to describe Michiels' moving fictions, in part because they are so associative, the reading process itself allowing for the signification. *Book Alpha* begins with three young brothers walking mud-covered roads, trying to reach a friendly farm before nightfall so that they might be handed something to eat. But the roads are so impassable that they find themselves in mud up to their hips, almost too tired to move on, but desperate to make headway before dark. The eldest, who has promised to take care of his brothers, is himself terrified of the trek, but is forced to be brave simply so that he will not frighten the youngest, who is already in tears. The "six-years of seven-years old boy," the second eldest, is so tired that he cannot even cry. Yet they must continue on, *left-right, left-right*, hoping that they do not encounter a dog before they reach a friendly house.

The very walking maneuver, *left-right, left-right*, quickly brings with it other associations, including the soldiers' marching through the city as sirens wail; and the crying of the small boy becomes the crying of everyone in the city:

> In this one moment, this one indivisible long moment, the world shrank, the no-world, the no-longer world, within the small square of his field of vision: then the small crying of the little boy triumphed in the large crying of the street, the city, of the roads toward the city and away from the city, of the roads toward the city and away from the city and to the cities beyond, the small crying in the

crying of the streetcars, still jolting past as always, of the army trucks, honking as they drove into one another, of the baby carriages and handcarts and under the carts the dogs and on the other side of the dogs the rumble of a crumbling wall somewhere, the large crying of the sirens to which no one listened any longer....

From there, Michiels moves us through the narrator's memories through the community, from South Square to Calendar Street, naming the people of the now-destroyed village: from Schram the butcher to Haling and his little girl, from Brand and Vanna and Pacco to, finally, An, a major figure in this book since she represents the beloved of the narrator, a girl who he never bothered to ask for sex.

But there is a long and painful series of memories, experiences, conversations, and terrors before we get to that place in the work, and the small ignominious childhood punishments of the narrator speak volumes about how the seemingly well-meaning and structured society has come unglued.

One of the most moving scenes concerns a boy who is commanded to put his face into a bowl of glue in order to pull up a coin from the bottom—a horrific inversion of the innocent children's game of bobbing for apples that is applauded by the whole community. In the

 same scene a drunken priest is forced to sell his last sacred book of scripture so that he can afford a few more drinks. Even the child, humiliated just a few moments earlier, joins in the horrific laughter of the drunken elders as they mock the suffering priest. One quickly recognizes how humiliation is quickly transformed into a sense of superiority and even hate.

Book Alpha ends with the narrator, now himself a soldier, possibly attempting to abandon his post—and certainly abandoning it through the ruminations of his mind—as he marches through the now nearly abandoned city, seemingly attempting to revisit his old house.

> In the square the marching drone jolted to a halt, a few brief commands were shouted and then the final trumpet call sounded. Then the colors were lowered and soon no guards would be needed any longer, not here. With pounding heart he pushed the key into the lock as he waited patiently for the order to move on he turned around once more to the street and to the sun which stood white and high in the sky like a drum that could not be heard but hurt, hurt the eyes.

 If *Book Alpha* is about pain, about crying out in horror and suffering, *Orchis Militaris* takes us further into a kind of sadomasochistic world beyond even pain, where sex and violence, tenderness and brutality are inextricably intertwined. A group of people sit in total darkness in a train car stopped until the shelling finishes, quietly and breathlessly waiting, pushed together like sardines, some sleeping, some having sex, others simply hunkering down in terror as the sky around them lights up with bombs and searchlights.

In another scene, two soldiers, one German and one Belgian, engage in an absurd conversation wherein they describe the lives and activities of their villages, a kind of set piece that would be almost perfect as a radio performance or even a staged play:

> Do you know, he said, in my town it is market day every Saturday, all the year around. They put stalls up in the square in front of the town hall. The town hall dates from the eighteenth century. Or maybe it's the nineteenth.
>
> Do you know, said the soldier beside him, in my town it is market day every Wednesday, all

the year around. They put stalls up in the square in front of the town hall. The town hall dates from the seventeenth century, or maybe it's the eighteenth century, I'm not sure.

There are also stalls in the narrow streets leading off from the square and at the other end of the little streets there is another square with more stalls. This square is smaller than the one in front of the townhall.

There are also stalls in the narrow streets leading off from the square and at the other end of the little streets there is another square with more stalls. This square is smaller than the one in front of the townhall.

This passage goes on like this for several pages, so long that you begin to see these two men less as different soldiers than as echoes. Yet, when the German later bends to retrieve a cigarette stub, he is mercilessly beaten.

In another scene, a wounded soldier seeks solace with a nurse, whom he bribes into his room with stockings and other gifts. She pretends to comply, but ends by forcing him to repeat after her a litany of curses that shows her detestation for him and his people. In retaliation, he beats her, while perceiving it as the action of another man, not himself.

Over and over again in the moving pages of *Orchis Militaris,* we witness the folly of Marinetti's paean to violence, as person after person crumbles in despair and, once again, unbearable pain. There may be a kind of beauty in Michiels' final description of these horrors, but it is a vision of something almost impossible to bear:

> ...he saw, the bodies red and the pavilions around flooded in red, but already he had become part of the stream of men and women that thronged toward the gate, arms stretched and eyes wide, on his lips always the words—: the child, he cried. Aah, he cried. Help, he cried. Jesus, he cried.

---

*Clearly also important to Michiels' concerns in these books is a horrible event that occurred in Mortsel during World War II. On April 5, 1943, the Minerva car factory in the city, used as a repair place for Luftwaffe planes, was the target of Allied bombing. The target, however, was missed and the bombs hit, instead, a nearby residential area, resulting in the death of 936 citizens, including 209 children. In fact, the city seemed cursed: on March 27, 1945, in one of the last V2 launches, the bomb missed its target, Antwerp, and fell in Mortsel, killing 27 people.

LOS ANGELES, APRIL 22, 2011
Reprinted from *EXPLORINGfictions* (April 2011).

 *On March 29, 2012, my friend Tom Van de Voorde wrote me a letter from the small village of Le Barroux near Avignon, in the south of France. He had been visiting with Ivo Michiels, talking that afternoon, as he reported, with the great author about his former neighbor, René Char, as well as his friend Lucio Fontana, and his readings of Gaddis, Pound, Beckett, etc.*

"I cannot repeat it enough how happy the Green Integer edition and the award [The America Award] has made him. You made him promptly feel 20 years younger!" wrote Tom.

Michiels still had not, however, received any books, but Tom passed on Michiels' email, so that I might respond.

I wrote Michiels immediately, relaying to him how happy I was to have been able to publish the two volumes, and telling him our intention of doing the other volumes of the Alpha Cycle. *I would immediately send him copies if only he could pass along his address.*

For a week or more I heard nothing, until Tom wrote me again on April 4, 2012. Michiels had been in the hospital, and had not been able to write. He suggested that I send an email to Michiels' wife.

Unfortunately, my own health matters made me postpone my response until April 21, when I wrote:

Dear Christiane Faes,

I heard from Tom Van de Voorde how delighted Ivo was with the US publication of the first two volumes of his Alpha Cycle. I wanted to immediately send him copies and wrote him on March 30th, hoping to obtain his address. I have recently heard back from Tom, however, that Ivo was in the hospital. I am very sorry to hear that. How is his health? I hope by this time he is back at home.

My sincere regards,

Douglas Messerli, Publisher
Green Integer

On October 12th of the same year, Michiels died at the age of 89:

Veldonick—The Scream

HUGO CLAUS **DE VERWONDERING** (AMSTERDAM:
DE BEZIGE BIJ, 1962), TRANSLATED FROM THE DUTCH BY
MICHAEL HENRY HEIM AS **WONDER** (BROOKLYN, NEW
YORK: ARCHIPELAGO BOOKS, 2009)

LATE IN 2009 Archipelago publisher Jill Schoolman
sent me a copy of their translation of Hugo Claus' important fiction, *Wonder*. It wasn't until March of 2010
that I could get a chance to begin reading it, and I finished it only in early April.

Like the other fictions and poems by Claus (who
died in 2008), *Wonder* is an extraordinarily powerful and original work. With its numerous shifts in
time and tense—often within the space of a few para-
graphs—and in its uses of dialect and an internal, almost privatized language, *Wonder*, as I confessed to my
friend Michael Heim, the translator of the book, must
have been nearly impossible to translate. "Claus writes
brilliantly," he observed, "and he writes like no other

writer." I might have even gone further and declared Claus' writing as somewhat eccentric, in the positive sense of that word.

Indeed, even the story of this wondrous work is purposely as strange as a story can get. A middle-aged school-teacher, bored with the bourgeois proprieties of his job and the mediocrity of his peers and superiors, is slowly moving toward a mental shutdown. Despite a life of subservience to all and impeccable obedience, he has sex with one of his underage students, and soon after carefully arranges to marry her. But the young girl, predictably, is frustrated with her life with the confused pedant, and leaves him.

On the day in which the fiction begins, the teacher, Victor-Denijs de Rijckel, is asked by the principal to introduce him that evening at a lecture he is giving on "the function of classical music in our society" to

the Association for Flemish Culture Friends of Music. Unpredictably, de Rijckel misses this event, instead wandering, somewhat drunkenly, into the midst of the hundreds of revelers come to town for the annual costumed White Rabbit Ball. There he passively watches and speaks to a beautiful

woman who ends the
evening by walking
into the ocean along
the beach, doing a
kind of dance in the
moonlit waves.

Claus' fiction
moves suddenly into a
future time, where de
Rijckel is evidently locked away in a house recovering
from the mental breakdown by, in part, keeping a daily
journal. But we quickly discover the facts behind this
breakdown as Claus, almost like a magician drawing a
rabbit out of a hat, introduces the teacher to a young
male student who has evidently witnessed de Rijckel's
behavior at the ball, and who tells the teacher that he
knows where the mysterious woman of the night before
lives. Before the reader can even assimilate this strange
encounter, the two are off by train to Veldonck, a small
village where the young woman, Alesandra Harmedam,
lives in a castle.

Neither teacher nor his unusually clever guide
know what they intend to do if they can reencounter
the woman. And as they take stock of the situation,
it appears that the castle, backed by a series of strange
sculptures, is highly fortified; they escape a possible attack with their lives, retreating to a nearby inn, where

the teacher pretends he is the boy's uncle.

On the second day, they take a more conventional approach and are greeted as if they were expected, even toured about the place. Soon we realize that the castle is preparing for a significant gathering of supporters of an obscure Flanders wartime figure, Crabbe, who, siding with the Nazis, fought a kind of individual war based on nationalist beliefs. De Rijckel and the boy are thought to be a doctor and his son from the Netherlands come for the event, and, accordingly, Alesandra readily entertains them. Yet suspicions are clearly aroused by some of de Rijckel's comments, and a former aide to Crabbe, Sprange, who lives at the castle, looms as a fearful skeptic.

The local villagers who visit the bar at the inn each evening are suddenly suspicious of the new guests, particularly since they are now associated with the Harmedams and Sprange; and when it is revealed by the hotelier that they are not father and son, but uncle and nephew, their suspicions turn prurient. The boy is forced to sleep in the hall.

Strangely de Rijckel's sexual instincts seem to have been right; Alesandra is attracted to him and the two clumsily engage in sex. But the teacher's instincts for self-survival diminish as he loses his glasses which blurs his vision. Intellectually, he dangerously toys with the now-gathered fanatics of Crabbe and their ideas. Before long they reveal that they know he is a pretender, threatening him with death. De Rijckel and the boy attempt to escape, with both the figures from the castle and the villagers, angry with him for other reasons, chasing the two down in a cornfield where they are hiding.

The house where he is now incarcerated is apparently where Sprange, after torturing him, has taken de Rijckel, who is so incapacitated by events that he even allows other inmates to piss upon him in the small derelict nook wherein he sleeps.

Claus' story, in short, is so absurd, so illogical, that the reader really does not have a sense of any one truth, much the way the Flanders locals had no coherent picture of the war. Villagers clearly lived out the war supporting any side that seemed momentarily about to win, sometimes even hiding Jews and others from the Nazis less out of principle than financial gain or plain stubbornness. And there is also in Claus' preposterous plot a great deal of humor, just as there is in the dark and dangerous activities of Crabbe, who believes in principles so hard to understand that he is either a mad fanatic or a ridiculous hero.

Like Flanders during the war, de Rijckel ends this fiction so confused that even his escape from his confines is half-hearted, and he is returned to imprisonment, weakly imagining alternatives: "I was thinking of phoning the principal from the telephone booth by the Hazegras Bridge as soon as I went out. I would have told him I was alive and hoped he had cancer or polio. And I might have gone to school afterwards as if nothing happened. Nothing. No boy."

That, so Claus suggests, is just the problem. There is no outrage in the society—for anything or anyone. There is no righteousness, no fury. Things simply happen, and even the strangest of events are unflappably assimilated.

> We in our country of two hundred and ten airplanes and two submarines, we work hard and have a good reputation abroad—ask anyone—because we are flexible in our transactions and give our all. On Saturdays we'll go for a spin in our big American cars (ninety percent of which, my good man, are bought on credit) to the coast, our coast. We study the rim of West Flanders that lies on the sea.... Circumstances, if we are to be believed, are in the hands of others....

Yet this little man who has so willingly engaged the catastrophes that have befallen him, finally does act; ultimately he rises again, if nothing else, to explore his own imprisonment; and in the process and despite possible punishment, de Rijckel lets out a long righteous scream against the perverted Ensor-like landscape surrounding him:

> A gray-haired mother sitting on a terrace opposite the esplanade said to her son, "Did you hear that, darling?"
>
> Her son, though fully grown, was wearing shorts. He was in a wheelchair, and saliva dripped from his lips onto his pink, hairy thighs.
>
> "No, no, no!" he said, swinging his heavy head. She carefully dabbed his lips.

LOS ANGELES, APRIL 17, 2010
Reprinted from *EXPLORINGfictions* (April 2010).

Brussels—Into the Congo

ON THE AFTERNOON of June 3, 2010, the group of publishers with whom I was exploring Flemish literature were taken by bus to the small, but lovely town of Mechlin, where at the bookshop De Zondvloed we were fed wine, cheeses, sliced meats, and good bread. The bookstore was a large, two-storied place with a reading occurring, even as we dined in another part of the building. One cannot imagine such a well-stocked busy bookstore in small-town America, but Mechlin is midway between Antwerp and Brussels, and perhaps can depend on travelers scurrying between the two cities. It was certainly a perfect stop along our route.

After lunch, several authors, including Stefan Brjs, Rachida Lamrabet, Yves Petry, and Annelies Verbeke, spoke about their work, read short passages, and were interviewed (quite incapably, I felt) by the Flemish journalist Elke Vandersypen. She sounded more like a provincial American journalist, without a clue of what a writer is and does.

We left Mechlin around 3:00 p.m. and continued to Brussels, where at the beautiful Grand Place we were given about an hour to simply tour alone or together. I chose the former, and quickly walked through the tourist-filled streets near the great square, indulging in some famed Belgian fries along the way, after clearly disappointing the chef by refusing any of the dozens of sauces provided in which to dip them. I've never liked fries with sauces, but in Belgium it is almost a requirement, and, clearly, etiquette demands it.

After finishing as many of the fries as I could, I sought out a bar, in this case a gay one, to get a drink and wash my hands. Although I personally liked all of the publishers, the fact that we had been compelled to be with each other for so many days, and that I was now completely surrounded by tourists who milled around the streets in large, laterally sliding gangs, made me seek out a place of silence where I might catch up on my daily diary and even possibly write. A gay bar at 3:30 in the afternoon would be as still as a tomb, I thought to myself. And, yes, it was quiet, perfectly delightful with only the bartender who might speak.

When I rejoined the group at a large restaurant nearby for coffee, Brussels waffles, and ice-cream, they asked me where I had been, and I told them. Some were confounded. How did you find a gay bar? "Well," I paused, "it was called L'homo erectus! But I would have sniffed it out even if it had had a less ridiculous moniker. Gays know how to do that by habit." In truth, I hadn't been to a gay bar in decades and probably would never have discovered an appropriate place for such delicious silence in most cities, where gays and straights now drink together in what had formerly been exclusionary places.

Our guest at this high-caloric gala was the author David Van Reybrouck, whose *Congo. Een geschiedenis* (*Congo: A History*) some of us had perused at our publisher meetings a few days before. It was a hefty-looking, beautifully produced tome that had received raves in the Flemish press. David was a quite charming and brilliant man, a philosopher and archeologist by training. He'd gone to the Congo to research this book, living there for a long period of time and befriending an ancient but clearly entertaining man who had lived there as a child under Belgian rule. Van Reybrouck's history, beginning from a time before Stanley's arrival, brought his readers up-to-date with the country's current economic crises.

Van Reybrouck read a chapter, and discussed the book as a whole. But immediately after, I interrupted, "You know, David, this is clearly a marvelously brilliant work, but—and I say this with some hesitation—perhaps with the exception of Ascheoug and Luchterhand—you are trying to sell this book to the wrong people. I would love to publish such a book, but it would be a huge and very expensive undertaking, and we are all primarily literary publishers!"

Barbara Epler, from New Directions, agreed. "I was very honored, in fact, that the book was offered to us, but we are not your kind of publishers, and we could never do it properly. You need some university press, like Chicago or the University of California Press," she concluded.

"Or even a large commercial publisher," I added. "I

don't see why a larger commercial publisher wouldn't want to publish this book. It's looks to be wonderful!"

Both of us and others suggested some publisher names and agents. And he seemed appreciative, if a little taken aback by our inabilities to consider his work.

But the interchange made for a kind of momentarily intense relationship, and I couldn't help but tell him about my childhood experiences writing musicals in my family's basement. "When I was...I must have been 12 or 13...after I'd fallen in love with Broadway musicals, I attempted to write my own musicals in the basement of our house. We had a small piano there, and, although I couldn't really play it, I'd tap out tunes, and sing them and dance. Yes, it had to have been when I was 13 because it was 1960, the year of the Congo's independence from Belgium. I wrote a work entitled *Rain on a Lonely Street*, about a Midwestern family that had gone to the Congo as missionaries (I was big on missionaries as a child), and gotten caught up in the battles of February 1959. The father, a minister, was killed, and the mother and son had a difficult time in leaving Brazzaville, in part because they had no way to travel and also because they were committed to the people with whom they had so long lived. I still remember the major song, sung by the stranded son:

Rain on a lonely, lonely street

Will it never stop, this sleet.
The mud up to our knees, please
God, let it ease.

For me then, it was a great, romantic symphony. I now perceive it as a really ghastly piece. Why rain, and why was he so lonely? Perhaps because of the death of his father. But at the time, in my imagination, it represented a significant intercultural relationship.

Everybody laughed heartily. But Van Reybrouck was astounded. Had some young American Iowa boy really been so moved by the Congo and the events there that he had written of it way back then? "Yes, it seemed startlingly real to me, the news of the revolution and its aftermath. I must have read some place that missionaries had been stranded and murdered."

Soon after came the cakes and waffles and various ice creams and silence as we sat consuming them in delight.

I recently read that David's book has been accepted for publication by Ecco, an imprint of HarperCollins.

Again, we were given a bit of free time before we were to all meet up at the amazing Passa Porta bookshop. On the roof of the shop, we were served an excellent dinner, afterwards moving down into the large store itself. Passa Porta, much like its name, is a hub for international writing, serving not only as a seller of

 books but as a kind of literary center which provides grants, with the support of the Flemish government, to foreign artists to come and stay for periods of time near the bookstore, allowing them time to write and perform. Among the artists have been Richard Powers, Tod Wodicka, Phillippa Yaa de Villiers, and Alan Cherchesov. It is, in short, the kind of bookstore that I would have had for Sun & Moon and my nonprofit Contemporary Arts Educational Project, accomplishing a mix of publishing, bookselling, and direct literary support. However, in the context of US funding, we could never achieve that.

On the evening of our attendance there were readings by four prose writers, Gie Bogaert, Elvis Peeters, Peter Terrin, and the intensely handsome Dimitri Verhoulst, and, also, two poets who I planned to publish in a Flemish poetry anthology I was preparing with help from the Flemish Literature Fund and their poet-expert, Tom Van de Voorde. Both of the poets, Paul Bogaert and Peter Holvoet-Hanssen, were wonderful writers. While Holvoet-Hanssen was involved with a kind a loony narrative work, performing with puppets and objects, Bogaert was a more abstract maker of language, with hilariously funny tropes that were present-

ed with a straight face. After the readings we drank quite late into the night,
and I talked with enormous pleasure,
primarily to the poets.

We reached Antwerp long after
midnight, all seeking out the rather
lowlife bar across the street from our
hotel. After only two beers it became
apparent that my now dear friend Barbara Epler was getting quite tipsy, and I
offered to accompany her back to the hotel, the two of
us staggering across the street and through the lobby.
The clock in my room read 2:30 a.m.!

LOS ANGELES, MARCH 25, 2011
Reprinted from *Green Integer Blog* (March 2011).

It took three years to finally receive the book on Congo by David Van Reybrouck in English, and several weeks, thereafter, to read it. I was astounded by its quality and breadth of coverage. Finally, in October 2014, I was able to write the review printed below.

The Dead are Not in the Ground

DAVID VAN REYBROUCK **CONGO: THE EPIC HISTORY OF A PEOPLE**, TRANSLATED FROM THE DUTCH BY SAM GARRETT (NEW YORK: ECCO, 2010, TRANSLATION 2014)

IT WASN'T UNTIL page 500 of David Van Reybrouck's astonishingly moving *Congo: The Epic History of a People* that I finally broke down in tears. Not that there weren't dozens of emotional passages previously in this very personal book, but after having traveled through pages and pages that recounted the lies and violence the Congo natives had suffered from nearly every major country (and many minor ones) as well as from their own kind; after years of having suffered internal wars, sometimes more related to the tribal battles of the Hutus and Tutsis of nearby Rwanda, Burundi and

Uganda than to issues directly linked with their fellow countrymen; after finally having been able to free themselves from the madness of the longtime despot Mobutu Sese Seko Koko Ngbendu Wa Za Banga; and, finally, for only the second time in the more than a century-old history recounted in the pages in this book, having obtained the opportunity to vote, the fact that their major choices were the mostly brutal former rebels Joseph Kabila, Jean-Pierre Bemba (whose soldiers had practiced cannibalism in rebel attacks), Azarias Ruberwa, Antoine Gizenga (who had once served as deputy prime minister under Patrice Lumumba), and even Mobutu's son, Nzanga Mobutu, overwhelmed me. Despite those seemingly abysmal choices, however, nearly everyone who could in that far-flung country—larger at 900,000 square miles than any European country except Russia, and the 11th largest country in the world—came together in the hundreds of outlying polling places to vote without incident. In isolated jungle areas, Van Reybrouck reports, the votes were counted by "candlelight in a hut, [the poll-keepers] having eaten nothing all day." When the lights failed, the fatigued men and women counters fell asleep, "their arms around a sealed ballot box, as though it were a shrine or a child," to protect the ballots. Even the author seemed astounded by the facts!

The choice, ultimately, was Kabila—in part because he bought the votes of the Gizenga and Mobutu parties by promising the candidates important government posts—despite the fact that the capital city of Kinahasa had voted for Bemba. The important thing, in hindsight, seems to have been less a matter of who was chosen than the fact that the elections occurred with basic calm and lack of fraud. "Were things really going to change?" the author himself asks. How could they, we perceive, in a country in which its citizens were never given a chance to learn about let alone experience any truly democratic government. For more than a century generations of intelligent Congolese had been isolated, imprisoned, enslaved, maimed, tortured, and killed, always in the name of others' definitions of progress, of others' determination of what was best for the people. Even, in those brief moments, when the citizens of this vast land were tolerated, cared for, educated, nursed, and healed, the values imbued were always imported from somewhere else.*

Van Reybrouck quotes the cleric-activist Abbé José Mpundu in connection with his question about hope: "From 1990 to 1995 I fought for elections that would

not be like the charade we got this time. It was a parody, orchestrated by the international politico-financial
Mafia! I wanted to vote for Tshisekedi, but he had rel-
egated himself to the sidelines, so I just voted for Bemba. They let us play a bit part. It was one big, worth-
less Mafia gambit. For a lot of money, the international
community bought itself the president it preferred; we
would have been better off passing the hat around to finance the elections and building our own ballot boxes.
At least then they would have been our own" (p. 503).

Even if Kabila had been a brilliant leader, a financial wizard, and a liberal political voice—none of which
he was—he would have found it nearly impossible to
live up to the dreams of his fellow countrymen or even
his own dreams for his country which he parroted in
his acceptance speech: "There will be punctuality, and

discipline. I will take up matters again with determination and regain 100 percent control of the situation." Without a real military, without a stable and educated community to man governmental positions, and, most importantly, without any money—in debt, in fact, for billions of dollars from loans siphoned off into Mobutu's own pockets and which the IMF (International Monetary Fund) still refused to forgive—how could even the most enlightened of leaders have been able to give its people the things they had been shown by the formerly ruling white leaders who had for so long refused them? Just as Joseph Kasavubu had turned to Belgium, as Lumumba had reached out to the United Nations and, when that failed, to the Soviet Union, as Mobutu had turned to the United States, so Kabila reached out to China for help. And like all of the leaders before him, he once again sold out, many argue, the rich resources of the African nation—its ivory, coffee and other foodstuffs, palm oil, copper, diamonds, coal, uranium, and coltan—for practically nothing in return: a few promised highways, a railroad, a few new buildings. It's enough to make even a cold cynic cry.

If history alone reveals the full picture of the epic battles that time and again the Congolese citizens lost—and Van Reybrouck's *Congo* details this history with an almost encyclopedic thrust (as his 22-page small-print listings of source materials and another 22 pages of references representing a virtual library of Congo materials reveal)—the author gives us something that no other work about the Con-go, to my knowledge, has done, a feat perhaps impossible to repeat. Van Reybrouck tells his story not only from the eyes of a sympathetic ex-conqueror (he is, after all, a Belgian himself, his own father having been one of the ruling class who helped to create the original railroad lines), but through numerous astute and intelligent voices of the Congo citizens and storytellers. The voices range from the earliest days of King Leopold's mad creation (the King not only haphazardly created the borders of the country, but was originally the sole owner and emperor) to the book's last reports of young Congolese entrepreneurial efforts in China, taken from dozens and dozens of interviews with the individuals directly involved with these historical events. Leave it to Van Reybrouck not only to seek out a person whose own history begins with the Belgian involvement in redefining the area now called the Democratic Republic of Congo, but to actually *discover* such a being in the figure of Étienne Nkiasi, born sometime around 1882, three years before Leopold created the country we now call Congo, Étienne lived until the book was finally published in 2010 to the age of 128—and this in a country where the life-expectancy is currently a little less than 56 years of age. The tales this elder relates make the history of the early Congo come eerily alive—including his first encounter with the early missionaries, among them the American Baptist active from 1893 on, Mister Ben (Alexander L. Bain), and, perhaps, British-American Methodist Bishop William Taylor. And Étienne personally knew Simon Kimbangu, the founder of one of the largest African religions, Kimbanguism. He also knew authors such as Disai Makulo, who, after being captured and taken prisoner by slave traders, actually met up with Henry Morton Stanley and joined his entourage before being left with Stanley's friend Anthony Swinburne in the new station Stanley had created in Kinshasa, where the boy learned how to read and write.

But Van Reybrouck does not merely employ the memories and texts of these ancient figures living and dead, he goes on to interview hundreds of others, including politicians, musicians, both male and female aid workers, religious figures and spiritualists, students, soccer players, boy soldiers, and even local terrorists. These stories create a skein of incidents that lend his work a startling sense of coincidence that, in turn, helps the reader to feel as if he or she were really living at the heart of this vast and somewhat mysterious world—convincing us that "the dead are not in the ground," as Nkaisi's son quotes Senegalese poet Birago Diop.

By book's end, in fact, if we still feel in awe of the enormous diversity, we also come away with an intense sense of knowledge, as we gradually discover that despite Belgium being overrun in World War I, for example, the *Force Publique*, the black internal police force of Congo, suddenly having been transformed into soldiers, won the War in Africa, conquering even German-held territories such as Rwanda and Burandi. In World War II, Congo troops, trained in Liberia and Ghana, helped as soldiers and doctors to liberate Eritrea and Ethiopia, and worked in makeshift hospitals as far away as India and Burma.

Amazing facts begin to pile up. Without Congo uranium, the US would not have been able to drop the atomic bomb on Japan: fearing capture of their mines, Belgian mine owners had dug up their uranium deposits and shipped them, unknown to American authorities, to a warehouse in Brooklyn, so that when the Americans began the Manhattan Project they suddenly discovered what they most needed at their own back door. A large part of the Cold War was fought between the US and the Soviet Union over the politics and geologically created products of Congo.

How many of us recall that United Nations head

Dag Hammarskjöld died in a plane crash on his way to meet with Moïse Tshombe in an attempt to settle the violence in Congo? Sports fans surely remember the historic boxing battle between Muhammad Ali and George Foreman, the "rumble in the jungle," played out in the grand stadium in Kinshasa; Van Reybrouck interviews a Congo news photographer, Zizi Kabongo, to get a new perspective on that memorable event.

Just this past Sunday (October 7, 2014), *The New York Times' Science Times* reminded us that the dread Ebola virus was first uncovered by Dr. Peter Piot, a Belgian virologist, in Zaire (Mobutu's self-declared moniker for the country he ruled).

Who could have known that the strange black metallic ore named coltan (from which niobium and tantalum are extracted), plentiful in Congo, would be necessary to produce electronic products such as cell phones and computer chips? If to Americans the history of Congo seems somewhat shadowy, gradually we discover how interlinked the country has been with our own and world history.

As I was reading the last chapter of this intense literary work, I suddenly overhead an advertisement in the middle of my morning CNN report, prodding Americans to invest in Congo, a country, so the pitchman declared, with a large rising middle class, a land of the future; the map of Congo which I had been

 surveying every night during my readings was suddenly cast as an image upon my television set with an inset of a beautiful new apartment complex. I was startled by this coincidence (or was it a coincidence, even if it was the first time I had ever heard this ad, and I've not heard it since?). I doubt whether things have changed that radically in the four years since Van Reybrouck completed his book, but who knows, perhaps the Chinese have come through with some of their promised commitments to the long-abused country by building some colorful new housing units.

Van Reybrouck has convinced me that, although by mid-century Kinshasa will be a city larger than New York and Los Angeles combined, it is not a beautiful place; that despite the shining skyscrapers just across the river in Congo-Brazzaville, Kinshasa is without color; a land, as the author puts it, in a world of "dream and shadow." For me that ad simply stood out as yet another pitch, like the thousands of previous worldwide attempts, to suck up the resources of this vitally alive world still in the dark about its own future.

Congo, it turns out, *is* a kind of "heart of darkness," an excitingly beating world in which its inhabitants are still struggling just for the necessities, let alone the riches they so palpably desire. It says something about Van Reybrouck's study that he mentions Conrad's great novel only once, and the author just another time in passing. You don't need fiction to show just how dark that great nation's history has truly been.

Yet, somehow, despite it all, the citizens of this hurt land keep singing and dancing, reaching out to another, laughing and endlessly talking, dreaming and imagining—hoping somehow that the land they inhabit might one day reward them for their enduring attachments to it. That *Congo*'s author can convey all this reveals he is not just a historian but a significant ethnographer who deeply cares about the people whose history he is narrating.

------

*For just one example, the author points to the moment when the Belgian country took over the vast territory from their King, Leopold. Well intentioned, Belgium immediately imposed a travel ban on isolated Congo natives in order to prevent the spread of numerous diseases, while simultaneously studying the native traditions (which the Bureau International d'Ethnographie published in compendious volumes) and teaching those values back to children attending the French Catholic schools. The result was that the Belgians helped solidify tribal differences and hegemonic values that, in reality, had never completely existed in pre-European days. Often dependent on commerce and trade for various different elements of their diets and daily survival, the Congo tribes had for centuries before been highly interlinked and intermixed. The results of such proselytizing ultimately revealed themselves in some of the horrific tribal battles (including those of Rwanda, which fell into Belgian hands indirectly after World War I) of the later 20th century.

LOS ANGELES, OCTOBER 7, 2014
Reprinted from *Rain Taxi* IXX (Winter 2014).

Ghent—Boating

I HAD PLANNED to spend my final day in Flanders in Antwerp, touring the city by myself, and finding a good restaurant for the evening. But when Tom van de Voorde invited me to his home, I really could not turn that offer down to see Ghent and, in particular, the Ghent Altarpiece in the Cathedral there.

I left the city early in the morning, again walking, this time back to the train station. But at least I didn't have my large "auntie" suitcase with me. I felt relatively lightweight and was prepared to enjoy the day.

Once in Ghent, I thought that I might be able to walk to Tom's house, but after asking a couple of people for directions, I realized it was quite a distance, and took the streetcar instead.

Fortunately, once I was told which car to take and at what stop to exit, the trip was an easy one, and I found Tom in his beautiful apartment which faced one of Ghent's many canals.

Tom served coffee and showed me his quite extensive poetry collection before we set off, stopping by a pleasant restaurant near the main center of Ghent where I had a salad and wolfish, also known as Seawolf.

Tom suggested that we take a boat trip around the center-city canals, and I, loving all sorts of water travel, didn't dare to tell him that such a trip in the hot sun would turn me bright red.

The tour, led by a friend of his and his wife's, was a beautiful one, and I thoroughly enjoyed it, however my face, arms, and other exposed body parts were all in a blush. Sites along the way included the old castle, the only wooden house in a city of brick and stone buildings, and views of the absolutely beautiful guild halls. There's something incomparable to slowly gliding along beside the streets, observing the city *en route*.

Next stop was the cathedral, where Tom told me a kind of horrifying story, funny nonetheless. Much of the beautiful white marble work, including the sculpture and tomb of Bishop Triest inside St. Bavo's Cathedral (Sint-Baafskathedraal), was created by the then-renowned Belgian artist Jérôme Duquesnoy (the younger). Throughout the period of installing his sculptures, he commanded that they be kept from public view by large hanging canvases and arras. One day, however, a guard dared to peek into the area where the artist was working, only to discover Duquesnoy sodomizing a young boy, his model and assistant. The city elders where outraged, and he was soon after tried, set upon a pyre, and burned to death in the large square outside the building.

The sculpture was lovely, as was the great Peter Paul Rubens painting "Saint Bavo Entering the Monastery." But when we attempted to see the better known *The Adoration of the Mystic Lamb* by Hubert and Jan van Eyck, we found only one small section of it on view; it was evidently being treated for conservation. Outside the cathedral, in the square, was a group sing-

ing English chanteys, attempting to stir up interest for the Ghent Opera's new production of Benjamin Britten's *Billy Budd*.

By this time I was

 quite exhausted, but Tom suggested we visit the nearby Flanders Poet's House, a wonderful library containing every book of poetry published in Flanders in Dutch and in translations. Not even the well-run Poet's House in New York can match the professionalism and complexity of this collection. I was enthralled and loved meeting the founder and the collection's curator.

I was nearly crawling by this time, so painfully did my legs hurt. I cursed my arthritic limbs, but I had enjoyed the entire day nonetheless. I took the train back to Antwerp, slowly transporting myself by foot, stopping along the way for a drink, to my hotel, collapsing into bed for a brief nap. I did venture out to De Markt, a nearby restaurant, later, where I inexplicably had a hankering for Italian food, and ordered up spaghetti.

LOS ANGELES, APRIL 27, 2011
Reprinted from *Green Integer Blog* (April 2011).

Bruges—Killing Time

MARTIN MCDONAGH (WRITER AND DIRECTOR) **IN BRUGES** / 2008

MARTIN MCDONAGH's 2008 film, *In Bruges*, is a movie that tries so hard to be likeable that it seems almost mean-spirited to say anything else. By combining a witty and tough dialogue, dangerously petty criminals who are tender at heart, and a story that walks a tightrope between a bloodbath and a tale of impossible love, the film pleads for its audience to find some kind of center to ground it.

It was hard for me, however, to believe in anything McDonagh had cooked up except for the beautiful streets and churches of Bruges where his preposterous plot takes place. The director's characters, no matter how many "fucks" they spew and no matter how insensitive they are to human life, seem more like Damon Runyon figures than the London murderers they are supposed to represent.

Ray (Colin Farrell) and Ken (Brendan Gleeson) have just blundered in a hit, intentionally killing a priest their boss, Harry Waters (Ralph Fiennes), has ordered dead, but also unintentionally killing a small child as the bullet passed through the priest's body. Together this unlikely duo are sent out of town to the Flemish city of Bruges until things cool down.

Ken, who has apparently been in the business for some years, is a slightly sophisticated and curious gay man who is delighted to get the opportunity to see the beautiful "Venice of the North," while Ray, who is the one who accidentally killed the boy, is a coarse and most definitely heterosexual, undereducated Dubliner who has no patience for touring and even less time for Bruges:

> There's a Christmas tree somewhere in London with a bunch of presents underneath it that'll never be opened. And I thought, if I survive all this, I'd go to that house, apologize to the mother there, and accept whatever punishment she chose for me. Prison...death...don't matter. Because at least in

prison and at least in death, you know, I wouldn't be in fuckin' Bruges. But then, like a flash, it came to me. And I realized, fuck man, maybe that's what hell is: the entire rest of eternity spent in fuckin' Bruges. And I really really hoped I wouldn't die. I really really hoped I wouldn't die.

Holed up in one room with Ken, Ray is a time bomb ready to explode, and he does fizzle, at least, several times, punching out a Canadian couple who complain about his and his lady companion's cigarettes, and, later, shooting out the eye of his girlfriend's cohort-in-crime (she picks up men after which he shows up to rob them). There are a lot of absurd subplots, one about a movie being shot throughout the city with a dwarf as the lead (Jordan Prentice); apparently Ray is fascinated by what he calls "midgets".

The important thing, however, is that a strange rapport develops between the two criminals, Ken and Ray, as they take in the city sights. Despite his tough-guy demeanor, Ray is truly haunted by his act, which Ken tries to ameliorate without success.

By the time Ken hears from Harry that he must kill Ray, he discovers Ray holding a gun to his own head, about to commit suicide. Ken saves Ray's life and sends him off by train to any other European town so that Ray can start over again, while Ken is left to face the

consequences.

The consequences, while at first cloaked in a sort of gentlemanly regard between Harry and Ken, quickly turn murderous, as Harry shoots out Ken's knees and, discovering that Ray has been returned to Bruges by the police for the incident with the Canadian couple, runs from the tower into the square intending to kill Ray himself. To warn Ray, Harry jumps from the tower, sacrificing his own life for that of his friend, who has become almost a son.

For a brief time, the film switches to an action-adventure tale, as Harry chases Ray down the narrow, cobblestone, Bruges streets. Returning to his hotel, Ray collects his gun and jumps from the window into a moving canal boat below, Harry on the chase. Harry's final shot goes through Ray's body, hitting and killing the dwarf, which Harry believes is a child. A man of deep conviction if not of moral values, Harry turns the gun upon himself.

We end the film not knowing whether or not Ray has survived, but his voice pleading for his life seems to suggest that he lived through the ordeal. The question is, which Ray? The murderous, crazy one? The boyishly good man at heart? The slightly clever con man? The drunken and drugged-out lunatic?

The problem with nearly every figure in this film is that they have no center—as well as no place in which to exist. Ray's disdain of Bruges—as beautiful as the city obviously is—seems justified. Why is this film called "In Bruges"?  You can almost hear McDonagh say, as might Harry, "'Cause I'd like to fuckin' go there; it's a kind of fantasyland."

But so too is his film a kind of garish fantasy world where no real human being dare show up. All are types, figures shifting in and out of various situations and set pieces, drifting always between the humorous and the downright ugly. Who could ever believe characters who converse as follows?

> RAY: What am I gonna do, Ken? What am I gonna do?
> KEN: Just keep movin', keep movin'. Try not think about it. Learn a new language, maybe?
> RAY: Sure. I can hardly do English. [*Pause*] That's one thing I like about Europe, though. You don't have to learn any of their languages.

From a sort of conscience-ridden, even if sentimental pondering, we quickly jump to the kind of advice one might receive on a cozy talk show, then on to a self-aware joke that seems incompatible with Ray's previous behavior, straight to the beat (1-2-3) before the punch line, a stale joke about the loss of European countries' identities, all in a few short sentences and interjections! McDonagh seems unable to keep any one character in his mind for more than a few lines, so that ultimately we lose all possibility of belief in anything but the writer's whims.

Next time I go to Bruges, it will be alone!

LOS ANGELES, APRIL 28, 2011
Reprinted from *World Cinema Review* (April 2011).

Amsterdam—Bicyling

WITH ITS OFTEN overcast sky, its tall houses reflecting into the canals, and with streets dedicated more to bicycles than either cars or pedestrians, Amsterdam is a nearly impossible city to experience. There seems to be no way, literally, "to see it."

When I checked into my hotel, the Eden—comfortably located in the midst of nearly everything—my room was not ready, so, tired as I was from the travel, I determined to take a look at the renowned red light district nearby. But hardly had I gotten out of the hotel door when a bicycle crashed into me, throwing both me and the rider onto the concrete. "Watch where you're going!" he shouted out in English.

"Are you okay?" I asked, checking my own pained limbs simultaneously. He stood, shook himself off, and sped away.

I had not noticed that what I thought was a walkway for human beings was the lane for masses of speeding bikes. At some points in the narrow streets, it was

safer to duel with the car than with the revered two-wheeler.

The red light district, so I discovered, no longer exists—except for heterosexual men desperate for a quickie. I should have realized that there is no longer any need for printed pornography since the computer stores images and even whole movies so conveniently. The entire area is on the remake, slowly gussying itself up as a tourist destination, with only some isolated back lanes of glass-covered booths wherein dreadful-looking prostitutes await, pounding the glass as any man passes. Busloads of tourists were told that "here you can get whatever you seek," but I no longer believed them. There were only a few gay stores left, and some of them were now sleek boutiques filled with Sadomasochistic costumes and machines for which I could not even imagine a use.

I visited a couple of lovely bookstores and returned to my hotel, which was certainly not elegant, but comfortable enough, even if I had to sit at the lobby-located bar to use my laptop. But then, I like to write and drink.

For dinner, I asked the concierge to suggest an old-fashioned Dutch restaurant that might serve fish, since

I was in the mood for it, and could only imagine that with all the water hereabouts, fish would be as bountiful as in Scandinavia. He suggested  Sluizer on Utrectsestratt, perfect for my taste!

I saw wonderful platters of fish being served, but inexplicably ordered Weinerschnitzel with *pommes frites*. What I hadn't expected, but quickly perceived, was that nearly any food in both the Netherlands and Belgium would be accompanied by mayonnaise and other sauces. I chose not to participate in the national passion for cholesterol.

The next day, I would be leaving by an afternoon train to Paris. After an early continental breakfast, I hiked about the neighborhood in search of another room, since I'd been told that, when I planned to return to Amsterdam for a few days after my travels in France and Belgium, the hotel would be booked up. Several other hotels looked suitable enough and were accommodatingly priced, but they also had no rooms available. Finally, I spotted a small hotel facing the same canal, opposite the Eden. The man behind the counter, who seemed also to own the small establishment, appeared to be gay, and rooms were available, so I booked.

Returning more than a week later, I was asked by the same gentleman if instead of a room I might like to stay in a nearby apartment that the hotel owned, or even on the houseboat docked in the canal in front. I was tempted by the latter just for the oddity of it, but the weather looked chancy, and a bobbing, rain-splattered night appeared in store, so I chose the apartment. It was not elegantly decorated, but certainly had a sense of student-like flair, with furniture, it appeared, like the kind you find at Ikea. A rather large living room faced the kitchen and dining room, with a commodious bedroom with large double and single beds behind sliding doors. It was perfect, I realized, since I was too tired to walk endlessly about the city in search of something to do. Most of the museums, I was told, were being restored, and had closed down large numbers of their galleries. Amsterdam still seemed bleak and difficult to get an image of.

I walked to the flower market, I marched through Rembrandt Square, I wandered to the opera house nearby, dropped into pubs, and met for lunch with Tom Möhlmann from the Dutch Translation offices, along with the vivacious Diane Butterman, who was translating the complete poems of Lucebert for us. At that pleasant lunch, on the top of a department store, I could, for the first time, actually glimpse  a vista of the city. Perhaps I should have visited several churches, seeking out their bell towers. But I was happy at the large, circular table the hotel had provided for the apartment, upon which I had placed my laptop.

I wrote several pieces and, in pausing, stared down from the flower-laden balcony at the mobs of soccer fans below, totally pleased with myself.

Bicycles spun down the streets with an abandon I no longer had to dodge.

One evening I ate what amounted to a feast at a nearby Indonesian restaurant, a delicious meal. I returned to Sluizer, this time to eat the previously proffered fish. At Flo Brasserie the next night, I dined upon an overly rich meal of French oysters followed by veal medallions smothered in a sauce of mushrooms and sweetbreads with mashed potatoes patterned into small, dumpling-like mounds. An economics professor and his psychologist wife conversed with me from the next booth over. Hearing I was a poet, he informed me that one of his colleagues uses Robert Frost's "The

Road Not Taken" as the perfect metaphor for economic theory. I laughed, thinking to myself, "Oh, those clever Dutch. They've found the perfect role for Frost!"

The next morning a taxi appeared, the driver helping me carry the big suitcase I'd come to call my "maiden aunt" down the stairs, maneuvering it into the trunk, then whisking me away to Schipol Airport where I was charged $100 for the burdensome aunt.

AMSTERDAM, JUNE 8, 2010
Reprinted from *Green Integer Blog* (June 2010).

Men in the Streets

BERNARD-MARIE KOLTÈS (ORIGINAL TEXT),
RADOSŁAW RYCHCIK (DIRECTOR) **IN THE SOLITUDE OF
COTTON FIELDS** / PERFORMED BY THE STEFAN ZEROM-
SKI THEATRE IN POLISH WITH ENGLISH SUBTITLES,
WITH MUSIC BY THE NATURAL BORN CHILLERS / THE
PERFORMANCE I SAW WAS ON SEPTEMBER 24, 2010 AT
REDCAT (ROY AND EDNA DISNEY/CALARTS THEATER) IN
THE WALT DISNEY CONCERT HALL, LOS ANGELES

BASED ON THE 1986 play *Dans la Solitude des Champs
de Coton* by French author Bernard-Marie Koltès, who
died of AIDS in 1989, *In the Solitude of Cotton Fields*
is an angst-ridden play about gay love and sex. The two
performers of this Polish production, Wojciech Niemczyk and Tomasz Nosinski, backed up by the neo-punk
techno band, Natural Born Chillers, begin the action
with a mesmerizing dance performance. Dressed in ret-
ro 1960s black suits, thin ties, and white shirts, the two
stunningly gyrate to the music, Niemczyk moving in

186

all-out abandonment, while Nosinski—already suggesting the character we soon encounter—dances in a series of more restrained, nervous twitches that suggests  an internalized psychological condition that won't permit him to "let loose." Both men are absolutely beautiful, completely aware of their lithe bodies and their youthful good looks. When they meet on the street after the dance, a gaze between the two sends them into a sexual interchange negotiated with an intense dialogue, as they play out the roles they describe as dealer and client.

Niemczyk is self-assured and insistent that he—a figure that haunts the dark world of the nighttime beasts—is a man who can discern what anyone is seeking and deliver. While Nosinski, covering any lust he may have with hauteur, claims he is a man of the light, never seeking out the dark; he, so he says, walks "straight," moving with the society as opposed to against it. The insistence of the one that sex is the territory of the hunted and haunted, and the other's apparent fear of involvement are the substance of the poetically-filled dialogues in which they engage, cautiously moving

toward each other as they verbally struggle, a psychodrama, in part, about sexual self-acceptance.

Of course, one might immediately (as do I) wonder why a normal sexual encounter of two gays on the street should result in these strange metaphors of Marxist politics, underlined by Sadeian issues of pain and pleasure. Koltès clearly saw sex as a battle between opposing forces and lived with a far greater sense of being an outsider than I, who joyfully encountered dozens of young men in my youth in just the manner these two do.

To be fair, however, it is not just sex that the author and characters explore, but the whole issue of what *through* sex they are seeking, the desire that Niemczyk claims he can fulfill and Nosinski is so ready to deny. The sensuality of both their positions is what makes this work so fascinating—and frustrating—as Niemczyk waits for the first drool of the mouth before pouncing and Nosinski struggles to bottle his sexual excitement and terror within his body. And what is marvelous despite Koltès' slightly empty and rather abstract thematic are the brilliant performances these two actors give. Unlike the American acting tradition where the body is made to parallel "natural action," the performances here propel mouths, faces, eyes, lips, hips, legs, and feet into constant motion, often revealing in their movements what words cannot express. One of the most explosive moments in the work occurs when, having painted his lips bright red, Niemczyk falls into a wailing scream that serves as a kind of siren song, a plea for love that no one can ignore, a music far more compelling than a written score.

Nosinski's thin frame seems controlled by wires more than nerves and blood vessels. The fear and horror he expresses in his every move explain, in part,  his absolute subservience to the more openly sexual being. At the moment when we feel he cannot survive without release, he slowly strips away his coat, shirt, pants, socks, shoes, and underwear to stand passively naked before his dealer.

Redressing, the men stand apart while a video collage of famous and unknown sexual encounters from movies, advertisements, and other sources is shown. I found this, mostly pictures of over-the-top sexuality, the least satisfying moment of the work. But when it

ends with both men's lips smeared in red, the three quick moments of their coming together are almost electric, a different kind of dance that reminded me, in part, of Robert Longo's homoerotic friezes of his 1981 performance piece, *Empire* (see *My Year 2005*); certainly the characters themselves also recalled Longo's male figures of *Men in the Cities*. I don't know how these actors were dressed in Koltès original play, but it would not surprise me if Longo, who himself was influenced by filmmakers such as Fassbinder, had been a source.

As the two men finally consummate their sexual act, it is still unclear whether or not they have fulfilled their desires. But for at least a few moments they have released the tensions between them, turning philosophical positions into softer, human acts, like sleeping in a field of cotton—although given the American history of such fields, that may involve an even more debilitating negotiation.

LOS ANGELES, SEPTEMBER 27, 2010
Reprinted from *US Theater, Opera, and Performance* (Sept. 2010).

An Attack of the Heart

REYNOLDS PRICE **THE TONGUES OF ANGELS** (NEW YORK: ANTHENEUM, 1990)

AS I MENTIONED in *My Year 2004*, I met Reynolds Price only one time, when he appeared with a group of other Duke University professors, interviewing me for an assistant professorship. I think he asked me several questions, but only one remains in my mind, as he leaned forward to seriously query in his North Carolina dialect, "Mr. Messerli, do you intend to *abandon* Southern literature?" Yes, I did indeed intend to give it up, since I felt, having written significantly on Faulkner and Welty, that I had rather worn it out. And that was pretty much what happened until more recently, when working on essays for my cultural memoirs, I wrote on Tennessee Williams, Flannery O'Connor, and others.

But way back in 1978 I simply could not confess to that, and replied: "No, not at all. As you've noted, I've turned more recently to writing on what some might

describe as "postmodern" authors. But I still believe there's much to be written about on writers like Doris Betts (a professor at the nearby University of North Carolina) and you, Mr. Price." I don't know if he bought that or not, but the others seemed genuinely pleased by my reply. And, despite my own critical shift, I was speaking the truth.

Unfortunately, Price never lived to see the honesty of my statement. He died early this year on January 20th. Immediately I determined to write something. But the only book I had previously read was *A Long and Happy Life*, a few years after it was published in 1962. I would have been happy to reread it, but our local Beverly Hills Library did not own a copy. So I chose, instead, a fiction from Reynolds' mid-career, coming after some of his better known works, *A Generous Man, The Surface of Earth,* and *Kate Vaiden* and before the completion of his *Great Circle* trilogy.

Accordingly, I'm not sure that this book is truly representative of Price's work, but it does seem somewhat autobiographically based, filled with details of a

1954 boys' camp in the North Carolina Smoky Mountains, where the 21-year-old "hero," Bridge Boatner, takes on the responsibilities of caring for several rowdy boys living in large room in a summer camp. In that sense, Price's fiction might almost be read as an all-male version of his mentor Eudora Welty's long story, "Moon Lake."

Like Welty's story, wherein one young orphan girl, Easter, seems far more mature and daring than the other giggling schoolgirls, in *The Tongues of Angels*, one young boy, Rafe Noren, also a kind of orphan (he has seen his mother and her maid murdered), possesses talents and knowledge that awe both the other "reedy-voiced" boys and the young Boatner, a budding painter trying to lay to rest his own demons connected with his father's recent death.

Rafe, blessed with a beautiful smile, but also mercurial and far too deep of a thinker for a boy of his age, helps Boatner to find his way not only in his painting, spurring him to do far greater things and simply *to see* far more than he has before, but also helps him to deal with the past. Like most 21-year-olds, Boatner is, in several ways, no more mature than the boys whom he must teach and care for. First of all, he is still a virgin. Secondly he is—somewhat like the author of this book—a sentimentalist; as he describes himself, he is an "easy weeper."

My eyes tear freely at the least intensification of gladness, almost never at anger or grief. I fog up for instance at TV commercials that advertise long-distance phone calls—sons calling their mothers who drown in tears.

And finally, Bridge Boatner is simply unprepared for life. As an only child, he has been coddled and kept safe from the dangers that lurk in the corners of his young charges' eyes. A visit with another camp counselor to the Thomas Wolfe House in Asheville almost leads him to promise to marry the young country girl living within. His friend Kev pulls him safely away from self-destruction.

So it is no surprise that a figure like Rafe Noren, the son of a wealthy plantation owner, who quotes the Corinthians Bible passage behind the fiction's title—*"Though I speak with the tongues of men and of angels, and have not charity, I am become as sounding brass, or a tinkling cymbal."*—should be somewhat incomprehensible to his elder; and, while Boatner is able to save the boy from a poisonous snake bite, in the end he is unable to charitably give Rafe the love he truly needs.

There is almost a bitterness in Boatner's statement that the "really rich *are* different from you and me—they're starved. And what they crave of course is what we never give them. The way other people want peace and quiet, the rich want absolute love and loyalty in *spite* of their money."

It is in his inability to show his love to Rafe that Boatner truly fails. But in presenting this figure the way he does, Price also takes an easy way out. The story he tells, apparently, is told to the narrator's sons, years later, as an explanation of the painting upon his wall and a kind of confession for what he sees were his failures. Yet, it is just not believable, given the character Price has created in Boatner, that he is a heterosexual with a sensitive past.

I can well understand why the author, himself gay, did not wish to implant a gay man in a room with young boys for several weeks. The complications of what that might suggest and the critical reverberations would be more than painful. But yet, the way Price tells this story calls out for that explanation for both the deep bonding of the two and the later withholding of love. It is as if Price has refused the implications of his own tale. I cannot for one moment believe Boatner's desire for a young woman named Viemme, who, the one time he calls, betrays him by staying out all night in a place she cannot be reached. Everything that moves him, that energizes Boatner and pushes him into ecstatic delights, lies in the boy's camp, encapsulated in Rafe Noren and in the Indian lore taught by a Native-American named

Day, both representing something "outside" the normative community. Finally, it is difficult to comprehend why the painter's request to "draw the boy" should invoke such guilt as Boatner displays if that offer did not implicitly contain the sexual implications the phrase often suggests. There is no real connection between his request and Rafe's subsequently being bitten by a rattler—unless it's a symbolic one.

It seems to me that Bridge Boatner needed far more understanding of himself than his creator has allowed him. Certainly his sexuality, and his need to contain that in the situation in which he has found himself, would help to clarify the book's sad ending, in which the young beloved boy (seen as a true angel by everyone in camp) is found dead of a stroke at the sacred Indian prayer circle above their cabins. Price describes it as a stroke, while the reader understands it as an attack of the heart.

LOS ANGELES, MARCH 6, 2011
Reprinted from *EXPLORINGfictions* (March 2011).

Ready for Love

ANDREW HAIGH'S FILM *Weekend* begins quite inauspiciously with a family gathering in a home in what we later discover is Nottingham, England, where Karel Reisz's 1960 working-class drama, *Saturday Night, Sunday Morning,* was filmed. The major character in Haigh's movie, Russell (Tom Cullen), at first might seem little different from Arthur Seaton (Albert Finney) in that earlier film, a working-class bloke whose major activities include boozing and sex. Indeed, the first thing that happens when he appears at his friends' house—later than expected—is that Russell is handed a drink. Three males hover on the couch about the telly in much the way that straight Americans pray at the weekend altar of football and baseball games.

In part, that is just the director's point. Russell is not very different from the married couple for whom

he serves as their children's godfather. Despite that, we do sense something withheld, some reserve about him, and he soon makes an excuse about having to work early the next morning to slip out of their uneventful event.

Instead of going home, Russell drops in at the local gay bar, where, after quickly cruising the place, he picks out a handsome youth, not so very different in appearance from himself, following him into the bathroom. The chase is not successful, and, at first, the viewer becomes convinced that Russell will go home alone or with someone else. But we later discover that, although the other young man, Glen (Chris New), had hoped to go home with someone else, the two have ended up together, having evidently pleasurable sex before settling down to the uncomfortable conversation that inevitably follows such chance encounters.

Glen, however, is not like Russell's usual pick-ups. Before they can even began to reveal anything to each other, he has thrust a recorder in front of Russell, demanding he "talk about" the sex act they have just completed. It is a sort of "art project," he insists. "Say anything that comes into your head." The self-deprecating Russell, who works as a lifeguard, is more than taken aback, uncomfortable about talking on such a subject, something Glen argues is typical of gays, who, living in a heterosexual world, seldom feel comfortable about openly discussing their sexuality, even with one another. Taping such conversations, he argues, explores "a gap that opens up, when sex comes into play, between who someone really is and who he wants to be."

Arguing that his small film is not, primarily, a gay film, but simply a love story, Haigh often moves his camera in documentary-style shots to give his love story a kind of naturalistic quality. Yet the questions Glen poses, which, in turn, engage Russell throughout the three days of their short affair, are distinctly gay issues and their discussions are directly related to 1960s art films. Is gay life really different from straight life? Russell argues, no, that it is simply a matter of two people coming together, and, as he increasingly grows to love Glen, he becomes transfixed by the idea of a more-or-less permanent relationship. Despite the ridiculously short time he knows Glen, the idea of this man being someone permanent in his life seems to grow daily as they meet privately for sex and drugs, and publically with Glen's  friends. At first Glen purposely lies to Russell, but finally admits that on Sunday he is planning to leave for the US for two years to study art.

Against Russell's gradual "coming out," so to speak, to the idea of a long-term gay relationship, Glen argues that gays are habitually trying to imitate straights, that marriage is just a way of denying what is different in their lives, their open and sometimes abandoned sexuality. For Glen, all socialized behavior pushes the individual toward what he describes as a life in "concrete," a life lived locked in set behavior. Even though we perceive that he has been terribly hurt by the failure of an earlier relationship, he insists that he didn't really care that his mate cheated, just that he hated that he had lied.

Much of the film, to its credit, deals with the awkward little things—the dishware one has chosen, the clothes one puts on—that any "couple" must assimilate in order to discover each other. But just as Russell

 perceives, for the first time perhaps in his life, that he is "ready" for love, Glen increasingly pulls away, although we can see that in so doing he is putting himself in a corner that is worse than a concrete bunker. The problem with Glen's riffs is that most of them are just hot air, which one might easily juxtapose with Russell's repeated baths in hot water. The desired purity of the one is faced with the literal consumption and disappearance of the other.

On the day of Glen's departure, Russell has promised to attend a birthday party for his goddaughter at the house where the film began. Observing his sad and almost haggard look, his married friend queries him about what is wrong. Russell steers the conversation away, suggesting it's just a gay thing, but his friend fires back that he has never discussed his sexual life.

I was struck by the comment. Only a few days earlier, at lunch with straight friends, the woman, an art critic, commented that although several of her gay artist friends were very close to her and had been friends for years, few of them ever spoke of their sexual lives, as if somehow that was a territory no straight person could ever enter. I laughed, suggesting that Howard and I might be perfectly willing to discuss anything, but that since we had been together now for nearly 42 years, it probably would not be very interesting.

In the movie, Russell finally opens up, if just a little, to describe Glen and his feelings about him. As in the film *Notting Hill*, where Will Thacker (Hugh Grant) chases down Anna Scott (Julia Roberts) as she is about leave the country—a film actually referenced in Russell and his friend's conversation—the two rush off to the train station to see Glen.

Like all lovers, Russell and Glen briefly argue, but in the end kiss and make up in public—a first for the shy and less effusive Russell. Yet the film does not end happily, as Glen enters the train and is swept off, leaving Russell with a truly broken heart as he returns to his apartment—shot on the very spot where Albert Finney stood alone at the end of *Saturday Night, Sunday Morning*.

LOS ANGELES, OCTOBER 9, 2011
Reprinted from *World Cinema Review* (October 2011).

Sidney Lumet's death this month, on April 9th, sent me back to review his 1975 film, Dog Day Afternoon, *a work I remember with great fondness.*

Anything for Love

FRANK PIERSON (SCREENPLAY, BASED ON AN ARTICLE BY P. F. KLUGE AND THOMAS MOORE), SIDNEY LUMET (DIRECTOR) **DOG DAY AFTERNOON** / 1975

FOR THE FIRST HALF of the film, it appears that *Dog Day Afternoon* might be weighted down with the thematic concerns that are so dominant in Lumet's oeuvre, focusing on the moral, political, and social issues as in works such as *The Pawnbroker, A View from the Bridge, Serpico,* and *The Verdict.* These films are all admirable and well-directed. But for my taste there is something almost lugubrious about many of them, as they slowly uncoil, revealing their characters' moral fibre and the social conditions which define them. In some respects, many of Lumet's works never seem to be completely transformed from stage plays into cinematic creations, although that is precisely what I love about his *Long Day's Journey into Night* (see *My Year 2017*).

 *Dog Day After-noooon* begins simply as a badly bungled bank robbery, with one young partici-pant abandoning his cohorts even before the two central robbers, Sonny Wortzik (Al Pacino*) and Sal (eerily played by John Cazale), can notify the manager and tellers what they are undertaking. When they do demand to be taken to the vault, they discover that there is no money, since it has just been picked up for deposit elsewhere.

The only takings that Pacino has for all his trouble are the teller's drawers, which he carefully empties, making sure that he does not pull all the bills out at once and trigger the alarm. When offered, by one teller, the wrapped new bills, he refuses, noting that they are marked. Yet for all his carefulness, he is soon called to the phone where a policeman wants to talk to him, the bank having been already surrounded.

Suddenly we perceive the absurdity of the whole event. The inept robbers are now forced into a stand-off with what appears to be, as Sonny later announces, "the fucking militia." Indeed, there are so many police-men setting up camp across the street, blocking off cars, swarming the roof and the back of the building, and hanging from fire escapes that one would think they were responding to an international terrorist threat. He is now forced to take the tellers and manager as captives, but proclaims: "I'm a Catholic, I don't want to hurt anybody." Even the dense-minded Sal insists he doesn't smoke because "the body's the temple of the Lord."

Before long a large crowd has gathered, and the movie appears to have shifted into a work dealing with police brutality, particularly when, on one of his sidewalk discussions with the police coordinator, Det. Sgt. Eugene Moretti (Charles Durning), Sonny invokes the Attica prison riots of 1971, when, after days of negotiations, police killed or caused the deaths of over 39 prisoners. Pacino, brilliantly over-the-top, whips up the crowd for his cause—and assured safety:

> Tell them to put their guns down! Put the fucking guns down! Put 'em down! Put the fucking guns down! Put those guns down! Attica! Attica! You got it, man! You got it, man! You got it, man! You got it! You got it! (pointing to different individuals in the crowd as they shout, "ATTICA! ATTICA!")

Moreover, when Lumet briefly inserts scenes showing Sonny's mother (hilariously played by theater director Judith Malina) and his overweight, beleaguered, and not very bright wife, we begin to fear that the film may attempt a psychological explanation for his acts.

But even early on, we suspect that the story has something important yet to reveal, particularly when, after being lied to by Moretti, the two have the following interchange:

> SONNY: Kiss me.
> MORETTI: What?
> SONNY: Kiss me. When I'm being fucked, I like to
>   get kissed a lot.

Everything soon shifts, in a delicious twist of reality, when we discover the wife Sonny has asked for the police to bring to him is another man, Leon Shemer (Chris Sarandon), and the reason for the bank robbery is Sonny's attempt to get enough money for Leon's sex-change.

Even stranger, it is not Sonny demanding the sex-change—who seems to be perfectly in love with Leon as a gay man—but the psychiatrist's idea:

> LEON: I couldn't explain why I did the things I did.
>   So I went to this psychiatrist who explained to
>   me I was a woman in a man's body. So Sonny
>   right away wanted to get me money for a sex
>   change operation: but where was he to get

that? 2500 dollars! My God, he's in hock up to his ears already.

Before long the gays have joined the crowds surrounding the absurd stand-off, Sonny becoming a kind of ridiculous folk hero in an era in which police were hated for their abuse. And Lumet has sent his film on a loony and, quite frankly, bravely outspoken path where I am sure some members of the original audience had not been prepared to go. One must remember that the only major American film that had seriously and openly dealt with homosexuality was William Friedkin's *The Boys in the Band* of 1970, a film so based on gay stereotypes that, even after I had served for a few nights as an usher during its New York run, Howard and I, along with other members of the newly formed gay liberation group at the University, picketed the film outside the Madison, Wisconsin theater where it was shown.

Lumet was not only taking on the issue of homosexuality in *Dog Day Afternoon*, but transgender sexuality, and, even more complicated, the subject of bisexuality, since Sonny was also heterosexually married with two children! Yet Lumet allows this subject

 to be treated seriously by including the scene where Sonny dictates a will, leaving most of his money to Leon, with only a small amount going to his legal wife.

Even though he is, as he admits, "a fuck-up" and "an outcast," Sonny is also a caring and loving man. As he admits to Sal, "I got all these pressures!" and, at another point, "I got to have all the ideas!"

And strangely and absurdly, he takes those ideas to their logical extension, planning to use the hostages to get an airplane traveling to, of all places, Algeria! When asked to what country he might like to go, Sal replies, "Wyoming." We know, accordingly, that there can now be no turning back, and there will be no way of returning to whatever they might define as normality for these poor, sweet outcasts. The only element of the plot still unrevealed is whether the two will be brutally murdered or simply arrested.

Both happen, as the limousine driver pulls out a gun and shoots Sal, the police arresting Sonny.

In real life, John Wojtowicz served 14 years in prison for the attempted robbery. The $7,500 he received for the movie rights went to his lover, Ernest Aron, for the sex change. Aron became Elizabeth Eden, dying of AIDS-related pneumonia in 1987. Wojtowicz died of cancer on January 2, 2006.

———

*I might note that there is a wonderful irony in Pacino's performance, for which he was nominated for Best Actor by the Academy of Motion Picture Arts and Sciences. In real life, Wojtowicz and his co-conspirator Salvatore Naturile had seen *The Godfather*, in which Pacino also played, earlier in the day and planned their robbery based on events in the film. John Cazale performed alongside Pacino in *The Godfather* as Fredo.

LOS ANGELES, EASTER 2011
Reprinted from *World Cinema Review* (April 2011).

Embedded Trio

EUGÈNE SCRIBE AND CHARLES-GASPARD DELESTRE-POIRSON (SCREENPLAY, BASED ON THEIR PLAY), GIO-ACHINO ROSSINI (COMPOSER) **LE COMTE ORY** / NEW YORK, METROPOLITAN OPERA, *LIVE IN HD* BROADCAST, APRIL 9, 2011

ROSSINI'S 1828 OPERA, *Le Comte Ory,* is one of his most memorable and truly humorous works. However it is seldom performed. The Metropolitan Opera of New York had never before mounted a production of it until April 2011, an excellent rendition directed by Bartlett Sher which was presented in a *Live in HD* broadcast on April 9, which my companion Howard and I attended.

For one of the first times in my memory, the opera began without a curtain, further attempting to recreate the theatrical conventions of the age by allowing the Prompter to be observed throughout, and using cast and chorus members to enter and exit openly with sets and props.

We are in Touraine around 1200, where most of the men of the community have gone off to fight in the Crusades. Outside the castle of Formoutiers, the  women, who have pledged a vow of chastity in the absence of their men, gather outside the castle where they have moved in with the Countess Adèle to protect themselves and serve her.

In love with the Countess, the irresponsible Ory (Juan Diego Florez) has disguised himself as a hermit, sending his friend Raimund ahead to announce his arrival. The women, hearing of the hermit's legendary ability to grant all their wishes, bring him a bounty of food and gifts, each hoping to get a chance to speak with him, and reveal their desires. Since the women have been so long in solitary, they are desperate for the return of their husbands—or, at least, the attentions of a man, all of which Ory, when he appears, turns to his advantage. One of the great joys of this slower moving and somewhat less invigorating first act (the music of the act repeats many of Rossini's songs in his earlier opera *Il Viaggio a Reims*) is Florez's comic miming as, in

his long beard and dingy clothing, he greets each of his supplicants with numerous promises and strokes of their body and hair.

Meanwhile, Ory's tutor (Michele Pertusi) and his page, Isolier (Joyce DiDonato), have coincidentally arrived in the same area, hoping to find the missing Ory and bring him home before he does any damage. When the tutor hears of the presence of a noted hermit in the area, he is certain that it must be his student, as he proclaims to Isolier in the long lament of his "honorable" role in life.

When Isolier encounters the hermit, he also asks the "holy" man for advice, admitting that he is in love with the Countess and that he has a plan to enter her retreat dressed as a female pilgrim. Ory, as the hermit, encourages him, proclaiming that he will do everything in his power to help.

When the hermit meets up with the despondent Countess, his advice to her is that she must find love and embrace it immediately to rid herself of her melancholia. When the Countess sees Isolier nearby, she quickly falls in love, as Ory tries to warn her to beware of his former page in hopes that he himself may ultimately be the object of her love. Her paean to Isolier ("En proie à la tristesse") turns into a wonderful tussle between the two wooers as they vie for the Countess' favors.

The tutor arrives just in time to see through the hermit's costume, revealing his student's reprehensible acts, as the women, in horror and dismay, retreat once again into the castle, vowing to remain in isolation.

If Act I is charming, Act II, although much simpler in terms of plot, is the heart of this opera, and Rossini wrote new music for it. As villainous as always, Ory determines to employ Isolier's plan to lay siege to the women of the town and to seduce the Countess. Dressing as nuns, he and his numerous followers, arrive at the castle in the middle of a stormy night, proclaiming that they too have been attacked by Ory, pleading to be allowed protection within the castle walls for the night.

The Countess eagerly permits them into her company, finding rooms for the entire group, and speaking with Ory in nun's habit as the representative of the group. Florez plays his role of Soeur Colette with great vigor, alternating between a shy and frightened pilgrim and a woman in need of love and its caresses, thoroughly confusing the Countess. But that is only a warm-up for further mischievous acts.

Raimund, having found a cache of wine and liquor, passes out the bottles to Ory's group, as they sing a drinking song ("Buvons, buvons") between the entrances and exits of the Countess' servant Ragonde, who is suspicious of the noises coming from the kitchen. The song is completely extraneous to the developments of the opera, but the very idea of a group of bewhiskered nuns drinking bottles of wine creates a sense of hilarity that is a perfect introduction for the next scene, in which Ory attempts to break into the Countess' bedroom to rape her.

Fortunately, Isolier, come with the news that the women's husbands will soon be home, realizes that the hairy pilgrims are Ory and his band, reporting the news to the Countess, who, together with him, plans her revenge on the Count.

In the Met production, the bed was lifted somewhat vertically so that we can witness the absurdity of the event as, in the dark, the Countess courts Ory, while Isolier lies silently between them, receiving most of the attentions of Ory's bodily press, and planting kisses on the lips of his beloved. It is an absurdly funny scene, given the fact that Isolier is played by a female mezzo-soprano. Accordingly, if you perceive the situation as it is in the fiction, Ory is making love to Isolier, with two men and a woman upon the bed; but if you perceive the work in terms of their actual sexes, it is two women lying upon the bed with a man, all eventually becoming wound up and around each other as if in orgiastic joy that is either gay or lesbian. Sher has directed this so flawlessly that when the deception is finally revealed, Ory stands with a slight smile upon his face, as if he has not at all minded the confusion of sexual identities, singing out in praise of marriage which brings home the man. With the help of Isolier, he makes a final escape, presumably to seek out others to trick into love.

Just a short while before the show began, Florez was at his wife's bedside, having just witnessed the birth of his new son. He reported between acts that he had not slept all night.

LOS ANGELES, APRIL 18, 2011
Reprinted from *Green Integer Blog* (April 2011).

Criss-Cross

CZENZI ORMONDE (SCREENPLAY), LISTED WITH
RAYMOND CHANDLER (WHO DID NOT WRITE THE FINAL
VERSION), BASED ON AN ADAPTATION BY WHITFIELD
COOK OF PATRICIA HIGHSMITH'S NOVEL, ALFRED
HITCHCOCK (DIRECTOR) **STRANGERS ON A TRAIN** /
1951

STRANGERS ON A TRAIN has long been one of my favorite Hitchcock films, and with the news yesterday of the death of one of the film's stars, Farley Granger, I felt it was time I wrote about this work.

I have seen this film dozens of times, and over the years I often mused about a silly game I might undertake, suggested by the phrase "criss-cross," which Bruno Antony (Robert Walker) uses to describe his plan for murder. Applying a version of "six degrees of separation," I felt I could link all the characters of this film to people whom I had met or known. For example, Robert Walker was married to Jennifer Jones until her

Bruno's meeting, there is no escaping each other, reiterated when Haines meets up with his wife, who refuses to grant him a divorce. Haines' fury as he calls back to Anne Morton in Washington, D.C. again points up a kind of receptivity to Bruno's mania : "I could kill her!"

Bruno's acquisition of Guy's lighter along with his murder of Guy's selfish wife doom the tennis player to be entrapped within Bruno's perverted universe. Suddenly Bruno is everywhere, talking to Guy's friends at the tennis courts and even attending the senator's parties, where we truly experience Bruno's madness:

> BRUNO [*to the senator*]: How do you do, sir? I'd like to talk with you sometime, sir, and tell you about my idea for harnessing the life force. It'll make atomic power look like the horse and buggy. I'm already developing my faculty for seeing millions of miles.

By the end of the evening he has almost unintentionally strangled one of the senator's guests, making the senator's daughter (Ruth Roman) suspicious that there is a link between her lover and the interloper, which she expresses to Guy almost in a jealous anger:

> ANNE: How did you get him to do it?
> GUY: I get him to do it?

affair with David O. Selznick. In 1971 Jones married art collector and philanthropist Norton Simon, with whom my companion Howard met several times when the Norton Simon Museum was contemplating loaning some of their contemporary art to the Los Angeles County Museum of Art. Four separations.

One of Farley Granger's earliest performances was in a play by Lillian Hellman, who helped support Djuna Barnes in Barnes' later years by slipping envelopes of money under her door. I had met and interviewed Barnes in 1973, a few years before her death. Three separations.

In his autobiography *West Side Story*, Arthur Laurents writes of his affair with Farley Granger while working on Hitchcock's film *Rope*. Tony in the film version of *West Side Story* was played by Richard Beymer, who attended my literary salons several times. Three separations.

Another of Granger's lovers was composer-director Leonard Bernstein, who personally encouraged my friend Charley Wine to become a composer. Three separations again!

The year after *Strangers on a Train*, actress Ruth Roman played in *Young Man with Ideas* with Nina Foch, who taught acting to and befriended Howard's Aunt Lillian (whom I've met several times). Three separations. My parents once reported that they, too, had

met Nina Foch in a 1956 visit to Los Angeles, when she was at work on *The Ten Commandments* (although I have no idea how and why this meeting took place). In any event, this linking could go and on, although as one must ask, to what purpose?

I suspect that my desire to interconnect this way has something to do with the structure of *Strangers on a Train*, where several different individuals cross paths, echoing and affecting one another. Indeed in the case of the two major figures of the film, Guy Haines (Farley Granger) and Bruno Anthony, there is no separation. Once Anthony has recognized Haines on the train, intruding upon the famed tennis player, ("I beg your pardon, but aren't you Guy Haines?") the two become almost inseparable, dining together in Anthony's small train compartment, and conversing about all things from tennis to Anthony's strange philosophical views ("I have a theory that you should do everything before you die"). Although we know from the beginning that Haines is dating and hoping to marry the lovely senator's daughter, Anne Morton, as soon as he can divorce his wife, Hitchcock plays out this strange encounter as a kind of gay pickup, clearly toying with Granger's

real-life bisexuality and his astonishing good looks. Why else would Guy allow himself to be literally swept up by the foppish mama's boy Bruno (who in some scenes looks nearly as handsome as Guy), ultimately consumes him in the vertigo of his mur[ous intents? Before Guy can even display his dis[fort, Bruno has outlined a plan whereby he wil[Guy's wife if Guy will kill Bruno's father, an inge[game he describes as "criss-cross." Guy's inadequa[sponse—"I may be old-fashioned, but I thought[der was against the law"—reveals both his inabil[comprehend this absurdity and suggests a darke[sibility, that he is not at all adverse to the idea.

In Highsmith's novel, Guy does go throug[his part of the crime and is imprisoned; in an[script by Raymond Chandler, a script which Hitc[hated and tossed into the wastebasket while h[his nose, the film ended with Haines in a strai[The doppelganger aspects of Haines and Anth[pear to be innately within the structure of the[suggesting a kind of fused being with a Dr. Jek[Mr. Hyde personality. From the moment of G[

ANNE: Bruno Anthony. He killed Miriam, didn't
he? It wasn't you, it was him.
GUY: Yes....
ANNE: Tell me the truth, how did you get Mr. Anthony to do it?

The "doing" obviously is murder, but it suggests
another "doing," the sexual act, (con)fusing the two. By
film's end, Guy is forever wed to Bruno. What he says
of the detective following him might also be said of his
"double": "He sticks so close he's beginning to grow on
me—like a fungus."

When Guy refuses to participate in his half of the

"bargain" with this devil, he precipitates a series of events wherein almost everyone in Guy's company is swallowed up into the secrecy and anguish facing him, including Anne (who, visiting Bruno's mother, tries to convince her of her son's guilt) and the senator's other daughter, Barbara (Patricia Hitchcock), who, up until now has taken the whole thing as a lark, suddenly realizes it was her face on which Bruno was fixated while nearly asphyxiating the woman at the party; her glasses cause her to resemble Guy's wife Miriam. It is as if Bruno is a kind of whirlwind force that sucks all those whose paths he crosses into his insanity.

Accordingly, it is no accident that, in his attempt to implicate Guy in the murder of his wife by planting his lighter at the scene of the act, he and Guy are swept away in a battle upon a carousel, whirling out of control, where innocent children are hurt and possibly killed as well.

Even as he lies dying, Bruno will not give up the evidence of the lighter or the truth, keeping like a fetish the links he still has to Guy Haines' identity. Only in death will he free his "other."

For good or bad, this movie reveals, we are all intricately intertwined. Is it any wonder, in the final moment of the film when another stranger asks of the tennis player, "Aren't you Guy Haines?" he and Anne get up and move away. Perhaps, teases Hitchcock, it's better *not* to know your neighbors, an issue this director will take up again in his 1954 movie, *Rear Window*. At the same time, to be accused of something you did not do, merely through association, brings up issues that were boiling over in the public sector when *Strangers on a Train* was made, namely what was later described as the "Red Scare," including the arrests of Julius and Ethel Rosenberg in 1950. That same year a connection between homosexuals and communists was laid out in the government-published report *Employment of Homosexuals and Other Sex Perverts in Government*— some issues of which Hitchcock would explore in his 1956 film, *The Wrong Man*.

LOS ANGELES, MARCH 30, 2011
Reprinted from *World Cinema Review* (March 31, 2011).

In the room in which I sleep when in New York at Sherry Bernstein's Central Park West apartment, there is a high shelf of books collected from childhood to the high school-student days of her son, Edward. Edward is now a teacher, and evidently his own apartment can no longer hold all of these early wonders. When I visit, I often peruse those books, and have read some of them over the years.

On the morning of May 5, 2011, I decided to check out his yellowing and dog-eared Dell/Laurel Drama series, consisting of several volumes of plays from the 1920s, the 1930s, the 1940s, etc. I had had some of those same volumes in my basement hideaway in my parents' house as I grew up.

For some reason, the 1940s volume particularly interested me. What a strange selection, I thought to myself. I could understand the choice of Thornton Wilder's The Skin of Our Teeth *and Arthur Miller's* All My Sons, *even Carson McCullers' lovely play* The Member of the Wedding, *but Maxwell Anderson's* Lost in the Stars *was a very strange selection. The final play, Arthur Laurents'* Home of the Brave, *his first work, was a modest success with a run of only 69 performances, but I'd never read it, so it attracted me most. I began reading a few pages, and before long I had finished the first act.*

I went out for breakfast and, soon after, took a taxi to mid-town, where in a few hours I was about see the first of five plays I was planning to attend during my stay. Suddenly on the taxi television, I saw a news flash: Arthur Laurents, New York playwright, has died at age 93. For a few seconds I sat in some shock, since I had not only seen in the past year his new directorial rendition of West Side Story, *but had just been given, by my companion Howard, the DVD of Hitchcock's* Rope, *for which he wrote the screenplay; and I had only a few weeks before written about Laurents' one-time lover Farley Granger in* Strangers on a Train. *I might not have been so surprised, given that this kind of coincidence is nothing new for me, this sudden chance relationship with larger events; but I was shaken, nonetheless, by the facts. Surely it meant that I now had to finish the play I had begun that morning; and over the next few days, between my own writing and my theater attendances, I finished the reading as a private salute to him.*

The Coward's Hand

ARTHUR LAURENTS **HOME OF THE BRAVE** / ORIGI-
NALLY PRESENTED AT NEW YORK, BELASCO THEATRE,
1945

ARTHUR LAURENTS' first play, *Home of the Brave*, is
the story of a young soldier, Peter Coen, who is part of
an engineering division of the US Army during World
War II in the South Pacific.

By the time the curtain rises, Coen, called by his
Army companions Coney, has already endured a mis-
sion in which he and four others penetrated an island
held by the Japanese, secretly surveying and mapping
the landscape to prepare for an invasion and the building of a small airport. Just as they finish their jobs and
prepare to evacuate, Japanese soldiers discover their position and shoot, hitting Mingo and, later, wounding
Coney's best friend, Finch, who has temporarily forgotten where he put the maps. By the time Coney retrieves
the maps, Finch is too hurt to move ahead with him

and the others, and they are forced to leave him behind with the hope that he will eventually make his way to them before they leave the island that night.

Events do not go well, and the soldiers are horrified when Finch is found and tortured by the Japanese at a distance close enough to where the others are hiding so that they can hear his cries and suffer his torture. As they move off to dig up their canoes, Coney is left alone to protect the gear. Finch crawls into the small clearing, dying in Coney's arms.

Coney attempts to bury him so that the Japanese cannot dismember the corpse, but by the time his friends return, he finds himself unable to walk, suffering an inexplicable paralysis. He is carried away by a fellow soldier, waking to find himself in a military hospital under the care of Captain Harold Bitterger, a sympathetic psychiatrist.

In December 1945, the date this play appeared at the Belasco Theatre in New York, the events of World War II were still so fresh that the audiences who attended the performances would have felt the circumstances of the play had occurred only yesterday. The play's events are described as just a year earlier, and only five months before the play's opening the US had bombed Hiroshima and Nagasaki.

If today much of the psychological jargon and the treatments used to help Coney seem obsolete and naïve, one must remember that, although Freud had perhaps been assimilated by the intelligentsia, even a couple of years earlier a major character in *Guys and Dolls* had been told by his girlfriend, "Nathan, you got psychology, everybody's got it!" Certainly the ideas of postwar syndrome and psychological hysteria were startlingly new concepts for the general public; treatment by "narcosynthesis" must have seemed almost futuristic.

Any sensitive reader today, in our cure-all culture, might be able to discern that the problem with Coney was a terrible feeling of guilt for not having protected his close friend Finch, the only one of the group for whom his being Jewish seemed to have no significance. The discovery later that Finch, in a moment of duress, turned on his friend, parroting the statements of the other men—"you lousy yellow..." stopping before he finished the word "Jew," and transforming it into the word "jerk"—helps us to further understand Coney's guilt. The hurt Coney momentarily endures in that statement results, a few minutes later, in a momentary flash of pleasure when Finch gets shot. And we realize that his regret for that momentary sensation is entangled with the hundreds of racial and religious epithets Coen has had to endure not only throughout his life but, more particularly, while he has put his own life on the line for his prejudiced companions.

Laurents has created a painful and revelatory play

about how racial slurs and prejudices affect all Americans who must suffer them, whether in civilian or military life. But the situation upon which Laurents focuses, where Americans such as Coen were helping to battle just such hatred in Europe and elsewhere, makes such disgusting behavior even more insufferable.

Only two years later, in 1947, the film *Gentleman's Agreement* would even more interestingly reveal the ugliness and prevalence of American anti-Semitism and its effects on good families and human inter-relationships, including Gregory Peck's relationship with the liberal WASP Kathy Lacey (played by Dorothy McGuire) and, even more evidently, the job aspirations of Dave Goldman (John Garfield). In that sense both of these works, *Home of the Brave* and *Gentleman's Agreement*, should be understood as works that helped, if all too slowly, alter standard American prejudices with regards to being Jewish, prejudices which my own father, fighting in World War II, thought he was challenging as well through his actions as an Air Force bombardier flying over Germany.

Yet I cannot help but feel there is something "more" going on in Laurents' play that is not at all an issue in *Gentleman's Agreement*, another matter that renders the central subject of *Home of the Brave* somewhat diffuse and incomprehensible. The good psychiatrist perceives the "central" issue, so it seems, and "cures" his patient by helping Coen to realize that every soldier, of necessity, feels, when another soldier is hit, a momentary sense of relief. As another of Coney's group, Mingo, puts it, "Thank God, it's not me!" Coen is made to understand that he is like everyone else, no matter how men like the intolerant T. J. describe him. That, in turn, frees Coen to forgive himself, to comprehend his flash of anger and hatred towards his dying friend as an instant of justifiable self-protection.

Even the psychiatrist, however, laments that he cannot go further, in the short period he has to work with his patient, into Coen's past in the comprehension of his mental issues. By play's end, now with Mingo's help, we can hopefully believe that—unlike T. J.'s suspicions that one day Coney will go "off" again—he will survive in the civilian world as a productive human being. Yet Laurents, we feel, or at least *I* do, has left something out. Why has Coen gone "off" in the first place? It is hard to believe that a Jewish man living in the anti-Semitic society of the 1930s and 1940s, fighting in a War that, at least in the European scene, occurred in part *because* of the German hatred for and determination to destroy all European Jews, would still be so utterly sensitive to what appear, at least in the context of the play, to be a few racial slurs. Yes, they would be painful, angering, particularly, when uttered—or almost uttered—by a dear friend. But then, a moment before, Coen has referred to Finch as a "dumb Arizona bastard," perhaps to Finch just as painful an epithet. Of course, there is a radical difference: one is a statement dismissing one's home state and the conditions of life there; the other is a complete dismissal of belief and cultural identity, not only one's *own* identity, but the identities of one's father and mother and all the generations before that. Yet both demean and belittle the individuals to whom these slurs are thrown.

Throughout one of the earlier scenes, moreover, Coen calls Finch a "jerk" numerous times. A few minutes later he describes Finch to Mingo as "the Arizona tumbleweed." So Coen himself is not above handing out a few epithets that suggest his friend's backwardness, lack of education, and cultural isolation. What exactly does Coen's over-sensitivity to slurs he must have heard much of his life suggest? I am reminded of an important scene in *Gentleman's Agreement*, when Phil Green (Gregory Peck) reveals to his Jewish friend, Dave Goldman, that he is pretending to be Jewish in order to write a story about anti-Semitism:

> PHIL GREEN: I've been saying I'm Jewish, and it works.
> DAVE GOLDMAN: Why, you crazy fool! It's working?
> PHIL GREEN: It works too well. I've been having

my nose rubbed in it, and I don't like the smell.

DAVE GOLDMAN: You're not insulated yet, Phil.
The impact must be quite a business on you.

PHIL GREEN: You mean you get indifferent to it in
time?

DAVE GOLDMAN: No, but you're concentrating a
lifetime into a few weeks. You're not changing
the facts, you're just making them hurt more.

So too does Peter Coen seem to be concentrating all his
hurt into a single incident having to do with a young
Arizona boy named Finch.

Of course, it helps to know that he and Finch are not
just *friends*, but are planning, when they are discharged,
to open a bar together in...Finch's "whistlestop home"
in rural Arizona. A Pittsburgh Jewish boy in Arizona?
Something is wrong with this picture. Or, I should perhaps say, something is quite right—if you comprehend
the situation. The two men are clearly in love, whether
or not they know it or the author is willing to express it.
The very fact that Peter Coen, who keeps Kosher and
is religiously observant, would be willing to abandon
city life and move to a small town in the Southwest in
the 1940s—long before that area's startling growth—in
order to open a bar where "married men" will feel comfortable speaks volumes. The two men are suggesting a
long-term relationship completely off the beaten path,

which was a way of saying, in those days, that they were committing themselves to one another.

Of course, Laurents cannot speak of this, and why should he? His central issue was painful enough. To have illuminated it as a story of their love would have completely overwhelmed any other concerns he might have wanted to express. Or, to put it another way, if Laurents had centered the work on gay sexuality in 1945, the play would never have been produced. While it *was* the time to discuss, finally, the issue of anti-Semitism, gays would have to wait through the blistering attacks on homosexual writers, composers, and other figures of the early 1960s until later in that decade to even bring up the issue. Laurents would be one of the earliest to suggest these issues in his 1948 screenplay *Rope*, where he and Hitchcock created a situation where two gay men simply lived together, without making anything of it in the story; but then, they were murderers, based on the real-life figures Nathan Leopold and Richard Loeb.

I know there are a few readers who, after reading

several of my essays, will say that I find these issues in too many plays, films, fictions, etc.—and they are right. My response is that for much of the 20th century, writers who wanted to consider these issues had no choice but to bury them in other narratives that opened for those who understood and were sympathetic to the situations but remained closed or oblique to those who were not.

Moreover, I want to make it clear that I am not diminishing the obvious concern of Laurents' play. It's simply that the love between these two soldiers, sexual or not, intensifies and clarifies everything!

Laurents, moreover, takes this issue even further. Once Coen has regained his sense of self and purpose, he goes off with another man—this time Mingo—perhaps the kind of married man for whom Finch and Coen had planned their bar. Mingo suggests he is willing to partner, at least for the bar, with Peter. A man whose wife has abandoned him, Mingo even likes poetry (perceived by many in this decade as a woman's avocation), which he claims throughout the play his wife writes, but which we suspect, given the appropriateness of the lines he quotes, he himself might have written:

Frightened,
you are my only friend.
And frightened, we are everyone.

Someone must take a stand.
Coward, take my coward's hand.

The ending is a bit like Rick and Louie's last lines
in *Casablanca*:

CONEY: Hey, coward.
MINGO [*turning*]: What?
CONEY [*coming to him*]: Take my coward's hand.
[*He lifts the bag up on MINGO's back.*]
MINGO: Pete, my boy, you've got a charming
memory.
CONEY [*a slight pause, softly*]: Delightful!...

And it is...charming, delightful, as the one-armed survivor and the formally paralyzed man walk off into the
sunset.

NEW YORK, MAY 8, 2011
Reprinted from *US Theater, Opera, and Performance* (May 2011).

Sideshows and Carnival Barkers

THE UNITED STATES, in its history of political campaigns, has surely had its share of outrageous behavior, hypocrisy, and outright lies. There's something in particular about running for president that brings out the worst in some of the men and women who seek that elusive and, to my way of thinking, undesirable job. Thank heaven there are still megalomaniac men and women who want to run our country. And occasionally one argues persuasively that he or she has the best interest of the US citizens at heart—whether or not that turns out to be a fact.

I feel Obama, despite all of his failures (which, after all, are complicated by the failures of our legislative government), has convinced me that he is less interested in his own voice than in reforming government policies. However, his necessary commitment to the center has defeated his own best attempts at accomplishing anything. But I am not going to attempt here a deconstruction of how the President and the Congress together have failed an often-uninformed and sometimes near-idiotic public. We are undergoing one of the most difficult times, with regard to the federal and even state governments, that we have ever faced as a country. Trust in public office seems to be at a new low, and those outside of government seem to be increasingly ignorant of what politics is about. The trouble with playing the center, as Obama has attempted to do, is that there may no longer *be* a center in American culture, which makes the President's position an extremely lonely one. If his approval ratings continue to decline as they have, I think we can chalk it up to the fact that there is no longer any way for a leader to appeal to both the left and the right, in part because both sides have too often let their extremist voices speak for them.

What concerns me most is that, while we face dire issues of health care, global politics (particularly with regard to the new North African and Arab populist challenges), ongoing warfare in Afghanistan, and financial debt which may collapse everything we have worked for, we are evidently unable to focus on these dilemmas, rather we are transfixed by peripheral and quite meaningless issues. One of the most egregious of these, it seems to me, is the "birther" issue, long festering since Obama's election, in extreme right and religious groups, and more recently whipped up by potential presidential candidate Donald Trump. At the beginning of this week a *USA Today* and *Gallup* poll found that, among Republicans, 43% felt that Obama was not born in the United States; and even among the general electorate, 15% said he was "probably" born abroad, with another 9% saying that he was definitely born on foreign soil. Perhaps one should not take these polls too seriously, since, as an article in the *Los Angeles Times* this morning mentioned, about 45% of those polled questioned the American birth of Donald Trump.

However, that this stubborn perception of Obama still persists is shocking after Hawaiian officials, both Democratic and Republican, have stated over and over that Obama was born in their state, and there is biographical evidence that his mother, Stanley Ann Dunham, an American citizen, lived in Hawaii at the time of Obama's birth, August 4, 1961.

As Janny Scott reports in a fascinating essay, "The Young Mother Abroad" (*The New York Times Magazine*, April 24, 2011):

She dropped out of school (the University of Hawaii), married him (Barack Hussein Obama) and gave birth shortly before their union ended. In the aftermath, she met Lolo Soetoro, an amiable, easy-going, tennis-player from the Indonesian island of Java.

Dunham and her son moved to Seattle, where she enrolled at the University of Washington from September 1961 to June 1962, afterwards moving back to Hawaii, where she resumed her education at the University of Hawaii. Soetoro and Dunham married in 1964, and in 1967 Ann Dunham and her son, Barack, joined Soetoro in Indonesia, to where he had been called home the previous year because of political events. The future president was six years of age. So what's the problem?

Of course there are numerous conspiracy theories suggesting that Dunham somehow managed to fake the birth in Hawaii, but that an unknown young mother would want to illegally register her son as a native-born American seems a rather odd supposition to me. How she might have accomplished this is even more perplexing. Could she have even imagined a young boy with a black Nigerian father might someday be president?*

But then the very idea of the need to be born in the US in order to run for president, from my point of view, seems equally absurd. I suppose the early founders must have feared that a man born in another country might have conflicts of interest and influences from that other country which might stand in the way of US interests. Of course, many of us are very much influenced by the homeland of our forbearers, and, since we are a country of immigrants, one might suggest that no one but a Native American would have no possible influences from abroad.

When I was 16, I lived for a year in Norway; and over the years, I have found some of the most pleasurable moments of my life in France. Might I not, if I were to run for president, be described as having special interests in these countries? It all seems rather tribal to me. I have always felt that just being a citizen ought to be enough.

Accordingly, I basically ignored the "birthers'" concerns, seeing those who supported the question primarily as crackpots. When an aunt of mine, a fundamentalist, born-again Christian, emailed me bigoted texts that argued for Obama's illegality, I simply deleted them, until one day, after receiving several of these unwanted epistles, I wrote her, asking to be taken off her mailing list. Good Christian that she is, she replied that she would never talk to me again. And she has kept her word.

Despite my disdain for the whole issue, however, I realize that it is the current law that the President must have been born in the US, and the problem is that for some apparently illogical souls—a great number

240

of them actually—
Obama must be ex-
cised from his Ameri-
can heritage. Many
intelligent observers
have suggested, and
I strongly agree, that
this position is sup-
ported by strong racial animosity and outright xeno-
phobia.

Why, accordingly, when Trump began talking
about this issue—and others equally disturbing ("We
need to seize Iraq's oil." "The Chinese are our enemies!")—didn't some of the few clear-headed Republicans speak out? Of course, some may have, their voices
drowned out by an equally crass media who allowed
Trump to capture the stage, where he claimed, at first,
that the President's birth may have happened in Africa,
and later said, on March 17th, "The reason I have a little
doubt, just a little, is because he grew up and nobody
knew him." I gather that Trump had never heard of or
refused to believe Hawaii Governor Neils Abercomb-
rie's memories of Obama's mother and his celebration
with them of Obama's birth.

A few days later Trump described hiring his own
private investigators who, "at a certain point in time,"
will reveal some "interesting things."

Finally, Trump told CNN interviewer Ali Velshi, "When I started, two months ago, I thought he [Obama] was [born in Hawaii]. Every day that goes by, I think less and less that he was born in the United States."

Whatever information Trump was privy to, we never discovered. It is clear to me that it was simply another "trump," a play of the cards to keep the public focused on his confused and obscure political positions. In any event, the tactic paid off as far as he was concerned, if only because it forced the President to finally produce his own birth certificate, which indeed states his birth to be on August 4, 1961 in Honolulu.

One might have imagined that finally this piece of dirty folklore could be laid to rest. But Trump, turning everything inside out, claimed that he was "honored" to have helped get the certificate's release. He was "proud of himself" for having had a role in settling this matter finally so that we could move on to other issues. Repeating himself, Trump declared that he was "really proud" and "really honored," before suggesting that the document had to be looked at carefully, as if to hint at new doubts.

In truth, Trump's major role was precisely what the President spoke of that morning, namely that of playing a part in the sideshow as a carnival barker with the pretense of saying something important about American politics. It was he, not the president, who had stirred up new doubts for an issue that might have been laid to rest years ago, given the statements from the State of Hawaii, released early on as Obama announced that he would run for President.

Obviously, the issue will not disappear. As Hendrig Hertzberg righteously suggested in *The New Yorker* of May 2, 2011.

> The dismaying truth is that birtherism is part of a larger pattern of rejection of reality that has taken hold of intimidating segments of one of two political parties that alternate in power in our governing institutions. It is akin to the view that global warming is a hoax, or that the budget can be balanced through spending cuts alone, or that contraception causes abortion, on a par with the theory that the earth is six thousand years old...."

Hertzberg goes on to suggest that, as Trump has proclaimed, "the world laughs at us." What Trump doesn't comprehend, however, is that if the world *is* laughing, it is at his own buffoonery, and at others like him. It is a sad *commedia* repeated by the thousands of so-called leaders and individuals in our country who cannot deal with the realities that Hertzberg suggests, and other truths such as the fact that the US is one of the few

 civilized and wealthy countries that provides no healthcare for vast numbers of its citizens, and is apparently determined to take away even the insufficient benefits provided by Medicare and Medicaid; or the tragic fact that public education in our country is in shambles, with states and cities less and less able to provide high-quality teaching.

As if this recent circus had not been enough, a couple of days later Republican Committee Chairman Reince Preibus, like a flying trapeze artist, turned everything on its head once more:

> We're borrowing four and half billion dollars a day and this president is more worried about birth certificates, Oprah Winfrey and fundraisers at the Waldorf Astoria. It's maddening and I just wish the president would engage in the real issues that are affecting America.

When asked why, then, he hadn't suggested Trump alter his rhetoric, Preibus argued that his role was not to serve as censor. Yet Preibus would clearly censor the President for even responding. The most maddening thing of all is *not* the President's inability to engage in real issues, but the Republicans' inability to even comprehend what any "real" issues might possibly be, or how to communicate them within the political forum, which would mean to do precisely what Preibus refuses to do, to sit down with his constituency to determine a sane beginning to a dialogue.

More recently, Trump has publically mused why Obama hasn't released his grades from his Freshman year at Occidental College in Los Angeles—as if one of the best-educated and most intelligent Presidents in decades needed to prove something.

Before I could even revise this essay, that wonderful political spokesman Donald Trump again attacked the Chinese: "Listen, you motherfuckers, we're going to tax you 25%!" Even a suicide bomber might be reminded that the Chinese own $755.4 billion of the US Treasury securities against American debt. Do the Republicans—so determined, as they insist, on balancing the budget—really want to risk a complete and total financial collapse, all in the name of Trump's entertaining, family-unfriendly expletives? *La Commedia è finita*! And I haven't even mentioned Sarah Palin!

*Scott does report that Ann Dunham, amazingly, *did* think that her son, as he got older, could even become President of the United States. What a wonderfully determined mother she must have been.

LOS ANGELES, APRIL 29 AND APRIL 30, 2011
Reprinted from *Green Integer Blog* (May 2011).

Being There

EDWARD KIENHOLZ, RESTORED BY NANCY REDDIN
KIENHOLZ **FIVE CAR STUD** / LOS ANGELES COUNTY
MUSEUM OF ART, OPENED SEPTEMBER 4, 2011 / I SAW
THE INSTALLATION ON SEPTEMBER 2, 2011 AND AGAIN
ON SEPTEMBER 3, 2011

ARTIST EDWARD KIENHOLZ gained enormous notoriety as far back as 1966 for his "Back Seat Dodge
'38," an assemblage that included part of a Dodge car
with the back seat door opened, within which mani-
kins portrayed a couple "making out." Today one can
hardly imagine the furor it caused upon its Los Angeles County Museum of Art showing, when the Los
Angeles County Board of Supervisors declared it "por-
nographic" and attempted to shut the show down. A
compromise was reached wherein the back seat door
would remain closed, to be opened only by a guard
when requested and no children were within the gallery! The uproar determined that the piece had to be

seen by everyone, and opening day more than 200 people lined up to see it.

In September 2011, Kienholz, who died in 1994, is sure to cause some controversy again with the presentation of his 1972 piece "Five Car Stud," viewed publicly in Germany at Documenta that year, and never again seen. The piece, purchased by a Japanese museum, has been hidden away in storage, and only recently, through LACMA and the Getty Museum's collaboration, has been restored by Kienholz's second wife and collaborator, Nancy Reddin Kienholz.

If the earlier piece shocked some with its sexual content, this piece should stun us all for its portrayal of violence. Certainly there are sexual elements; a black man who has obviously been discovered in a truck with a white woman has been pulled from the car by six men, who, when we look closely at the scene, are in the process of castrating him. But the horror of this as-

semblage is not just the act, but the dramatic terror of the entire scene. The men are more bestial than human, their faces covered with horrific masks: one, pulling the ropes taut, has his face covered with a mask that will remind some of the great circus clown Emmett Kelly; another, standing beside the victim's truck, wherein a white woman sits vomiting, has a mask studded with horrific warts. It is difficult to stare too closely at each of these men, even though the audience of 15 individuals allowed into the room at a time must pass close to them in surveying the entire scene.

It is interesting that these men have chosen "clown" masks or something close to them to hide their identities. It reminds us of the role James Stewart played in *The Greatest Show on Earth*, in which he dressed in clown makeup throughout to hide his identity—

even though his crime was evidently an attempt to save someone's life. Further, it will bring to mind for some the serial killer of young boys, John Gacy, who worked as "Pogo the Clown," designing his own clown costumes, and sometimes enticing his victims through charitable events. Gacy's first assault took place a year before Kienholz's installation.

Remaining within the surrounding cars are not only the sickened white woman, but, in another, a young boy, whom Kienholz describes as "sissy boy," modeled, in part, upon the face of his own son. The horror which this child is witnessing, unlike the sexual acts of Kienholz's earlier piece, is truly devastating, a nightmare that we recognize will never allow this fearful boy to live anything but a haunted life. These men are not only destroying a man and a woman, but robbing joy and innocence from the entire society in which they exist.

The victim himself is no longer a man, his torso having been transformed by the artist into a receptacle of fluids, a trough of water in which float the letters that occasionally spell out the word through which these men have justified their torture: "nigger."

Walking through this darkened exhibition, I was terrorized, awed even, by the devastating act I was observing in tableau. But for me, even worse, was my own "being there," the sense of my voyeuristic fascination with the observation of it all. I could not bring myself to turn my eyes from the series of tragic events being played out before me, and I walked again and again around the circle of the five cars, peering into them, listening to the soft Delta music emanating from one. This behavior can be understood as something good or bad. Perhaps in witnessing such a scene I could serve as a sensitive historian of such events in our past, reminding others—those who even today might wish to harm people for racial or political differences—of what these actions mean to the individual and the society at large. Yet I might also simply be seen—in my inability to change history, in my own viewer passivity—as an unwilling participant to such events. Only my actions in life can determine which kind of witness I might be. But I was there and cannot hide that fact. On the gallery floor the artist has laid down a carpet simulacrum of a dirt road, into which each viewer's footprints are embedded. I saw my own!

LOS ANGELES, SEPTEMBER 4, 2011
Reprinted from *Green Integer Blog* (September 2011).

It was a Sunday, Mother's Day 2011. I often end up in New York City on Mother's Day, since it is the weekend my distributor, Consortium, generally chooses to host sales conferences.

I remember one such Mother's Day, waiting for a play to begin in a bar on 45th or 46th, when I overheard a head usher from one of the nearby theaters discussing the horrors of the day, describing how numerous middle-aged couples had celebrated the event by taking their elderly mothers and fathers to the theater and simply dropping them off, then picking them up later, sometimes long beyond the end of the production, presuming that the theater staff would take care of the parents until they arrived from wherever they had gone in the interim.

"They treat us as if we were babysitters or schoolteachers," the salty professional complained, "leaving their poor parents to sit in their theater seats for hours sometimes after the play has ended, like it were a playground superintended by us."

"Several times," she continued, "we've had to call the police to report missing families for these dear old folks. I hate Mother's Day!" she concluded.

I was startled to hear of such events. I never imagined that the theater might be used as a kind of dumping ground for the elderly, but I've seen it several times since. On Mother's Day I try not to attend popular musicals or comedies that might attract these inconsiderate middle-

agers as the perfect place for their mothers and fathers to spend the day, as if it were a Chuck E. Cheese's playground for the agéd.

I knew that the intensely serious play Jerusalem and, even more so, the off-Broadway production of the Belarus Group's Being Harold Pinter, the pieces I was planning attend, were unlikely venues for such abuse.

What I hadn't prepared for is that both of the plays I chose for a Mother's Day celebration were very much centered on violence and, more succinctly, blood. Hence, my title "Sunday, Bloody Sunday," an echo of the terrible events of the Bogside Massacre of 1972 in Derry, North Ireland, the song from the U2's 1983 album War, and the movie of 1971 about the Jewish family doctor, Daniel Hirsch (Peter Finch), and the divorced working woman, Alex Grenville (Glenda Jackson), who share the same lover.

My "Bloody Sunday" was "bloody," fortunately, without real bullets or actual deaths.

I decided to grab a quick bite near the theater in preparation for the likelihood that I would not be able to eat dinner, given the fact that Jerusalem ran until 6:00 and Being Harold Pinter, way downtown at 4th Avenue's Ellen Stewart Theater, began at 7:30.

I chose, quite by accident, but most felicitously, an Italian restaurant, Lattanzi, on 46th Street in Hell's Kitchen, one of several Italian restaurants on the block.

For my taste, I couldn't have chosen better, given that Lattanzi serves Jewish Italian, the kind of food I'd grown to love in Rome's Trastevere, the old Jewish ghetto of the city.

Because I arrived early, the restaurant was nearly ghostly, but the hostess and waiters were most friendly, as I decided to sit at the bar at the other end of the restaurant from the entry. I had a gin and tonic before ordering the primi, *Coarciofialla Giudia*, artichoke with garlic and olive oil cooked in the Jewish manner. What this means is a crispy brown outer series of edible artichoke leaves with the pointed, thorny stalks just to remind you of the mass of the vegetable that had to be cut away to get to the heart, that tender green, olive oil-infused center that literally melts in your mouth.

The balance of the two, the braised outer, thorn-like leaves with the luscious green circle of the center, is a perfect balance of the fruit of this nearly impenetrable fortress, which Americans generally serve after boiling or braising all the taste out of them, and smothering the slightly edible remainder with butter and salt. The artichokes at Lattanzi need little but the oil and a good appetite.

Before the artichokes the waiter had brought me a basket of breads far different from the usual Italian fare, although a more traditional chewy sliced bread lay under the treat of the matzo, incredibly thin, slightly grilled, and topped with garlic oil! Unlike the packaged holiday matzo, this was almost like an Indian naan or even Puri, deliciously flavored and light as a feather, but recognizable as matzo nonetheless.

The waiter suggested a secondi, Trigliette all'Embrice, a Red Snapper sautéed in garlic and onions, with olive oil, pine nuts, white raisins, and vinegar. To compliment this, I chose their champagne, infused with orange and ginger, the perfect match for the sweet and bitter under flavors of the fish. I couldn't imagine a tastier or more healthy dish. I felt it was the perfect food to fortify myself for the five hours following of intense drama I was looking forward to.

I have to go back to taste their dozens of other menu specialties which I might have ordered under slightly different circumstances.

LOS ANGELES, MAY 11, 2011
Reprinted from *Green Integer Blog* (May 2011).

Sunday, Bloody Sunday (1)

JEZ BUTTERWORTH **JERUSALEM** / NEW YORK, THE
MUSIC BOX, 2011 / THE PERFORMANCE I SAW WAS A
MATINEE ON MAY 8, 2011

JEZ BUTTERWORTH'S PLAY *Jerusalem* begins with
a blindingly blaring party in a small wooded clearing
inhabited primarily by a Waterloo trailer. In the quick
glimpse of the strobe-lit bacchanalia it appears that the
celebrating group is made up mostly of young teenagers.
But the next morning we gradually perceive, as court
processors arrive to post a demand to clear the property, that the main celebrant and owner of the trailer
is a burned-out, alcoholic, drug-consuming, former
bicycling stunt artist, Johnny "Rooster" Byron (Mark
Rylance), whose woodland trailer plot serves as a kind
of open house for any and all discontent beings near
the small town of Flintock, not far from Stonehenge in
Wiltshire County, England.

Among Rooster's several regulars are his wan-

nabe "mate," Ginger (Mackenzie Crook), a young man who has never outgrown this world of Peter Panism; a former Professor (Alan David) who drops by mainly for the alcoholic beverages freely proffered by the host; an overweight and under educated butcher, Davey (John Gallagher, Jr.); a soon-to-be traveler to Australia, Lee (Danny Kirrane); two silly and rather unattractive teenage girls, Pea and Tanya, the latter quite desperate to give up her virginity; and, upon occasion, the former Queen of the Fairies, Phaedra (Aimeé-Ffion Edwards), gone missing from the home of her violent stepfather, Troy Whitworth. These and others help keep alive the myths surrounding Rooster, and, in turn, boost his morale as he carouses daily, in battle after battle, straight into the jaws of death.

In the context of Butterworth's play, Rooster is represented as something akin to a figure of Druid or Nordic history, or, at least, a kind of Falstaff-like celebrator, a larger than life "hero," who stands against the staid and boring behavior of the small-town bourgeoisie surrounding him, so desperately desirous of ousting this outsider from the environs so that they can quickly build up a few more suburban-like houses or apartments.

Given the goings-on in this little "Jerusalem," the loud, late-night parties, underage drinking, drug consumption, and sex, I think it's safe to say that nearly every member of the elderly Sunday audience who tumbled into The Music Box, mostly from New Jersey, Connecticut, and Bucks County, Pennsylvania, like the good citizens of Flintock, would have just as readily signed the petition to remove Johnny "Rooster" Byron from his little plot—although given what we later discover about the hypocritical, alcoholic, and drug-hungry adults we encounter from the community, it is doubtful my audience would venture to live in Flintock either.

So why do audiences like the one I joined sit through the assaults on their sensibilities and, at the end of it, after a series of ridiculous plot developments I will soon reveal, applaud, not just politely but enthusiastically, cheering on these obvious misfits?

There are, perhaps, a number of reasons, but the most obvious one bears the name Mark Rylance. For Rylance is not just a good actor, he creates and inhabits the character of Rooster so fully that we are in awe as we watch a thing of words, a literary character, grow, bit by bit, into a monstrous yet humanly pitiable being with whom we have no choice but to contend. I sat in the front row of the theater, where I and the others there not only suffered some of the slings and arrows of spit, beer, sod, and blood, but watched his towering performance as he stood often just in front of my seat, since the characters claimed it was the spot where they smelled the wonderful wafts of wild garlic and where Rooster drew his ex-wife and other figures to look into his eyes, whereupon a deep rumbling sound shook the theater at its roots. Rylance is so convincing, so commanding in his role, that I believed in his dark powers even without that stage device.

For much of each act Rooster creeps round his "Jerusalem"—nearly crippled by all those "slings and arrows," the Evel Knievel-like jumping stunts, the numerous bar fights and beatings, and his advancing age—covered in layers of sweat, beer, liquor, wine, and other liquid ablutions, spinning off remarkable myths to his spellbound, if skeptical, merry band. The eldest and least imaginative of Rooster's protégées, Ginger, particularly struggles to restore some rational logic to Rooster's larger-than-life proclamations; but in that very act we foresee that, having stayed on beyond his time, he is soon to join the failed and flailing folk of Flintock adults.

Rooster may be a pied-piper, but his powers have little effect upon his own small son Andy, who has to suffer torments from his fellow schoolmates just for being the man's son. And as much merriment as Rooster provides his young teen friends, he has few gifts for the very young and no comprehension of how to nurture.

Throughout this endless turbulence, Rylance, if at times going a bit over the top (how could he not in such an operatic role?), literally takes over the stage with a sort of Medea-like dance of revenge against all the hundreds of offences he has suffered and committed himself.

One seldom witnesses these days such a complete theatrical abandonment of an actor's own self into that of his character, so that by play's end one almost feels the character and his body might collapse as the actor goes flying through the high canopy of trees imported onto The Music Box stage, a feeling reinforced by Rylance's compulsion, during the curtain call cacophony, to jump and up and down a couple of times as if to prove he was not really as crippled and bound to earth as was Rooster.

I wish only that the story were half as convincing. Beyond the bad boy behavior of its characters, Butterworth presents little else to suggest that Rooster is heir and kin to a long tradition of English, Druid, and Nordic brutes, including St. George, the slayer of dragons, on whose celebratory day the events occur. Rooster, the author hints, is one of the giants of English lore, who must battle against the petty societal demands that he faces, including a trio of dangerously violent brothers

who are convinced that he has had sexual intercourse with Phaedra, and, of course, against the court decree with bulldozers waiting nearby to shatter his castle come morning.

After a bloody beating and brutal branding by the Whitworth brothers, Rooster pours gasoline across his yard, curses the earth about him for anyone who touches it, and calls out the names of his family genealogy as he beats the drum he has told the children will bring out the giants. Rooster has also revealed to his son that he bears within a kind of "royal" blood, obviously of Blood group O, for which each month Rooster is paid for donating, the source of his money for all the good times.

Royal blood, giants in the earth, blood kinship, curses, and revenge—all the tribal and clan claims that have so plagued Asian, African, Middle-Eastern, and European cultures, are the forces that Johnny "Rooster" Byron finally calls up! Except for a few stuck-up descendants of Plymouth Rock, the USA has nothing quite like this, which explains our absurd fascination, I suppose, with English royalty, along with so many Americans' Anglophile obsessions, and, probably, some of the audience members' rapt appreciation of this play.

Despite Rylance's wondrous performance, however, I was not convinced that those curses, the drumbeats, even the sonorous rumbles, would bring anyone to his rescue to save his sacred green garden from the bulldozers about to descend. The gasoline might set one such machine afire, but there are others—there will always be others—behind it, and the people of Flintock and environs have already been cursed by the contingencies of contemporary life. But then, I never believed in the regeneration by rain in *The Waste Land* either, a poem written by another Anglophile equally invoking hierarchical myths of tradition. If Rooster is Faust, so is any passing thug.

I'll put my faith in the young Lee, the boy who perceives that it's necessary to escape, and has a number of intelligent and silly reasons for having chosen Australia. Even his desire to change names—completely incomprehensible to the leaden-brained Davey—suggests Lee seeks a new identity and life, free from all the things that Rooster attempts to conjure up. If that is Butterworth's point, I toast *Jerusalem* as a play as well as a great vehicle for Rylance's talents. But if we are to suppose that the man who once died will rise again, next time I'll root for the dragon.

NEW YORK, MAY 9, 2011
Reprinted from *US Theater, Opera, and Performance* (May 2011).

Sunday, Bloody Sunday (2)

VLADIMIR SHCHERBAN (ADAPTOR AND DIRECTOR)
BEING HAROLD PINTER, BELARUS FREE THEATRE / NEW
YORK, LA MAMA ELLEN STEWART THEATRE / THE PER-
FORMANCE I SAW WAS THE EVENING OF MAY 8, 2011

THE MOMENT I left the production of *Jerusalem*, I
caught a taxi downtown to the East 4th Street La MaMa
Theatre. I was looking forward to seeing the highly re-
spected Belarus Free Theatre's *Being Harold Pinter*, in
part because I am a great admirer of Pinter, but also because I feel a great sympathy with this theater company
that speaks out about political issues, a company who
currently cannot return to its homeland.

I should have realized that this production would
also show a great deal of blood: from the very first moment of the work when Pinter writes in his memoirs
about falling on the street, the actors holding up bloody
hands as evidence, straight through to a gripping series
of confrontations between prisoners and prison guards.

 This production, which begins by speaking of Pinter's method of creating characters, uses the playwright—himself an increasingly politicized figure as he aged—as a kind of lightning rod with whom and against whom the actors play out their various notions of what makes theater political, or, in their eyes, something of value.

They begin with the openness with which Pinter creates his figures, first setting them off from each other as alphabetical numbers which, as they react to one other, grow ultimately into full-blown characters. The company is intent, it appears, upon revealing the domestic violence of Pinter's figures, displaying their relationships and language alongside their own renditions of absurd prison interviews and punishments by officials and guards.

Certainly anyone who knows Pinter's plays well, along with his later critical writings and his Nobel Prize acceptance speech, will realize that this playwright is a political figure, and his plays, while sometimes moving into more and more abstract territory, became increasingly insistent about the nature of human torture and suffering. Using scenes from "Mountain Language,"

"One for the Road," and "Ashes to Ashes," the group helps the audience to perceive just how similar and, yet, how different Pinter is from the company's own presentation of Abu Ghraib-like stories of life in Belarus prisons. "Ashes to Ashes," in particular, points up Pinter's own dramatic use of dialogue between a jealous lover and a woman who is haunted by torturous memories that may never have happened.

Yet there is a sense among these actors, also, that what they love in Pinter is something they will rarely be able to reach, for they are out to present political realities, no matter how absurd the situations may be, while Pinter is far more interested in human relationships between good or bad. His characters often seem to torture one another less for what they see as mistaken ideas and actions as for the simple joy of it.

Particularly when these Belarusians performed scenes from Pinter's earlier play, *The Homecoming*, the group somehow got it all wrong. Yes, as they point out, the play begins with a hostile conversation between a father and a son, but the heavily brooding way in which they performed it is not, thank heaven, a standard reading. Often behind the hate expressed in Pinter's interrelations is an enormous amount of wit, a dark humor which cloaks and confuses the meaning, allowing us to see new aspects of each character's personality. In Pinter there is no simple good or bad. We may be morally

disgusted by both Max and Lenny, but we also have to recognize the fabulous energy behind their never-ending duels and laugh at the absurdity of life.

The Belarus Free Theatre performers—Nikolai Khalezin, Pavel Gorodnitski, Yana Rusakevich, Oleg Sidorchik, Irina Yarshevich, Denis Tarasenka, and Marina Yurevich—are all very serious minded, which, given the difficulty of their artistic lives, is completely understandable. And Pinter, even they admit, is not truly what their theater is all about. The prison scenes they play out may be equally absurd, the characters using language as a torturous device to break down the individual will, but there is little wit and joy behind it, and we recognize in that difference why political theater is often so predictable. The company was brilliant in its performances of those political scenes, and the substance of their criticism truly moved me. But then I have seen that play over and over again in the pages of newspapers and books of history, whereas each time I see a play by Harold Pinter it is as if I am discovering it for the first time.

LOS ANGELES, JUNE 6, 2011

Fixing Things

JOHN LOGAN (SCREENPLAY, BASED ON *THE INVEN-TION OF HUGO CABRET* BY BRIAN SELZNICK), MARTIN SCORSESE (DIRECTOR) **HUGO** / 2011

SCORSESE'S 3-D *HUGO* begins in Paris' Gare Montpar-nasse with the camera, slightly above the actors' heads, speeding through the crowds. It is a slightly dizzying and cinematically impressive start that also made me fear that the movie was going to be closer to anima-tion than human drama. But, in the end, after the very satisfying human drama that *Hugo* is, one realizes that that first scene was simply presented as a kind *tour de force*, as Scorsese's way of showing off: "Look what I can do now that I'm filming in 3-D." Indeed *Avatar* direc-tor James Cameron has been quoted as telling Scorsese that *Hugo* represented the best use of 3-D he had ever seen.

One might argue that that first rush of filmmaking is part and parcel of what the movie celebrates. Like Mi-

chael Hazanavicius' *The Artist*, *Hugo* concerns itself with the history of silent film; but while *The Artist* can be said to truly celebrate the form, *Hugo*, even in its devotion to the films of Georges Méliès, uses that history as a celebration of cinema in general and, by extension, as a hurrah for directors like Martin Scorsese. As Scorsese has admitted, the father-son relationship in *Hugo* reminded him of his own childhood experiences with his father sharing films.

Well, why shouldn't Scorsese celebrate himself? Although he has never been my favorite director, for years he has produced some of the most watchable movies of male vulnerability, from *Taxi Driver*, *Raging Bull*, and *After Hours,* to *Good Fellas*, *Cape Fear*, and *Shutter Island*. In *Hugo* he has marvelously worked against that type of film to produce a lovely fable that both children and adults can admire.

Young Hugo Cabret (Asa Butterfield) is an orphan—a kind of 20th-century Oliver Twist—due to the death of his mother and beloved father (Jude Law), as well as, we soon discover, the drowning of his constantly drunken uncle (Ray Winstone), who worked as an unknown employee in a train station. His father, a museum worker who died in a fire, was a tinkerer who restored toys, clocks, and other machines, and, just before his death, attempted to bring to life a marvelous metal automaton which he had rescued from the museum's vaults of unwanted art. Upon his father's death, Hugo is literally whisked away to the clock tower of Gare Montparnasse by his uncle, where the uncle now works as the official clock setter, winding up the huge clock and others each day at certain set hours. As we enter Hugo's world, the uncle has disappeared, and the boy has secretly taken over his position, stealing pastries and milk from the shops of the station in order to survive, living in the now-forgotten rooms originally provided for station employees.

The problem is that he has also been stealing bits and pieces, small mechanisms and springs, from a station toy shop owner in order to repair the automaton, and the shop owner (Ben Kingsley) is out to entrap him. Yet the major villain of Hugo's world is far more vengeful: the dreaded Stationmaster (Sacha Baron Cohen) whose central activity seems to be running down homeless urchins who frequent the station so that he can deliver them up to the orphanage, where he suffered much of his own childhood. The Stationmaster has his eye on Hugo as well, and some of the most remarkable scenes of the film are their amazing chases.

One day, however, Hugo is caught by the toy shop owner and made to empty his pockets, which contain not only the pieces of metal he has stolen over time, but a fascinating book, which we soon discover must have come with the automaton. Papa Georges, as the toy shop owner is known, seems more upset by the discovery of the notebook—which the child insists he return to him—than he does with the loss of metal parts. Georges announces to Hugo his intent to take the book home with him and burn it.

Why, we can only ask, is he being so vengeful to the boy? And what possible satisfaction might he attain by the destruction of this fascinating notebook? Like a forlorn puppy Hugo follows him home, continuing to demand the book's return, Georges attempting to rid himself of the nuisance. Once inside the house, Georges discusses the young annoyance with his wife. Hugo and the audience also discover in the house, a young girl, Isabelle (Chloë Grace Moretz), whom Hugo lures outside into the cold, pleading with her to help him regain his treasure. Isabelle agrees, at least, to keep the old man from burning it.

But the next day, the toy shop owner hands Hugo a small folded towel in which are only some ashes, evidence, presumably, of the book's obliteration. The child is in tears, and as some recompense, is offered part-time work in the shop. Georges is impressed as Hugo quickly fixes the mechanism to a small wind-up rat.

Reencountering Isabelle, Hugo discovers that the old man has not truly burned the book, and a tenuous friendship evolves between the two children. She is the more educated and forceful of them, he remaining, out of need, more secretive and fearful; yet they both gradually share their private worlds, Isabelle taking Hugo to a bookstore, he illegally entering a movie house with her through the back door. She has never been to a movie before, refused permission to attend films by Georges and his wife, her godparents, who have taken her in after the death of her parents. It is a day of great adventure for both; as they slip inside the movie house, Isabelle whispers: "We could get into trouble." Hugo declares, "That's how you know it's an adventure."

Yet when she demands to see where he lives, he backs away, forced to be protective of his hideaway and self-imposed job. That is, until he sees a necklace she is wearing: a piece of metal, shaped like a heart—the very "key" he has been unable to replicate in order to start up the automaton! Hugo is convinced that whatever the automaton might write will have a link to his dead father, revealing his course of life.

The boy can no longer resist showing Isabelle his clockwork's abode. As he brings her to his small room and to the automaton, the two of them putting the key into place, the machine rattles into motion. At first the metal man writes only a few unrelated scrawls in various positions on the page, a code that is impossible to crack. The child's disappointment is palpably displayed; after all, the hope of its message has been the only link he has left to his father.

Soon, however, the machine starts up once more, quickly composing a series of lines and images that reveal that the automaton does not write words but draws a picture: the very image which his father mentioned seeing as a child, a black-and-white version of the famed scene of a rocket crashing into the moon in Georges Méliès' 1902 film, *Le Voyage dans la lune* (*A Trip to the Moon*).

The automaton even signs the piece with the name of the film's director, Isabelle's godfather. What, they can only wonder, is the meaning of it all? How has Hugo's automaton known anything about Isabelle and her life?*

That first half of Scorsese's film, filled with mystery, wonderment, and adventures, is, frankly, the best part of the movie, and the heart of its charm. The second half, filled with sometimes flat-footed explanations and historical recountings is less convincing, as we gradually discover that the bitter old man in the toy store is actually the great early filmmaker, painfully hiding out from his own past life after having been rejected by the post-World War I generation, his over 400 films having all been destroyed, some of them melted down for their cellulose.

Scorsese's attempt to educate both the audience

and the children about Méliès and his films is exemplary, and the images from the films themselves are, as always, a wonder to behold. But this section is overlong, with the morose tone of the disillusioned filmmaker dominating the work. Only the continued energy of its young actors and the frantic chases of the Stationmaster after Hugo keep the movie going. Having met up with a Méliès' historian, who has, perhaps, the only copy remaining of the great filmmaker's *A Trip to the Moon*, Hugo is determined to play the film again in Méliès' own home, hoping to reveal to Papa Georges that he is not forgotten and his work is still beloved, at least by a few. But his dreams of the night before are horrific, as he, discovering the automaton's key on the railroad tracks, jumps down to retrieve it while a locomotive comes barreling forward, and, unable to stop, plows through the station, mowing down numerous travelers, diners, and workers in its path—a reference to the horrendous Gare Montparnasse train derailment of 1895, which, in actuality, killed only one person, but injured hundreds of the train's passengers.

At first, the intrusion into the Méliès' home is unsuccessful, as Mama Jeanne (Helen McCrory) attempts to protect her husband from further piquing his long heartache and disappointment. But finally, the film historian convinces her to view, once more, the copy of the film, which so delights her (and the children, who also recognize Jeanne as one of its actresses) that the room is transformed into joy, Méliès himself coming forth after having apparently watched from the hall to answer some of their questions. Hugo, who sees himself as a fixer, has mastered a kind of miracle, as the old man recalls his wonderful life of the past. Jeanne summarizes it:

> Georges, you've tried to forget the past for so long,
> but it has caused nothing but unhappiness. Maybe
> it's time you tried to remember.

But Hugo has yet one more great gift to bestow upon the old director. He returns to the station to retrieve the marvelous automaton. This time, however, the Stationmaster discovers Hugo before he can re-enter his secret rooms, following him. The young child is forced to hide outside the window, hanging from the face of the giant clock, much like Harold Lloyd in the movie Hugo and Isabelle attended. Unable to find Hugo, the Stationmaster turns back, while the boy grabs up his treasure and runs; but this time, through the Stationmaster's maneuvers, the metal man is thrown into the air, crashing down onto the tracks. Hugo's attempt to retrieve him echoes his dream, as a train bears down upon the trapped boy, pulled to safety at the last moment by the Stationmaster. He hustles the

boy away, determined to finally send him off to an institution, just as the Méliès, Isabelle in tow, enter the station, claiming him as their own!

The story's ending is truly a kind of celebration of all that has come before, as Méliès is inducted into the French Film Society which, after having tracked down and reclaimed 180 of his films, presents a retrospective, the family and Hugo in attendance.

So has the film successfully embedded a real story—almost everything about Méliès is true—within a fable. But I must admit, although I love Méliès' magical art, in this case I prefer the magic of the John Logan fable!

---

*Although Méliès did experiment with automata, the one used in this film, I have read, is a kind of hybrid of two famous automata by the Swiss-born clockmaker Pierre Jacquet-Droz.

LOS ANGELES, DECEMBER 22, 2011
Reprinted from *Nth Position* [England] (February 2012).

Born Again

GEORGE SEATON (SCREENPLAY, BASED ON A STORY
BY VALENTINE DAVIES), GEORGE SEATON (DIRECTOR)
MIRACLE ON 34TH STREET / 1947

I'LL BEGIN BY ADMITTING that I absolutely enjoy
George Seaton's and Valentine Davies' holiday fantasy,
Miracle on 34th Street. I have probably watched this film
every year of my adult life on Thanksgiving day or during the Christmas season, and I get delight just imagining that I might have witnessed the premiere of this
film as a six-month-old baby.

This year, watching it just before Thanksgiving dinner, however, I had a different, more contrarian view of
the holiday chestnut listed in the National Film Reg-
istry.

Let me start by saying the obvious, a cliché spouted
each year by thousands of religious Americans, particularly, one imagines, by those who describe themselves
as "born again:" the Christmas season has increasingly

become commercialized, and most Americans have lost the sense of the holiday's true focus, the birth of Christ.

Admittedly, I am not among those religious or "born again" Americans, but even I was appalled when the Christmas shopping season, it was announced, would begin this year not on the Friday morning after Thanksgiving, but at midnight. A local radio station began 24-hour programming of Christmas carols (most of them centered on the holiday festivities instead of the child in Bethlehem) two weeks ago!

Generally recognized as the emblem of that pagan, commercialized Christmas is Santa Claus, the jolly, fat, Dutch, gift-giving *Sinterklaas*. You remember him, the one about whom your parents lied, leading you on to believe that he was the source of all of those lovely Christmas presents beneath the tree, until you grew old enough to appreciate the loving care they had been secretly showing you for all those years. As I have written elsewhere, I came to that realization, almost miraculously one morning, at a far younger age than most of my peers; it didn't bother me one little bit that there wasn't any Santa Claus and that my parents had been so nice to me for all those years. But my revelation of that fact to a school friend, sent her off crying into her mother's arms. I was told that I must never reveal the truth to anyone my age or younger. But even older children, I realized, might not like to hear my discovery.

 Seaton's work, however, begins almost at the opposite end of the equation. The young girl at the center of this story, Susan Walker (Natalie Wood), has been told by her level-headed mother, Doris (Maureen O'Hara), that there is no Santa Claus, without any noticeable effect in the child's demeanor. Mrs. Walker, who works at Macy's, coordinating the all-important Macy's Thanksgiving Day Parade, is apparently a practical woman who has, one imagines, tried to remove almost all fantasy and myth from her young daughter's life. She has been told that there are no giants, and the girl is discouraged from reading "fairy tales." Obviously, the mother has been hurt by what she perceives as the fantasies of her married life. One wonders how she has dealt with Christian myths, including the child born in a stable. But fortunately, for the survival of the film, Seaton has skirted that issue and, indeed, all issues having to deal with the season's real purpose.

The film begins with a seemingly persnickety old man scolding a young window dresser for putting the reindeer in the wrong places in relation to his store's depiction of Santa and sleigh. The man, Kris Kringle (the marvelous Edmund Gwenn), we soon discover, is very particular when it comes to all things about Santa. After all, he believes he *is* Kris Kringle, Santa. It is, as the doctor to the nursing home where Kris lives later assures us, a quite harmless delusion, one that only leads him to do good. But everything is soon made much more complicated when Kris accidentally encounters, during the early moments of the Macy's parade, that the man hired to play Santa Claus—the traditional star of the event (even today, as I watched the parade, the bands, floats, balloons, and other theater and vaudeville events, the parade culminated with Santa's arrival)—is absolutely soused! Reporting the man's condition to Mrs. Walker, Kris seems a natural to replace the drunk Santa. After all, he even looks like a well-trimmed and tailored Santa. It is almost inevitable that Mrs. Walker should invite him to *portray* Santa, since, he declares, he has certainly had experience.

Meanwhile, Doris' daughter, Susan, is watching the parade from a neighbor's window, from what we might presume is a Central Park West apartment. Today we might worry about the fact that she is watching this with an adult male, Fred Gailey (John Payne)—although we have been reassured by the Walkers' maid that she has been keeping an eye on the girl—who occupies an apartment across the way. The Santa Claus, declares Susan, is quite convincing, far better than the one of the year before. Gailey is a bit troubled by her mature dismissal of Santa, as well as giants, but is not beyond encouraging her to invite him to dinner in the Walker home. Mr. Gailey may be a happy man (the old fashioned meaning of "gay"), but he is represented as bit disturbing in his forward behavior. His "move" on the daughter, clearly, is also a move on her somewhat cynical mother. Nonetheless, he is invited to dinner.

Kris, meanwhile, not only looks the part of the perfect Santa, but is quickly hired by Macy's to become their department store Santa. Kris is delighted to be able to return to his rightful place, and everyone seems happy with his "acting," until it is discovered that he has been telling some parents to purchase their children's gifts at competing stores—even Gimbels. The scene where Thelma Ritter (in one of her first film roles) stops to thank the floor manager for their unusual new policy of putting the spirit of Christmas, so it appears, before their own financial gain is one of the most de- lightful of the film.

Such radical behavior is, expectedly, met with horror, until both the floor manager, Julian Shellhammer (Philip Tonge), and Mrs. Walker, summoned to Mr. Macy's office, discover that their boss loves the idea because it will result in even more paying customers. In another assault on the Walker family, Gailey encourages Susan to wait in line to see Santa before dropping her off at her mother's office. The girl is skeptical, until she hears Kris speak and sing to a young Dutch orphan in her original language. Doris' response is predictable: "Susan, I speak French, but that doesn't make me Joan of Arc."

To back her up, Doris summons their Santa, encouraging him to tell Susan that he is not really Santa Claus; but when he insists that he is, she demands his file, wherein she discovers that he goes under the name of Kris Kringle and declares his birthplace as the North Pole. A visit to the store psychologist is ordered for Kris, who passes all the tests with great aplomb, yet raises the ire of the psychologist, Granville Sawyer (Porter Hall), who throughout the interview pulls at his eyebrows (a trait shared by his secretary), by suggesting that something may be problematic in his home life. In retaliation, Sawyer suggests that Kris may have a latent hostility that could break out at any time. A call to the doctor who heads the Long Island nursing home where Kris has been living brings reassurances from Dr. Pierce (James Seay), who also suggests it may be easier if Kris can find a place to stay nearer to the store in Manhattan. Before you can say Kris Kringle, Gailey has invited the old man to share his bedroom, further insinuating his being into the Walkers' life.

As the old gent speaks to Susan, he is saddened to learn that she does not believe in his existence and that she has been spurned by her playmates for being unable to imagine herself as an animal. "But I am not an animal," she declares, after which he patiently teaches her how to pretend to be a monkey. It is clear that he has taken on the Walkers as a kind of test case:

> ...Christmas isn't just a day, it's a frame of mind... and that's what's been changing. That's why I'm glad I'm here, maybe I can do something about it.

Kris even repeats the sentiments I stated earlier in this essay, disparaging the commercialism of the holiday—a strange thing for that emblem of the commercial to do; but it is clear the director and writer want it both ways.

Soon after Kris discovers that a beloved young janitor, Alfred (Alvin Greenman), has also been see-ing the mean-spirited Sawyer, who suggests that Alfred has psychological problems simply for wanting to play

Santa Claus at his neighborhood YMCA. Furious with the abuse of this good-hearted boy, Kris charges into Sawyer's office, accusing him of malpractice and hitting him over the head with his cane. The violence Sawyer has predicted has, alas, become reality, and Kris is sent to Bellevue Psychiatric Hospital for evaluation, believing that Mrs. Walker has been behind the decision.

Despairing of the lack of faith she has shown, Kris purposely fails the psychiatric examination, and is destined to be locked away. Almost everyone knows the rest of the story, how Gailey takes on Kris' case, fighting to convince a disbelieving world and court that Kris Kringle is truly Santa Claus. Even Mrs. Walker and her daughter come round to support his cause.

The case is miraculously won, due, in part, to the political exigencies of the court. As the Pol Charles Halloran (William Frawley) puts it to Judge Henry X. Harper (Gene Lockhart):

> All right, you go back and tell them that the New York State Supreme Court rules there's no Santa Claus. It's all over the papers. The kids read it and they don't hang up their stockings. Now what happens to all the toys that are supposed to be in those stockings. Nobody buys them. The toy manufactures are going to like that; so they have to lay off a lot of their employees, union employees. Now you

got the CIO and AF of L against you and they're going to adore you for it and they're going to say it with votes. Oh, and the department stores are going to love you too and the Christmas card makers and the candy companies. Ho ho, Henry, you're going to be an awful popular fella. And what about the Salvation Army? Why, they got a Santa Claus on every corner, and they're taking a fortune.

So much for Kringle's dismay at the commercialism of Christmas! Perhaps no clearer statement of the relationship between the fat, jolly fellow and money has ever been made. Harper's children even hate him, and Gailey calls the young son of District Attorney Thomas Mara to testify that his father has told him, assuredly, that there is a Santa Claus.

Even more cynical are the US Postal employees, tired of all the unclaimed mail addressed to Santa Claus, who win the day for Gailey and Kris Kringle by forwarding dozens of sacks of letters to the courthouse, providing the Judge with an easy way out:

Uh, since the United States Government declares this man to be Santa Claus, this court will not dispute it. Case dismissed.

So, insists Seaton's film, Santa Claus, despite all evidence to the contrary, is alive and well. Yet Seaton and the original author go further, demanding of even the adult characters and viewers their utter belief in the commercial emblem. When asked what she might like for Christmas, Susan pulls out an advertisement for a suburban Long Island home. Even Kris Kringle is a bit stunned by her demand, and suggests, "Don't you see, dear? Some children wish for things they couldn't possibly use like real locomotives or B-29s." Her retort is the stubborn insistence of any spoiled consumer:

> If you're really Santa Claus, you can get it for me.
> And if you can't, you're only a nice man with a
> white beard like mother said.

The filmmakers hardly pause to take in the significance of what the child has just said, before Kris has sent the three traveling along a route that winds by the house of her dreams. Upon glimpsing it, Susan demands they stop and runs into the home as if she already owned it. How can Mr. Gailey and Mrs. Walker resist such a consumer dream, even if it means giving up their perfectly nice apartments, overlooking the parade route, and now probably worth millions of dollars? They will simply have to marry, move to the suburbs, and build onto the little family with which they have begun. The discovery of Kris' cane left near the fireplace

convinces them surely—as "born-again" Christians' zealous rediscovery of Christ—of Santa Claus' existence, just as the audience is bathed with consumer assurances that this is, in fact, the perfect house.

Perhaps never in the whole of Hollywood productions was there a more central pitching of consumer products. Even movies with thousands of "product placements" cannot match Susan's answer to Kris' question of where she had found the lovely sweater she is wearing: "My mother got it on sale it at Macy's."

During an ad between events of this year's Macy's Thanksgiving Day Parade, Macy's proudly quoted that line among other cinematic mentions of the august department store.

As Susan chants to herself: "I believe...I believe... it's silly, but I believe."

LOS ANGELES, THANKSGIVING 2011
Reprinted from *American Cultural Treasures* (November 2011).

Nothing but the Truth

OSCAR WILDE **THE IMPORTANCE OF BEING EAR-
NEST** / NEW YORK, AMERICAN AIRLINES THEATRE / THE
PERFORMANCE I SAW WAS ON MAY 7, 2011

THE CENTRAL PUN of Oscar Wilde's perennial comic
delight—the homophonic relationship between the
name Ernest and the word that characterizes "an intense
and serious state of mind"—is at the heart of Wilde's
work. While the lovely women of this play, Gwendolen
Fairfax (Jessie Austrian) and Cecily Cardew (Charlotte
Parry), can love only an "Ernest," a man of a serious state
of mind, the young men, Algernon Moncrieff (Santino
Fontana) and John Worthing (David Furr), immediately prove themselves be utter fakers and liars, both—
as Algy defines it—Bunburyists, men who lie to their
families about having a relative or friend elsewhere so
that they can escape into the city (in Worthing's case)
or into the country (in Algy's situation). And the first
scene of this play is nothing if not complete evidence of

these effete young men's triviality, each competing with one another with absurd aphorisms and often meaningless *bon mots*. Jack, we may argue, is the more serious of the two, but he is no more reliable in speaking the truth than is his friend Algernon, who besides being unscrupulous is represented as a kind of greedy glutton, particularly when it comes to cucumber sandwiches.

We find it somewhat hard to believe, accordingly, that Jack/Ernest is so smitten with love for Algy's cousin Gwendolen that he is ready to marry her on the spot; that is, until we discover that Gwendolen is just as frivolous, ready to marry him on that same spot because his name, she believes, is Ernest.

All of this is great fun, but would become tiresome were it not for the existence of Gwendolen's Gorgon-like mother, Lady Bracknell (magnificently performed by Brian Bedford), of whom Worthing notes:

> I don't really know what a Gorgon is like, but I am quite sure that Lady Bracknell is one. In any case, she is a monster, without being a myth, which is rather unfair....

A great believer in "natural ignorance," Lady Bracknell is a stolid column of English conventionality, ready to accept Worthing because of his lack of political beliefs, habit of smoking, and apparent wealth, but unable to

even fathom a man who has "lost both of his parents"—"To lose one parent, Mr. Worthing, may be regarded as a misfortune; to lose both looks like carelessness." She is absolutely flabbergasted when she is told that he was found in a black leather handbag in Victoria Station!

Bedford plays this most luscious of monsters absolutely straight, no winks to the audience, no loopy drag-queen flopping of hands, and no change of pitch in voice. Lady Bracknell, in Bedford's shoes, is, if anything, more of a lady than ever, muttering her ridiculous pronunciamentoes in a post-menopausal voice that seems made for the role. To watch him at work, although his "acting" is so flawless that one cannot comprehend it as "work," is a true joy, something that for me will be hard to forget.

The remainder of the play, as everyone knows, revolves around a series of hilarious coincidences and more outrageous one-liners than even Henny Youngman might crack in a single night. Wilde's play literally drips with wit.

As outrageous as it first sounds, Algy's suggestion that women only come to call one another sister "after

they have called each other a lot of other things," comes true when Gwendolen, curious about Jack's/Ernest's house in the country, comes visiting only to find another woman hosting tea. Their bitchy politeness crackles with firery hate.

Even Lady Bracknell's pronouncement of Jack's "carelessness" with regard to the loss of his parents is apparently close to the truth, when we discover that Miss Prism (Jayne Houdyshell)—currently Cecily's tutor—once worked for Lady Bracknell's sister, whose child she confused with her romantic manuscript, placed the romance in the perambulator and the child in her large black leather handbag—the act releasing a series of prismatic images of what this class-structured society has wrought.

The revelation suddenly makes the two men, Algernon and Jack, brothers—which they have spiritually been all along. Jack, who soon after discovers that his birth name was Ernest, can now marry his cousin Gwendolen, as Algy, although he must forfeit the baptismal name of Ernest, will now be permitted to marry the young Cecily. Thus all the characters can be said to have been incorporated into one large family, where everyone will live happily ever after...if they can remain earnest!

It is doubtful, however, in such a world of winding tales and deceit as this family has suffered, that deep seriousness will be long permitted. As Ernest (formally Jack) admits: "It is a terrible thing for a man to find out suddenly that all his life he has been speaking nothing but the truth."

NEWARK, NEW JERSEY AND LOS ANGELES, MAY 9, 2011
Reprinted from *US Theater, Opera, and Performance* (May 2011).

Being Married: Two Films by Pierre Étaix

PIERRE ÉTAIX AND JEAN-CLAUDE CARRIÈRE (WRITERS AND DIRECTORS) **HEUREUX ANNIVERSAIRE (HAPPY ANNIVERSARY)** / 1962, USA 1963

PIERRE ÉTAIX AND JEAN-CLAUDE CARRIÈRE (WRITERS), PIERRE ÉTAIX (DIRECTOR) **LE GRAND AMOUR (THE GREAT LOVE)** / 1969

ON NOVEMBER 16, 2011, the Academy of Motion Picture Arts and Sciences presented an evening of two films, a short and a feature, by the French director Pierre Étaix, a man little known in the US because his films were, for many years, tied up in copyright issues which also resulted in their deterioration. Through the help of several organizations, particularly the Technicolor Foundation for Cinema Heritage and Groupama Gan Foundation for Cinema, this director's films have been restored and will be released next year by Criterion on DVD. But it was a special treat to see two of them at the Academy's widescreen Samuel Goldwyn Theater.

The first of these "The Laughter Returns" films was Étaix's 1962 black-and-white short (15 minutes) *Heureux Anniversaire*, which reveals Étaix's roots in the circus, as well as his major cinematic influences, Charlie Chaplin, Buster Keaton, and Jacques Tati, with whom he worked on *Mon Oncle*.

This movie, which won the 1963 Academy Award for short films, is a kind of road picture—in which no one goes anywhere. The earliest frames reveal a loving wife, La femme (Laurence Lignières), setting a formal table, hiding a gift within the napery, and preparing a beautiful meal for her husband: it is, quite clearly, a special occasion, and when, soon after, we see Le mari (Étaix) with a wrapped package and champagne, we recognize that it is a shared holiday, in fact an anniversary. When the husband attempts to drive away from the shop where he has purchased the gift, he finds that other cars have locked him in. He honks one of the cars' horns, and a man, mid-shave, exits from the barber, politely moving the car so that the implacable Étaix can exit.

One major difference in Étaix's films from other comic works of their time is that they seldom focus on only one figure. For this poor man, whose space is immediately overtaken by another automobile, is forced for the rest of the film to circle the block, shouting out to the barber over and over that he will be right back.

The happy husband, meanwhile, gets trapped in a traffic jam, which the writers mock by showing various drivers engaged in every kind of activity—except driving—imaginable, from reading, playing games, dining, etc.

When traffic finally loosens a bit, our hero decides to stop by a flower shop. This time, he enters a narrow space, which, when he returns, permits him no entry into his car. For a few seconds, he even contemplates crawling through other cars to get to his own, but it is to no avail, and other trapped drivers berate him for the situation.

Meanwhile, the wife, patiently waiting at home, is growing tired, bored, certainly impatient, as she nibbles at a salad, nips at the wine.

The flowers are crushed by the time the hero is on his way again. Another visit to a shop, where he buys a ridiculous sunflower, ultimately ends with similar results: the flower is beheaded. By the time the poor man reaches his apartment door, the wife, having finished off the bottle and eaten much of the food, has fallen into a kind of drunken stupor, her hand lying upon the

dinner table. Le mari gently kisses her and rattles the little package she has hidden for him in the napkins' folds. He shall have to spend the night alone. Such is married life in the 20th-century urban world.

As Étaix himself describes it, *Le grand amour* is based on a vaudeville conceit, that of an older man attracted to a younger woman. If one wants to recognize just how adroit Étaix is, however, one might compare this film with an American equivalent, such as Billy Wilder's tepid comedy of 1955, *The Seven Year Itch*. Similar to *Le grand amour*, the male in Wilder's farce is fed up with married life and attracted to a young shapely woman (in this case, Marilyn Monroe), and like the Étaix figure, imagines all sorts of humorous scenarios of how to seduce the younger woman while his wife is away on vacation. Yet how much more coarse and, frankly, uninteresting is Wilder's version. Tom Ewell was a beanbag of a man, middle-age having spread to every muscle in his body. Perfect, I imagine, for all those frumpy American men who still might imagine that Monroe would swoon over them. But Étaix, still handsome in a comic way, has a true chance to attract this young beauty, his secretary Agnès; indeed she seems almost to flirt with him, and readily agrees to join him on a dinner date. In short, we know noth-

ing will ever happen between Ewell and Monroe; the idea is preposterous from the outset. But in *Le grand amour* there is actually a dangerous possibility that Pierre's attraction will take him further than an imaginary fling.

In *Le grand amour*, moreover, we also know the whole story of their lives, and witness how Florence (whose appearance is so close to her mother that she takes the frightening prediction—"like mother, like daughter"—to an entirely new dimension) has manipulated him. The family relationship is comically reiterated by the scene in which, after having heard gossip of her husband's philandering in the park, she packs up to go home to "mamma." The film brilliantly tracks her down the stairs, Pierre pleading with her as she goes, watching her enter a room below wherein her mother and father sit.

Florence's family have, despite Pierre's reluctance, been only too happy to marry their daughter off, and before he has even had the opportunity to think things out, he finds himself in the cathedral with a hundred sober faces behind him, determined to see him follow through with the event. The wedding is  made even a more hilarious when we discover the fact that Étaix later married the actress playing Florence (Annie Fratellini), several members of her circus-performing family serving as figures in the film.

The paternal business is a tannery, and before Pierre can even say, "I do," he is boxed into that family enterprise, each day facing the ugly visage of the father's capable secretary. Although outwardly playing the joyful married couple, dining several nights a week with Florence's family, the two, years later, are both dreadfully bored. No mere "seven year itch," Pierre is suffering from what might be described as an intense rash. He cannot even walk through the park on his way to work without arousing the interest of the provincial town's gossips, wonderful clowns and character actors whose antics carry this film into new comic dimensions.

It can hardly be a shock, accordingly, when a young, very young, beautiful girl turns up in Pierre's office to replace the former battle-ax. Goaded on by his friend Jacques (Alain Janey), Pierre suddenly begins to imag-

 ine, just as the Tom Ewell character in the Wilder film, all sorts of possibilities. But while Ewell's revision of his life is basically banal and ineffective, Étaix and Carrière draw their comic possibilities from the theater of the absurd, conjuring up (with Étaix's miraculous prop-man) beds that take to the streets, a spousal property settlement in which every object in the house has been split into halves, as well as a whole series of imaginary love scenes played out by the two men in a restaurant that cannot but convince everyone from the local gossips to the café waiter that Pierre and his friend Jacques are having a gay affair!

Whereas, Ewell attempts, in his imagination, to madly embrace his prey upon a piano stool, Pierre actually speaks out about his passion for his young secretary—without knowing, however, that he is pouring his heart out to the ugly secretary about to leave the company, who quickly locks the door to bar his escape!

Throughout all this ridiculousness, Étaix maintains an aplomb and grace that has been compared, with good reason, to the dancing of Fred Astaire. It is perhaps not accidental, the director reminisced after the film, interviewed by Leonard Maltin and translated by

Geneviève Bujold, that he works best with clowns and dancers. While Étaix perhaps sees his roots most clearly in the little tramp, I would argue that his personality is closer to the stone face and the choreographed agility of Keaton. And like Keaton (and to a certain degree Chaplin), the marvel of his movements are that they actually occur in real space instead of being recreated. As Étaix argues, "they were *real*, not something made up." The beds truly rode down country lanes. "We closed off the streets, but a car still came up to us as the bed flew past," he recalls.

Like Richard Sherman (the Tom Ewell character), Pierre does not go through with his imagined affair. In the American film, it is a combination of guilt, fear of discovery, and jealousy that finally extinguishes his passion for Monroe. In *Le grand amour,* it is his own being that finally reveals to him who he actually is. As he begins to talk to the young beauty over dinner, he speaks of nothing but the office. It is clear that, despite his seeming entrapment in Florence's world, it is precisely the place in which he feels most comfortable. He is a business man at heart, running a tannery, and as he begins to reveal himself, he grows older and older by the minute in her eyes—as well as in ours and, most importantly, in his own. Just as he has earlier wished that he were younger (in cinematic terms, *becoming* younger) before calling for his secretary, who arrives at his office door as a child of 10 years of age, so now he leaves the dinner comprehending the truth. "I have wanted to tell you something," he begins, "I no longer love you."

Florence returns from her vacation just in time, but he cannot find her at the station. When he does finally encounter her, she looks younger, refreshed; so too, she tells him, does he. She has disembarked with a young handsome man, who stands holding her bags. Pierre is outraged. Who is the young man? Does she give her bags up to just anyone? So the couple goes arguing down the street, their discussion clearly providing fodder for the gossips for months.

When asked why he turned the action away from their argument to the distracted clearing-up of the café waiter and the final shrug of a drunkard (another clown) who appears throughout the film, Étaix commented: "I did not want to 'end' the film with any conclusion, good or bad. It may be that the fight between the two is the first time they are really talking to one another. But I did not want to say that. I wanted to turn the audience's attention away from whatever they thought the ending might really be. There is no one answer, no one ending." The danger, that puts all of Étaix's characters on a kind of circus high-wire, remains. We can never know for sure whether they will balance themselves and walk across the tent-tops or tragically fall.

LOS ANGELES, NOVEMBER 17, 2011
Reprinted from *World Cinema Review* (November 2011).

*In 2011 the great Chilean filmmaker, Raúl Ruiz, died
of complications from a lung infection. At the time of his
death I had not seen any of his films. In 2013, I saw and
reviewed* Three Crowns of the Sailor, *which I included
in* My Year 2002. *I also saw and reviewed his* The Mysteries of Lisbon, *which I have included below.*

The Confessions

CARLOS SABOGA (SCREENPLAY, BASED ON *OS MIS-
TÉRIOS DE LISBOA* BY CAMILO CASTELO BRANCO), RAÚL
RUIZ (DIRECTOR) **MISTÉRIOS DE LISBOA (THE MYSTER-
IES OF LISBON)** / 2010, USA 2011

RAÚL RUIZ'S stunning costume drama of Lisbon, Por-
tugal in the late 19th century was first shown as a series
of television dramas before being combined into a 4½-
hour film in 2011. As one might expect for such a long
work (although there is no feeling of lethargy in this
rather exciting series of tales within tales), the movie
begins quite slowly, almost in a kind of catatonic state.
After the film's ongoing narrator sets the situation, an
elderly British woman is discovered to be drawing a
young boy, who reads nearby as if he didn't even no-

tice her. The camera
follows him into the
hall of the church
school housing or-
phans, where once
more, oblivious to
his fellow classmates,
the beautiful child,
named only João (João Luis Arrais)—without a middle
or last name, and rumored to be the son of the school's
priest, Father Dinis (Adriano Luz)—continues to read.
A young bully leaps out from the group of boys, grab-
bing the book from João's hands while insisting that
even if his classmate seems different and special, he is,
like them, only the son of a thief or horse trader. João
responds in the only way he might, offering the bully
the book but suggesting he might even teach him how
to read. The incident seems to end, but a few seconds
later a nun discovers João in the hall undergoing what
appears to be an elliptic fit.

It is at this moment, in its fevered hallucinations
depicting the child's ill mind, that Ruiz's brilliant film
actually begins. And although the child's mind ultimately stops its spin, the movie seldom does. Indeed,
one might describe *The Mysteries of Lisbon* as a kind of
hallucinatory fable in which ultimately it appears that
the inhabitants of Lisbon are interconnected to each

other, as in tale after tale in the work devoted to story-telling, we discover its figures living lives that are nested together a bit like Russian dolls, each containing each.

João's "fit" and illness summon to his rescue a woman of the nobility, Ângela de Lima (Maria João Bastos), who gifts the child a toy box theater (that reiterates the film's complex plot) and a portrait of himself, which reveals to the child that he does have a visage beyond the one he has created in his active mind. The woman, so Father Dinis explains, is his mother, who, married to a man other than his father, had to abandon him to protect his life. Although Father Dinis confesses this part of the story to the boy, throughout most of the rest of the film, he becomes, like Hitchcock's famous character, "a man who knows too much," having been the confessor of nearly everyone else in the complex grouping of characters. And little by little, first through the young boy's search for his paternity, and later through the interrelationships of other adjacent characters, we grow to perceive the nearly impossible series of coincidences that life often is.

João (whose real turns out to be Pedro) is the offspring of another figure of the aristocracy, D. Pedro da Silva (João Baptista), who like Ângela, alas, is a second-born child, which means in this hide-bound world of traditions that neither shall inherit any money, and  that both, accordingly, must marry into wealth. The fact that they fall in love can only be perceived as an unfortunate tragedy that must be righted by their parents by marrying them off to others, and, when it is discovered that Ângela is pregnant, we have evidence of the murder of her baby. Enter Father Dinis before his saintly avocation, a gypsy who convinces the would-be assassin, Alberto de Magalães, The Knife, to abandon his intentions by paying him a large sum of money. So does he take on the responsibility of the young boy, but, obviously, this is only the beginning!

If one were to recount all the dozens of miraculous—and, yes, still hallucinatory in Ruiz's almost always surprising camera work—interrelationships, I am sure it would sound much like a outsized soap opera. Indeed, it is, in terms of plot. But in terms of the fierce loves, hates, jealousies, gossip, treacheries, lies, and political machinations of the world in which these figures live, the interconnected stories seem almost inevitable, as each tale swallows up the others, so that we lose track

of the original figures only to have them reappear at unexpected moments, drawn back into the overall landscape as they age. In the process, Father Dinis, also an orphan, discovers his own paternity, and the now older João-Pedro reencounters the man that might have taken his life at birth, challenging him to a duel. Fortunately, the now-dashing pirate Alberto (Ricardo Pereira) cannot shoot well (a fact which we long ago witnessed in his attempt to kill Pedro's father years earlier), and settles the matter, somewhat comically, by himself confessing to the much younger man (who indirectly changed Alberto's life) how he came to love and abandon the beautiful Elisa de Montfort (Clotilde Hesme) before marrying Eugénia, formerly the mistress of Ângela's husband, the Count of Santa Bárbara! You see what I mean?

Ruiz, brilliant director that he is, does not at all attempt to maintain that these almost claustrophobic interrelationships are anything near realism. And besides, the figures themselves behave as if they were living in a grand theatrical work, women fainting on the spot for being called gossips, married women bawdily bedding any handsome man that comes their way. Men are killed and saved upon whims of fate and higher-ups. And children are tortured by the incompressibility of the world into which they have been born. The director maintains a Brechtian distance by simultaneously playing out these remarkable events in the child's theater box. In fact, when he again returns us to the sick boy's bed at the end of the film, we may even wonder whether the entire "mysteries" of Lisbon have truly been a hallucination of the young boy, lost in the imaginary adventures of his beloved books.

Has the child not only recreated a swashbuckling past for himself, but a future that resolves all that he cannot currently comprehend? Does it matter? Did the world of Scheherazade have to be true to enchant her listener night after night?

LOS ANGELES, NOVEMBER 4, 2013
Reprinted from *World Cinema Review* (November 2013).

Cleaning House

GIOVANNI RUFFINI (LIBRETTO, BASED ON A
LIBRETTO BY ANGELO ANELLI), GAETANO DONIZETTI
(COMPOSER) **DON PASQUALE** / NEW YORK, THE MET-
ROPOLITAN OPERA / THE PERFORMANCE I SAW WAS ON
NOVEMBER 13, 2010

A FUNNY THING happened on my way to this opera. I
had planned on my New York trip to attend the opera
the day it was being broadcast live via high-definition
video so that Howard could see the same production
back in Los Angeles as I sat in the theater. He might
even spot me in the audience as the camera scanned
it. The irony is that he would have a much better view
of the entire opera, plus backstage interviews that are
often entertaining, while I sat in a high balcony seat
squinting down at the small figures upon the stage. He
would also hear it, sung into microphones at the edge
of the stage, far better than I could hear from my vantage.

While I was in New York, I stayed with Sherry Bernstein, my poet friend Charles Bernstein's mother, to whom I told my plans. On Central Park West, her apartment is only a few blocks from the opera house. Oddly enough, Sherry also planned to attend...not at the Met but, just like Howard, at a live video showing in some movie theater.

Donizetti's comic opera is based very much on the stock figures of *commedia dell'arte*, so perhaps one need not be too serious about the ridiculous characters or the plot, which basically boils down to an attempt by two outsiders, Dr. Malesta (Mariusz Kwiecien) and his sister Norina (Anna Netrebko), to teach an old man, Don Pasquale (John Del Carlo), a lesson about life. Don Pasquale's young nephew Ernesto (Matthew Polenzani), in love with Norina, refuses to marry the woman his uncle feels is more appropriate. In reaction, Don Pasquale, on a suggestion from his doctor, Malesta, decides to marry Norina (pretending to be a convent girl, Sofrina) instead, disinheriting Ernesto. There is little else to the plot: the two are falsely married and Norina moves in, completely making over the house and her own wardrobe from top to bottom, as she prepares to head off to the theater without her new husband. Ultimately, the miserly Don Pasquale is so put out—literally of his own house—that he is relieved upon discovering he has been duped, and is happy to hand over Norina to his nephew, while agreeing to restore his inheritance.

This silly story makes for many delightful moments, including Norina's truly comical "See, I am ready with love to surround him," and the servants' hilarious confusion in Acts II and III, along with Norina's "Bring the jewels at once."

Yet I cannot help asking why this brother and sister team are so intent on teaching the old Don Pasquale a lesson, all for the sake of the rather meek and incompetent Ernesto? Norina is such a wicked flirt and liar that we can hardly understand her love for a boy who is so shocked by the announcement of Don Pasquale's marriage that he is ready to leave home and inheritance behind. Obviously, the two, brother and sister, do have something at stake. By pretending to marry Don Pasquale, the penniless Norina comes into great wealth, part of which most certainly will go, at the old man's death, to her lover.

But given her huge deceptions, even if they all turn out for the best, one has to wonder whether she will make such a poor boob a good wife. Certainly Ernesto is even more able to be hoodwinked than his uncle.

By the time of the finale, "Heaven, what do you say?" there is actually little to be said. The heaven that has been invoked is one in which Norina has metaphorically  cleaned the house of both men, who previously lived in a barren, cobweb-encrusted manor (at least in the Met production), existing, similarly, in lives basically empty and unused. I guess the question is, will Norina return the jewels or wear them to the theater each night?

NEW YORK, NOVEMBER 15, 2010
Reprinted from *US Theater, Opera, and Performance* (March 2011).

Not at Home

ALOIS HOTSCHNIG **DIE KINDER BERUHIGTE DAS NICHT** (COLOGNE: KIEPENHEUER & WITSCH, 2006), TRANSLATED BY TESS LEWIS FROM THE GERMAN AS **MAYBE THIS TIME** [READ IN MANUSCRIPT]

AUSTRIAN WRITER Alois Hotschnig's 2006 collection of short stories titled *Die Kinder beruhigte des nicht* (That Didn't Reassure the Children) is filled with empty people, shadow-images of life who haunt seemingly ordinary worlds, where no one seems to notice if these figures are present or missing.

In the first story, "The Same Silence, the Same Noise," a man rents a lakeside home, becoming entranced by the never-ending blandness of his neighbors, who each day sit peacefully on their deckchairs, staring into space. It is as if they have no other life, and he becomes so transfixed by this emptiness that watching them becomes a kind of mania. A first he watches out of the corner of his eyes or unseen from a window like a voyeur. But even when one of them turns to catch him in the act, there seems to be no recognition on their part. Gradually, accordingly, he becomes more and more open about his interest in their timeless stares into space, at one point boating out to their sundeck, struggling ashore with the intention of  sitting in their chairs in order to better understand the passivity of their lives.

Of course, in his mania, he too has become isolated and useless. He no longer sees friends, talks to few, and, like his neighbors, leads an idle life. When he finally grows disgusted with his actions, he discovers the previous tenant of his house has returned, and like him is intently staring at the couple, just as if he has been hypnotized. The current renter suddenly discovers a new focus of attention:

> He sat there now, in my place, and I watched him from the house, which soon I no longer left and I didn't take my eyes off him, but saw how he stared over at them, as they stared into the water, and I looked over at them every day, every night, always, until now.

In the eerie tale "Then a Door Opens and Swings Shut," Karl, a man on his way to visit friends, is lured into a neighbor's house, where a woman keeps a vast collection of seemingly handmade dolls. She shows him some of the dolls before she begins to talk about someone in the house who has been waiting for Karl, waiting evidently for years for his arrival. The *him* is a doll, also named Karl, who is the spitting image of the man, and strangely, meeting this doll, a feeling of peace comes over him; they become, somehow, *friends*.

Karl returns to the house several times, soon beginning to recognize some of the dolls as replicas of people of the village. The neighborhood children, whom the woman also tries to lure into her house, all fear her—with good reason. For, after several visits, the woman begins to make love to the doll Karl in front of the man, licking him obscenely. But as he watches the woman with the doll upon her lap, he grows more and more peaceful, reminded of the joys of his childhood. His relationship with his own wife begins to fray as he becomes more and more "used to the old woman's idiosyncrasies."

One day, however, he discovers in a cabinet different costumes for the dolls, shockingly coming across shoes, sweaters, pants, and other articles of clothing that he, too, wore as a child. And ultimately the man himself becomes one of her dolls, and through the doll is petted and cuddled.

Eventually, the licking, cuddling, petting are transformed into the woman's consumption of the doll:

> She kept licking tenderly and sucking, and now put the entire hand into her mouth, which also melted and vanished.... She ate and relished it, and, again and again, I sat there before her, watching as I disappeared into her and as she deteriorated more and more right before my eyes.

She begins to consume all the dolls, and when he returns, her eyes are no longer directed at him, but towards all. She has devoured her world.

Perhaps the best tale of this short but spellbinding collection is "Maybe This Time, Maybe Now," from which the translator has selected her English-language title. Here the numerous family members seem to be quite normal, gathering at holidays, birthdays, and other family events regularly in seeming joyfulness and celebration. Yet we soon learn that there is always one person missing, their father's brother Walter, who, although he often promises to attend, never appears. As the tale progresses we gradually learn that the family eternally forgives Walter his absences, but all are still convinced that "this time" Walter will appear. The narrator even attempts to skip these events, realizing that no one at these family gatherings is really important; only he, who is the focus of everyone's attention, really matters. Yet the narrator finds it hard to stay away, and returns to the pattern. Occasionally, Walter's wife visits, but never her husband, as she hurries away to discover what happened to him.

Walter, it gradually appears, is less a person than an unspoken desire, a desire different perhaps to everyone, but wished for always. While the family is surrounded by love and fulfillment, their focus remains on their emptiness. In short, the very reason for their gathering betrays their failure to live fully and love.

In the Kafkaesque "The Beginning of Something," a person discovers in the mirror "a stranger's face," and believes he is dreaming. But each time he arises to wash his face and rid himself of the dream's residue, he has more and more difficulty in returning to his own past, his own life. He has, in short, "escaped himself," and is unable to return to reality. He feels he has done something terrible, and realizes that those who seek him will never come; that he has become a living lie, an unreality.

Similarly, in "You Don't Know Them, They're Strangers," a man is called by another name and discovers things in his apartment that do not seem to be his. The neighbors, who he does not know, suddenly seem to know him. A stranger telephones, claiming to be a friend, arranging a meeting. But he doesn't know this "friend" either, who speaks knowledgably of the man's past.

The next morning he goes to work, but there he also is greeted by people he does not really know; although he goes through the actions, he is not sure what he is expected to do. A woman arrives at his apartment, "She'd come to pick him up as he was bound to have her waiting again or not to have shown up at all."

These events begin to happen regularly, and the man begins to wonder whether or not he has memory lapses or is totally distracted. But after a while, the pattern becomes familiar; his job changes daily. He never knows the people around him who claim his friendship. At least the apartment remains the same...but then it too begins to change, and a random visiting of other addresses surprises him with people who know him, or even enemies. Once, he is even mistaken for the man he was before all the changes took place.

Soon he begins to travel to other neighborhoods, even other cities, his key fitting into the lock of any door he chooses. He is greeted by people in other apartments as if he has arrived home. His own previous life, whatever it might have been, no longer exists. Like Woody Allen's Zelig, he has become a part of everyone else's experiences.

In each of these nine nearly flawlessly-crafted tales, the ego shifts or disappears, and with it people become something other than they were, or are revealed to never have been who thought they were in the first place. Identity in this rapidly shifting world, the author seems to suggest, no longer means anything. As everyone quickly adapts to becoming another or each other, no one is any longer "at home" and children can find no safe place in which to survive.

LOS ANGELES, MARCH 1, 2010
Reprinted from *EXPLORINGfictions* (March 2010).

No Body There

HENRI-GEORGES CLOUZOT AND JÉRÔME GÉRONIMI
(SCREENPLAY), HENRI-GEORGES CLOUZOT (DIRECTOR)
LES DIABOLIQUES / 1955

ONE OF THE REASONS that Henri-Georges Clouzot's
1955 film *Les Diaboliques* remains so compelling today
is that it lies to its audience, masquerading as a simple
murder film while actually being a kind of toxic horror
film / mystery.

If Venezuelan-born Christina Delassalle (Véra
Clouzot) is a wealthy heiress whose dream had been
to run a boarding school just outside Paris, she is also
a weak woman who has let her husband, Michel (Paul

Meurisse), abuse her,
evidently for years.
She is also naïve in
her beliefs, allowing
her husband's current
mistress to engage her

in something close to a lesbian alliance wherein the two plan to kill Michel. And although she resists going through with the convoluted plot several times, ultimately  she does successfully drug him (so she believes) and participates in his drowning in a bathtub.

Despite the deviousness of Christina's and Nicole's (Simone Signoret) plan, in which they supposedly lure Michel to his lover's apartment after his wife has demanded a divorce, the director somehow manages to allow his audience to side with their behavior, particularly given the fact that Michel has not only been brutal towards them but abuses the schoolchildren and his other colleagues as well. Indeed, it is a wonder that the whole school doesn't, as the children do at one moment, rise up in utter rebellion against its official Principal.

Clouzot manages, accordingly, to convince his audience that a murder is justified, making us cohorts, as it were, who continue to hope that the women get away with their dirty deed; and, in fact, we are led, like the naïve Christina, to believe they have carried it out successfully.

Gradually, however, the movie shifts to a kind of ghost-story, as we wait for the body which they've thrown into the dirty swimming pool to rise and be discovered. When some boys accidentally kick their soccer ball into the pool, threatening to send them into its waters to retrieve it, Nicole finally orders its draining. No body is discovered, and soon after, a young boy declares that the Principal—missing for several days—has confiscated his slingshot. A group school photo, showing us a shadowy figure above peering through a window, finally convinces us that something is horribly awry.

The sudden appearance of a private detective shifts the film again, at first convincing us that he is on to the actions of the two women, but finally forcing us to question our basic assumptions—just in time for Michel to appear in the flesh, resulting in Christina's heart attack and death.

Like her, too late we realize we have been tricked, that indeed Michel and Nicole have plotted *her* death.

In many senses, this rather clumsy plot twist is almost comic; in fact, Sidney Lumet used a similar plot device in his comic film of 1982, *Deathtrap*. But Clou-

zot ends his film with almost mock-seriousness, warning viewers not to reveal the ending.

That Clouzot's Brazilian-born wife, Véra, died of a heart attack only five years later, much like her character in this film, brought the film new attention, while sending its director into a deep depression.

LOS ANGELES, NOVEMBER 20, 2011
Reprinted from *World Cinema Review* (November 2011).

No One's Home

JEFFREY LANE (BOOK), DAVID YAZBEK (MUSIC AND
LYRICS, BASED ON THE FILM BY PEDRO ALMODÓVAR)
WOMEN ON THE VERGE OF A NERVOUS BREAKDOWN /
NEW YORK, BELASCO THEATRE / THE PERFORMANCE I
SAW WAS ON NOVEMBER 12, 2010

WOMEN ON THE VERGE OF A NERVOUS BREAKDOWN,
shouted Ben Brantley's review in *The New York Times*,
"needs—immediately and intravenously"—Ritalin.
The musical "is...a sad casualty of its own wandering
mind." *Los Angeles Times* reviewer Charles McNaulty
agreed: "all the frenetic activity—with Sven Ortel's
projections lending Michael Yeargan's fast-moving sets
the hyperactive feeling of a fashion video—can't con-
ceal the gaping flaws of the show any more than decorative icing can improve a cake made without enough
baking soda or eggs." "By midway through the second
act," observed the *Chicago Tribune*, "the audience can
no longer track the multi-character action through the

chaos suited only for film, and palpably checks out of the entire proceedings."

Anyone who has become acquainted with my theater writing will know that I have not always been kind to Broadway shows. But by the time I saw this original musical a week later, directed by the admirable Bartlett Sher, I could only wonder what all this critical hostility was about. Perhaps Sher had trimmed away some of his actors' frenetic motions since its opening, or perhaps these critics had simply gone to another play, for both I and the audience with whom I experienced this production thoroughly enjoyed the musical—a far better work, it seems to me, than most other musicals, originals, and revivals currently on Broadway. A woman in the row behind me gleefully admitted that she never reads the critics.

I presume these critics had all seen Almodóvar's film, on which the musical was based. McNaulty even attempted to compare the two. Yet it seems strange, having witnessed the campy hysteria of the film, that they didn't expect a fast-moving theater event. Indeed, the whole metaphor of both the film and the musical is that everyone, having lost or about to lose their sense of position or place (symbolized by love and home), is dropped into a whirling world of accidentally inter-related events. Accordingly, everyone is on the move: Pepa (Sherie Rene Scott), deserted by her lover Ivan (Brian Stokes Mitchell), wants to rent her penthouse and run off—unless she can convince Ivan to return—going so far as to burn her bed; her sexually active friend, Candela (stunningly performed by Laura Benanti), has fallen in love with a terrorist and is desperate for advice and fearful of being arrested; Ivan's ex-wife, Lucia (Patti LuPone), having recently returned from a mental institution, is intent on tracking down Pepa and Ivan for revenge; her and Ivan's son, Carlos, eager to leave his mother's troubled household, is intent on finding some new place where he and his fiancée might discover themselves. Add a passing telephone repair-man and the gossipy/prayerful concierges of Ivan and Pepa and one is certain to create a farcical entangle-ment of people on the run.

Only the sing-ing cabdriver Danny Burstein seems to truly comprehend the world in which he exists; prowling the streets to provide his services to Pepa

and others, he has stocked his cab with medicine, food, magazines, newspapers, and anything else his customers on the move may need. This is clearly a world where no one's home; the idea that constant motion should be reflected on the stage is exceptional. Few other musicals that I can recall—*Mahogony* and *Sweeney Todd* being obvious exceptions—have so thoroughly taken to the streets.

The only stop to all this action is, predictably, a Gilbert and Sullivan-like magic elixir, in this case Pepa's Valium-laced gazpacho. And it is in the arms of the sleep it awards them that Carlos and Marisa, Candela and the telephone repairman, and the Chief Inspector and his Detective can discover the joys of love and regain a sense of stability and peace.

The two strong women at the center of this work, Pepa and Lucia, must come to terms with their violent passions—and their accordant commitments to constant motion—realizing, in the case of Lucia, that her husband had been "invisible" all along, and perceiving, in Pepa's case, that she suffers from an "overdose of love." Lucia's song, performed in Patti LuPone perfection, is perhaps the most touching of the entire production.

And that *is* the real problem with *Women on the Verge of a Nervous Breakdown*. The singers, the acting, the sets and costumes, even the projections on the wall which some critics found so distracting are all quite

excellent in capturing the sense of this fast-moving, lovelorn 1980s Madrid. Although David Yazbek's lyrics and music at moments ("Lie to Me," "The Microphone," and "Invisible") rise to the occasion, overall they are simply not fetching and powerful enough to glue this musical into a coherent whole. And without these two central elements of musical theater, no production can long survive.

For all that, I think *Women on the Verge of a Nervous Breakdown* is an admirable failure, a larger-than-life statement of a culture that has lost its center and identity—clearly a subject that should have great significance for US citizens today.

NEW YORK, NOVEMBER 13, 2010
Reprinted from *US Theater, Opera, and Performance* (Nov. 2010).

Four Films of the 1960s

I have long argued that, although the 1950s culture has often been described as a period living within constrictive limitations, particularly for women, minority cultures, and the LGBT community, it, in fact, was far more culturally experimental and diverse than is now perceived. My essays "Three Children of the Fifties," "The Death of the Mother" (both in My Year 2004*), and "Between Who and What"(*My Year 2008*) consider these issues, suggesting that a far more culturally conservative period was the first three or four years of the 1960s, surprisingly during the "Camelot" years of John Kennedy's presidency.*

Suddenly, as I was working on the issues of this year, centered around the idea that "No One's Home," I realized that a great many movies of the early 1960s also contained stories of people being ousted from their homes or simply wandering through spaces, as in Antonioni's Eclipse, *for example. If mothers, as I propose, were suddenly banned from TV family series, so too did women and, on some occasions, errant men both suddenly find themselves without a family to embrace them, and even without homes to which they might return to be em-*

braced. Although I might have chosen dozens of such examples, I have selected just four films which support these observations.

Without coming to easy conclusions, on the surface it seems that there surely must be a relationship between the rising patriarchal controls that I observed during those same years, when the roles of women were first beginning to change and many males reacted with even further restrictions and rejections; certainly, for the first time as a young gay man—without even quite realizing that I was gay—I began to feel threatened by cultural and familial commentaries. Obviously by the mid-1960s this all changed, in reaction, I believe, to those very cultural restraints—or perhaps as an inevitable result of the changes that were already taking place. A culture that no longer felt it had a home to go to sought out communal societies or, often, took to the streets, as by the end of that decade I myself did in New York City.

LOS ANGELES, JANUARY 3-4, 2012

A Tear is the Fault of the Dress

MICHELANGELO ANTONIONI, TONINO GUERRA,
ELIO BARTOLINI, AND OTTIERO OTTIERI (WRITERS),
MICHELANGELO ANTONIONI (DIRECTOR) L'ECLISSE
(ECLIPSE) / 1962

IF WATCHING ANTONIONI's great films *L'Avventura* (see *My Year 2007*) and *La Notte* did not make it clear, then *Eclipse* of 1962 certainly reiterates that this director's films are not at all about narrative fiction. Plot truly does not matter, and the events of his films might often be somewhat shuffled. His films, rather, are psychological expressions—so psychological that Antonioni might almost have been a surrealist had he not chosen to use what appears as or pretends to be a realist world. Even Antonioni's rooms in these three films are mirrors of the owners' personalities rather than places to be actually inhabited.

Time and again, the characters move into spaces where the owners have gone missing. Landscapes generally are empty and barren as in *L'Avventura*, or pockmarked with the detritus of civilization like the half-devel-oped fields littered with preposterous constructions such as the mushroom-shaped water tower early in *Eclipse* or the seemingly never-to-be-completed new building near the female character's street. The characters, in turn, move around these spaces as if they were, in fact, sleepwalkers.

In the first long sequence of *Eclipse*, for example, Monica Vitti as Vittoria wanders backwards and forwards in and out of rooms while her lover Riccardo (Francisco Rabal) sits for long periods of time as if he were a statue. She smokes, drinks, and rearranges nearby objects, unable to properly express her intense emotions, while Riccardo serves as kind of Buddha, a figure mirrored by the nearby whirling fan, both frozen in the repetition of nothingness. No matter what has happened previously, we know the clash between the two is irredeemable. He is a publisher, a man of books and the words within them, she a creature unable to express her mind.

The director's camera, almost mimicking Vittoria's fidgety movements, darts around the same space, fragmenting furniture and faces, at moments moving to her legs beneath a chair before zooming up to a mirror or peering out, as she herself has a few seconds before, from the corner of a window. It is almost as if everything is moving in a languorous ballet, choreographed to express the uncertainty and awkwardness of the human beings within. Indeed it is this quite careful manipulation of movement that brings many viewers to describe Antonioni's filmmaking as "mannered." And in some senses, they are correct in their evaluation, for the entire scene is an expression "in the manner" of what we pretend are real experiences, but which, in truth, appear as something more out of Kabuki than our real everyday actions. Yet perhaps they reveal those everyday actions more faithfully than we might have ever imagined.

Antonioni, however, is not attempting to express the everyday, and never pretends to be. His "characters," as beautiful as they are, represent little more than stick figures, pushed and pulled through their daily actions by the rising industrialism, politics, greed, and, yes always, love without being able to solidly take hold of anything. They seldom make choices, and, even when they do, the choices are generally mistaken ones. For that reason none of them will find what we might call satisfaction.

Leaving her long-time elder lover, Vittoria is like a straw in the wind, her willowy body and diaphanous hair insubstantially tilting against the city backdrops, a sun ready to be blotted out by the bold black-and-white world in which she lives. She is obviously a figure of the wind, as her brief, exhilarating airplane trip through the clouds with her neighbor and her pilot husband reveals. Vittoria is clearly overwhelmed by the experience.

Yet there is also a kind of primitiveness about her, as her sudden determination to imitate a dancing Kenyan native in the apartment of her new acquaintance from Kenya reveals. But the same act also tells us that she has no comprehension of politics or even the dangerous implications of her spontaneous acts. Her friend Anita is quickly irritated by and embarrassed for her racist, "negro" mockery.

Time and again, Vittoria shifts in her tracks at the very moment she might actually be moving toward a destination. Suddenly, while trying to track down her new Kenyan friend's escaped dog, she is distracted by the sounds of poles blowing in the wind. Leaving the stock exchange after an awful day in which her stock-playing mother has lost a great deal of money, Vittoria follows an even bigger loser, who appears to possibly be contemplating suicide, only to discover a napkin on

which he has drawn several flowers. Vitti almost literally floats through the Rome of Antonioni's *Eclipse*.

Only one "thing," after her breakup with Riccardo, seems to temporarily catch her attention or offer even a location where she might briefly settle: the beautiful face and fierce intensity of motion she perceives in the stock trader Piero (Alain Delon). With his dark hair and long, almost feline eyebrows, Piero is exactly the opposite of Vittoria. If she wanders, he moves with the direct intention of a man who knows what he wants and generally gets it. The scenes of him and his peers at the stock exchange represent humans as a pack of lions frenetically pacing back and forth between the phone cubicles, where they get orders and glean information from other stock exchanges, and the bidding circle, where they shout out their stock purchases like desperately growling predators—which indeed they are! Money is an entry to the game played by those who hate and fear their fellow kind, a slightly paranoid reality expressed by Vittoria's mother (Lilla Brignone) as well.

The first moment this man of purposeless action spots Vittoria, it is inevitable, as so much is in Antonioni's world of coincidence, that he will stalk her. The very same day, Piero throws over his call-girl friend (a former blonde who has just changed into a brunette) and paces back  and forth below Vittoria's window, only to have his Alfa Romeo stolen by a stumbling drunk.

His reaction to the discovery of the car, the body of the drunk within, further emphasizes the differences between them. From a poorer family, Vittoria has no interest in finances, while he, the son of an obviously wealthy Roman family—who grew up in a house, we later discover, filled with great art and expensive furniture—excitedly uses others to make even more money and buy more possessions. He'll sell the Alfa Romeo, he boasts, for a better and newer car. Even a stolen kiss between them shows their differences when it ends with Vittoria's torn dress. Her passive answer: "A tear is the dress' fault."

We recognize that nothing can come of their explosive relationship, which ends in Piero's office, where he has temporarily removed all the phones from their cradles in order not to be disturbed.

As all lovers do, they promise to meet again that night, and the night after, until the end of time. But as Vittoria descends the stairs to leave, for a second turning to look back to what we know has become a pillar of salt, we can only doubt their promises.

Antonioni ends his Kabuki show, once again, with—from a realist perspective—an apparently mannerist conceit; but through the dream perspective of this nightmare vision of a world where humans increasingly feel dissociated, alienated, and displaced from each other and the world around them, he quite brilliantly conveys his major, and perhaps only, theme. Through a series of quick montages of various hours of the day from sunrise to sunset, the director takes us to all the spots where the couple has previously encountered one another. Strangers pass through the streets, going about their business, but neither Piero nor Vittoria show up. They too, like the unoccupied rooms and spaces they have throughout the film entered and wandered away from, no longer exist for one another. And even if they might ever come seeking each other out, there will surely be no one at home.

LOS ANGELES, JANUARY 2, 2011
Reprinted from *World Cinema Review* (January 2011).

Roman Holiday

CHARLES SCHNEE (SCREENPLAY, BASED ON A NOVEL
BY IRWIN SHAW), VINCENTE MINNELLI (DIRECTOR)
TWO WEEKS IN ANOTHER TOWN / 1962

A YEAR BEFORE *8½*, Hollywood director Vincente
Minnelli filmed a kind populist prequel, *Two Weeks in
Another Town*, to Fellini's far more complex and visu-
ally exciting masterpiece. Based on Irwin Shaw's pot-
boiler fiction, it's hard to explain even the title of this
work: why Rome is described as a town and how anyone might think the fictional filmmaker Maurice Kruger (Edward G. Robinson)—formerly considered an
important director—could shoot a film in two weeks
is inexplicable. But this, after all, is Hollywood—or,
better yet, Cinecitta Studios, the Italian home to thousands of badly acted melodramas, as well as great films
such as those made by the likes of Fellini and, soon after, Godard.

Indeed, at moments, Minnelli's Rome even looks

as if it were peopled by Fellini-like grotesques, and, as in Fellini's *La Dolce Vita*, all the beautiful people seem to be dining on streetside terraces, where everyone recognizes those who pass. Here, much as in *La Dolce Vita*, a jealous wife, Clara Kruger (Claire Trevor), has been joined by the cosmopolitan beauty Carlotta (played by Cyd Charisse, attempting a sort of Anita Ekberg imitation), along with a gentle Roman girl, Veronica (Daliah Lavi), and two has-been actors, the elderly Jack Andrus (Kirk Douglas) and a younger bad-boy version of him, Davie Drew (George Hamilton). We realize from early on in the film that there will be some wild parties and long nights ahead.

The film begins with an absolutely pointless series of scenes in a mental clinic where Andrus has gone after having cracked up, quite literally, by driving a car straight into a wall after a disastrous evening with his former wife, Carlotta. By the time we first encounter him, he's already been "cured" and is ready for release. With perfect timing, his arch-enemy, Kruger, cables him to come to Rome for a small part in his new film—once again a convenience of plot which makes little logical sense. No matter; once the cast has been assembled, we're finally in for some delights as the actors in this work, one by one, each try to prove that everyone in this world is a creative mess.

Indeed, if you look at Minnelli's film from this vantage point, as a kind of study in modes of bad and over-the-top acting or as a study in talent gone sour, it almost becomes interesting,

Trevor as Mrs. Kruger hisses and spits out her vindictiveness, mostly to her husband, before, at the end of the film, turning her medusa-stare to Andrus. Hamilton easily proves that, like his character Drew, he cannot seriously act (later proving that comedy was his real talent). And Kruger, whom the movie represents as a man who has lost any talent he once might have possessed, wanders around the set in Robinson's paunchy body like an old man, the script finally getting rid of him through the accident of a heart attack so that Andrus can take his place; after all, Kruger has long ago taken away even Andrus' small acting role. Lavi as Veronica does her best to be sweet, but the very idea that she has to make a romantic choice between either of the neurotic actors in the film makes her role nearly impossible.

Despite the preposterous shifts of intention and even genre—is this a love story, a study in psychological healing, a satire of filmmaking, or just a damn silly melodrama?—Minnelli, great filmmaker that he once was, does his best to detract us from what's going on through his richly-hewn metrocolor images and the spot-on framing of his scenes. A few of them might even hint that he is still at the top of his form; maybe he had simply lost his judgment about the projects he undertook.

At moments, it is apparent, Minnelli even tries to resurrect some of the fluidity and drama of screenwriter Charles Schnee's 1953 similarly-themed script, *The Bad and the Beautiful*. But actor Douglas, this time around, is trying to be one of the "beautiful" people, and doesn't have enough time in his role as a "director" to become the "bad" (but dramatically good) Jonathan Shields of that earlier work. Almost as if Douglas cannot find a way out of the stale story in which he's now trapped, his character, after another bender, tries once again to drive into a wall, this time with his ex-wife beside him in the car.

The fact that he doesn't succeed seems to imply—without logic once again—that he has truly been "cured"; for immediately after, he hightails it out of "town" to return back to the good ol' healthy USA, where he intends, apparently, to  convince someone of his newly acquired directing talents and, "when the time is right," to feature the slightly reformed Davie Drew in a new film. Now that I think about it, I think I prefer the circus he left behind.

LOS ANGELES, DECEMBER 31, 2011
Reprinted from *World Cinema Review* (December 2011).

Trading Up

PETER STONE (STORY AND SCREENPLAY), MARC
BEHM (STORY), STANLEY DONEN (DIRECTOR) **CHARADE**
/ 1963

STANLEY DONEN'S comedic thriller, *Charade*, begins
with a wealthy young woman, Regina Lambert (Audrey
Hepburn), ensconced at a ski resort (Megève) where
she admits to her friend, Sylvie, that she is soon going
to get a divorce from her husband Charles: there are
too many things she does not know about her husband,
too many secrets that he has seemingly kept from her.
A few moments later a handsome stranger, Peter Joshua
(Cary Grant), complains to her about her friend Sylvie's water-gun shooting son. The stranger is rebuffed
with a clever put-down:

> REGGIE: I already know an awful lot of people and
> until one of them dies I couldn't possibility
> meet anyone else.
> PETER: Well, if anyone goes on the critical list, let

me know.

When he turns to go, she chides him, "You give up awfully easily."

The scene sets up the movie in a nutshell: love, divorce, guns—or violence, at least—will be our focus for the next 100 and some minutes, along with, of course, some tuneful songs by Henry Mancini.

Upon her return to Paris, Reggie discovers her entire apartment has been cleaned out, her maid is missing, and, before long, she receives news of her husband's death, a man murdered and tossed from a train. She can now "meet" that new someone, and on cue Peter Joshua again shows up—a clumsy and basically unexplained plot element that nonetheless seems to make sense, for we already know that they are destined to fall in love.

But the reality of the tale is that Reggie has no choice now but to head to the streets, where she spends most of the film, or, at best, to check into a cheap Paris hotel, with Joshua, quite inexplicably, as her next-door neighbor.

Charade's ludicrously labyrinthine plot suddenly takes over as we are introduced, one by one—at Charles' funeral, no less—to the major characters, Tex Panthollow (James Coburn), Herman Scobie (George Kennedy), and Leopold Gideon (Ned Glass). These ex-soldiers, along with Charles and another figure, Carson Dyle, have robbed an OSS shipment of $250,000 in gold that was to have been delivered to the French Resistance, and the US government—so Reggie is told by embassy officer Hamilton Bartholomew—wants it back. He and, evidently, the three remaining robbers are convinced that, since Charles held the money, she must know of its whereabouts.

Once this ridiculous plot contrivance is set up, the movie settles back into a romantic comedy as Reggie and Joshua rush about Paris, threatened and harassed, from time to time, by the evil "gang."

Grant, so the story goes, was hesitant about being involved in a film where he (at 59 years of age) was chasing Hepburn (34), so the writers simply cut all of his lines that suggested his sexual interest in her and gave them to the character Reggie, the result of which is that Grant plays his character with the most laid-back diffidence of his film career. He seems more bemused by Reggie than sexually interested.

As the threats and acts of violence (a burning-match attack in a telephone booth, the kidnapping of Sylvie's son, a battle between Joshua and Scobie on the roof of the hotel) begin to pile up, it also becomes

 evident that Joshua is not who he seems, finally admitting that he is Carson Dyle's brother, Alexander. At first horrified at his lies (it is lying after all that separated her and her husband), Reggie quickly recovers her equilibrium and, even more incredibly, her trust in Grant's character, the authors repeating the same conversation that she had with Peter Joshua, as a standing joke:

REGGIE: Is there a Mrs. Dyle?
ALEXANDER DYLE: Yes...[*Reggie's face drops*] but we're divorced!
REGGIE: [*smirking*] I thought that was Peter Joshua?
ALEXANDER DYLE: I am just as difficult to live with as he was.

Despite the fact that she was ready to divorce her now-dead husband because he was not honest with her, off she now goes with the interloper for more adventures, these ending in several deaths, as the robbers begin to suspect each other. Once more, Reggie and, now, Alexander go through the contents of a small bag

Charles Lambert has left behind: toothpaste, a small calendar, a letter, a ticket to Venezuela, and passports in multiple names, etc., nothing that seems of value.

But now, following the instructions of the embassy official Bartholomew, Reggie finds herself in an even more terrifying situation, particularly when he insists that Dyle's brother died years ago, and soon after the camera pulls back to find the Grant figure in the room with the remaining "gang" members.

The former Peter Joshua, Alexander Dyle now admits he is simply a professional thief, Adam Canfield. The series of questions is repeated once again, her trust in the man amazingly intact.

As the body count rises, both Reggie and now Adam follow a clue in her husband's calendar where they encounter several booths selling stamps to collectors. In a simultaneous instant both she—who has given the letters on the envelope containing his messages to Sylvie's young son—and he realize the truth: the money has been used to purchase several rare stamps, which the boy, Jean-Louis, has unwittingly exchanged with a stamp dealer for a large package of international stamps. When they track down the dealer, he admits the rarity of the stamps, returning them to Reggie.

But now that they have the "money," Reggie is in even more danger, as Bartholomew, the embassy man, lures her to a square outside the Paris Opera, with Josh-

ua/Dyle/Canfield chasing after. Bartholomew, we discover, is really Carson Dyle, one of the original soldiers
who has stolen the gold, and he is now about to kill
Reggie. Hiding in the prompter's box, Reggie is stalked
by Dyle, as Canfield, high above, tracks his steps across
the stage, finally springing open a stage trap door which
sends Dyle to his death. I told you the plot was ludicrous and labyrinthine, now operatic.

No matter, Reggie is safe, has the money in hand,
and has fallen in love with Canfield. Crime seems to
have paid off, even if the stamps, now glued to the envelope, may not have the same net value. Oddly, despite
being a professional thief, Canfield, encourages her to
turn over the stamps to the US embassy.

As Reggie enters the office of the US agent, Brian
Cruikshank, the government official in charge of recov-

ering stolen property, she is suddenly greeted by—you guessed it—Canfield, who now admits his real name:

> REGGIE: Is there a Mrs. Cruikshank?
> CRUIKSHANK: Yes.
> REGGIE: But you're divorced.
> CRUIKSHANK: No. [*REGINA's face drops, CRUIKSHANK gets out his wallet to show her a picture*] My mother, she lives in Detroit, you'd like her, she'd like you too.
> REGGIE: Oh, I love you, Adam, Alex, Peter, Brian, whatever your name is, I love you! I hope we have a lot of boys and we can name them all after you!

So, it appears, she has traded in the stamps—which presumably had formerly been the contents of her house—for a new husband. And so many people have died or simply been extinguished in this story that she will now clearly have room to meet many others in her future life.

LOS ANGELES, NOVEMBER 10, 2011
Reprinted from *World Cinema Review* (November 2011).

Bed to Bed

JOHN OSBOURNE (SCREENPLAY), TONY RICHARDSON (DIRECTOR) **TOM JONES** / 1963

ALTHOUGH WE OFTEN speak of the 1960s as if it were a coherent age of political and sexual openness and experimentation, having been there I can assure you that 1963, the year of Tony Richardson's joyous testament to youthful debauchery, was not yet part of the liberated culture that followed it. As I have written elsewhere and reconfirmed by many studies, the early 1960s—at least in the US—was in many senses, particularly for gays and those who might soon after seek out open sexuality, a very conservative period. Although President

Kennedy might have been living a quite satyric life, Jackie sat with her pillbox hat in a room separate, perhaps whispering

nice appreciations into Leonard Bernstein's ear, and even, at times, enjoying the euphoria of drugs, but living in a world that no one might have perceived as "liberated." Life in the early 1960s for the vast majority of Americans was not what the later 1960s might offer up to them.

How remarkable, accordingly, for the culture at large to encounter Richardson's bawdy revelry, hidden behind its faux 18th-century moral narrative lectures. Albert Finney, portraying the naughty boy antics of the Henry Fielding hero, literally giggling along with composer John Addison's spritely harpsichordal refrains, permitted nearly anyone without dour religious convictions to give themselves up to the sin of the flesh without actually having to admit it had anything at all to do with their own daily personal lives.

No wonder the movie made millions and won over nearly any Brit and American living through those days, winning several Academy Awards, including Best Picture, while being described by popular journals such as *Newsweek* as "The best comedy ever made."

Finney portrayed the rapscallion Tom as the kind of figure who neither woman nor man could possibly resist—unless you were the foppish half-brother Bifil (David Warner), who uses his faked religiosity as a cover for his greedy desires. Even the well brought-up Sophie Western (played with an innocent lustiness by

Susannah York)— who has been raised by her priggish aunt (Edith Evans) and her gout-suffering, hunt-loving, and woman-izing father (Hugh  Griffith)—could not abide Bifil, the supercilious man, promised to her for marriage. She chases, along with a pack of women, young and elderly, after the virile, handsome, young Tom.

That the usually anguished, working-class spokes-man John Osbourne was so brilliantly able to whip up a screenplay out of Fielding's encyclopedic original satire is truly amazing—akin to the possibility that American playwright Arthur Miller might have been able to cre-ate a comic masterpiece, which that sincerely-serious writer was clearly incapable of.

And just as startling is that the director of works like *Look Back in Anger, A Taste of Honey, Luther,* and *The Loneliness of the Long Distance Runner* could possi-bly stir up the delicious pot of Keystone Comedy antics and the gluttonous sexual orgies of this film. Those who worked with him, including cinematographer Walter Lassally, report that Richardson, out of personal dissat-isfaction with the results, almost boiled the frothiness of this work away to a stale stew. Fortunately, finances

and temporal limitations prevented his further stirring. The accidental results are absolutely memorable.

No one who has seen it can forget the intense flash of Mrs. Waters (Joyce Redman, the hero's possible mother) and Tom's eyes as they fathom the feast of birds, raw meat, and human flesh: no sexual act could possibly match the fulfillment of those eyes, mouths, and jaws consuming everything in sight. Lust has never before or since been so perfectly embodied.

The mad chase of Squire Western and nearly everyone else of good will in this cinematic fiction to save Tom from his much deservèd swing from the gallows is the glorious summation of hundreds of cliff-hanging endings of early cinema serials.

For years after, in my literature classes, I used this exuberant film to demonstrate narrative strategies that were employed only by the most experimental of 20th-

century fiction writers, including the intrusive narrations, the direct address of characters to the reader/viewer, and the authorial interventions that so delighted 18th-century readers—until, one day, I realized that most of my students were not even born when this popular film transformed its audiences.

Along with The Beatles and The Rolling Stones, Richardson's film represented a part of the British cultural revolution that soon would change everything in American society, punching American artists and audiences to transform the arts on an even larger scale. If Richardson, as his later films reiterate, was hardly a cinematic visionary, in 1963 he was able to create a work that suggested he might possibly be one, and helped to extend what the French New Wave filmmakers had already intimated.

Two years later Godard would offer up, in *Pierrot le Fou*, the same sort of self-conscious and self-destructive fool that Tom Jones was in Richardson's and Osbourne's droll cinematic representation—but, even then, without Finney's sexual exuberance, Godard's hero had no solution but finally to completely destroy himself. Only in Penn's 1967 *Bonnie and Clyde* did we discover characters as openly able to flaunt social and sexual conventions as Fielding's handsome foundling—yet they too were necessarily destroyed by the surrounding society.

By that time, however, everything everywhere had already changed, and the society of the late 1960s began to realize that death was not a necessary result of sexual and political transgression; yet, perhaps, given the 1970s and 1980s struggles with AIDS and other versions of social and sexual scourges, that recognition came too late.

Perhaps, coming as it did before we even expected it and could assimilate its radical message, *Tom Jones* should be perceived as a kind of self-enchanted trumpet charge into a new generation, a work that had no idea where it was going, but gracefully went there none-theless. If Rick and Elsa will always have Paris, I and millions of others of my generation, will always have the light-tripping antics of nightshirted Tom, merrily traipsing off in utter confusion from bed to bed.

LOS ANGELES, DECEMBER 12, 2011
Reprinted from *World Cinema Review* (December 2011).

Artful Deceivers

SCOTT ALEXANDER AND LARRY KARASZEWSKI
(SCREENPLAY, BASED ON MATERIAL IN *NIGHTMARE OF
ECSTASY* BY RUDOLPH GREY), TIM BURTON (DIRECTOR)
ED WOOD / 1994

TIM BURTON / CURATED BY RON MAGLIOZZI,
JENNY HE, AND RAJENDRA ROY BY THE MUSEUM OF
MODERN ART, NEW YORK / I SAW THE SHOW AT THE LOS
ANGELES COUNTY MUSEUM OF ART ON OCTOBER 27,
2011

BY COINCIDENCE Howard and I attended a showing
of the art of Tim Burton at the Los Angeles County
Museum of Art just a few days before Halloween, the
perfect time to take in the drawings, films, photographs, sculptures, puppets, and other artworks of the
film director. Including work from the early 1970s to
forthcoming work of 2012, one easily recognizes that
the somewhat surreal, gothic, sci-fi, and just plain
strange images of the young Burbank, California boy
(born August 25, 1958) almost naturally transformed

into the images Burton later used in his films, particularly in *Beetlejuice*, *Batman*, and *Edward Scissorhands*. Indeed, the show includes work from all his films, both early sketches and drawings by Burton himself as well as clips, objects, and drawings by his associates that were used for and in those films. Even the Angora sweater worn by both the characters Ed Wood and Dolores Fuller in Burton's film was on view.

Some of these works, particularly the puppets and other strange constructions, as well as entire visual environments that function somewhat like carnival sideshows, are quite arresting—and strangely beautiful. But after a short while, the fact becomes clear that what may have begun as classroom (and clearly after class) doodles turned into a lifetime activity. In short, the boy never grew up, and remains, at least in his own mind, a complete outsider even today. There is something embarrassing in witnessing room after room of the same thing, sometimes more interestingly rendered, but always with a similar mix of Edward Gorey, Dr. Seuss, and Edward Sorel imagery transformed into outlandishness.

Do we really need a showing of over 700 objects

from this filmmaker? The show is less an art presentation than it is a shrine to Burton's vision. And on the day we attended it was filled by people, some of whom looked like Burton's ghouls, staring wondrously at the walls as if witnessing images of the outsiders they see themselves to be. Personally, I felt a bit uncomfortable in the company of these works and people—less because of the strangeness of the images and the artist's fascination with death than because of the ultimate lack of true significance. Feeling like an outsider is perhaps common to most individuals, in particular the young; but to celebrate it as Burton does somehow makes it absolutely ordinary and, in the long run, representative of a kind of nostalgic desire for assimilation. Perhaps that is why most of Burton's figures seek what they cannot have, the placid lawns punctuated by the streets and driveways of American suburbia, the world in which I grew up, but where I never wanted to live.

Nonetheless, Howard and I have enjoyed several of Burton's films, and that same night we again watched *Ed Wood*, my favorite of his movies to date.

Ed Wood, like most of Burton's figures, is a true outsider, a born loser without the ability to capably write, to create narrative, or to direct either theater or film, as well as being apparently unable to artfully think—although he clearly loves film, or at least the *image* of

Orson Welles. In a sense Wood is the apotheosis of Burton's outsiders. Less skillful than Edward Scissorhands, without the burning revenge of Sweeney Todd, nor the ghostly cleverness of *Beetlejuice*'s Maitlands, he is a product of and believer in the American Dream, and, accordingly, is so removed from reality that he perceives himself as a true winner. Wood is an American dark optimist in a long line of such figures dating back at least to Poe and Melville—a confidence man who swallows his own story.

In fact, Ed Wood is so pathetic in his lack of vision that he is absolutely crazy, the way all great poets, as William Carlos Williams insists, "must go crazy." And in that fact he is as lovable and endearing as any American hero. Johnny Depp, who could probably charm the Devil himself—and perhaps already has—is a perfect actor for Wood, confidently smiling his way through all adversities (even without his dentures) as if he had been immersed in Dale Carnegie's theology. His pathology is, in fact, a kind of religiosity; he is utterly unable to see anything but the bright side of life. Facing a negative review of his first directorial effort of a play he has written, Wood observes:

> Look, he got some nice things to say here. "The soldiers' costumes were very realistic." That's positive!

To which his gay, cynical friend, Bunny Breckinridge (excellently realized by Bill Murray), replies: "Rave of the century."

Later, when told by a producer that his film was the worst he has ever seen, Wood comes back: "Well, my next one will be better."

Such utter faith may be a kind of madness, but it, nonetheless, draws people to him, even though every last one of his friends are unusual and perverse. Evidently Dolores Fuller—who died this year in May—was, as she described herself, quite conventional. In reality, she evidently loved Wood, helping him immensely in his career, but was uncomfortable with his transvestism. She was determined to have a successful career herself and did just that, writing several songs for Elvis Presley, Nat King Cole, and others. Burton correctly perceived, however, that the character in the film had to be a kind of foil for all the other strange figures with whom Wood surrounds himself, turning Fuller (Sarah Jessica Parker) into a kind of vengeful, shrewish scolder who, herself, is a failure.

Given Wood's friends, one wouldn't blame anyone for reacting as does the film's version of Fuller. Wood, a heterosexual transvestite, clearly surrounded himself with gay and transvestite figures such as Bunny Breckinridge, whose great desire throughout the movie is to have a sex operation—"Goodbye Penis!" His attempts are hilariously unsuccessful.

Wood's attraction to actor Bella Lugosi—particularly at a time in Lugosi's life when, seen as a has-been, he was addicted to morphine—is nearly inevitable. As the chance meeting quickly turns into an affable friendship, Lugosi (skillfully performed by Martin Landau) finally finds someone who will pass no judgment upon him and give him his last feeble opportunities to act.

There is something fateful, moreover, about Wood's strange entourage, including the absurdly inaccurate psychic Criswell (Jeffrey Jones), the Swedish professional wrestler Tor Johnson, Maili Nurmi (Vampira), and Conrad Brooks, who played in Wood's early movies and almost every really bad B-movie after. Wood's inversion of the outsider, his perception that the unusual was a kind of normality, or at least a gift that would help him in his artistry, clearly served as a magnet to the

strangest of beings. The idea, moreover, that Wood could convince a pragmatic huckster such as Georgie Weiss and churches of the Southern Baptist Convention to support his outrageous projects is testimony to his dynamic personality. In real life he cannot have been that far apart from Depp in his convincing performance.

That the films he directed—spliced together with stock footage, bad sets, bad acting, and near-illiterate scripts—may have been some the worst films ever made. But conceived, as they were out of such a passionate desire for filmmaking, they are, in the end, redeemed, artful creations even in their own clumsy artlessness. That is, I suggest, Burton's major theme here, as in most of his films portraying losers such as Wood, the physically challenged such as Edward Scissorhands, and even the dead as artful deceivers.

In this instance, Burton has accomplished his goal less with fantastical images than with a kind of realist euphoria, transforming the black-and-white world that serves as a backdrop usually for dramatic or even tragic events into a kind of comic ecstasy. Even Howard Shore's score, with its references to Wood's original films, gets into the spirit of things, zithering up Theremin chords that tickle the eardrums.

In the end, one wishes that the world were more like what Wood wants it to be. After just having suffered a terrible premiere of his failed movie, Wood asks his current girlfriend, Kathy O'Hara, to marry him:

> ED: Right now. Let's go to Vegas.
> KATHY: But, Eddie. It's pouring rain and the car top is stuck.
> ED: Phooey. It's only a five-hour drive and it'll probably stop by the time we get to the desert. Heck, it'll probably stop by the time we get around the corner. Let's go.

How can you not go along with him? Edward D. Wood, Jr. is a solid lunatic, just what the world most needs.

LOS ANGELES, OCTOBER 31, 2011
Reprinted from *World Cinema Review* (October 2011).

Six Degrees of Insanity

ALICE GOODMAN (LIBRETTO), PETER SELLARS (DI-
RECTOR), JOHN ADAMS (COMPOSER) **NIXON IN CHINA** /
THE METROPOLITAN OPERA, NEW YORK / THE PRODUC-
TION I SAW WAS A *LIVE IN HD* SCREENING AT THE RAVE
THEATER, WESTCHESTER, CALIFORNIA ON FEBRUARY 12,
2011

ALTHOUGH MOST OF THE CRITICS who I read (Mark
Swed in the *Los Angeles Times*, Anthony Tommasini in
The New York Times, and Anne Midgette of *The Wash-
ington Post*) agreed that the Met's new production of
Nixon in China was excellent and long overdue, there
was a sense between the three that the plot of the work
was static and that one character in particular, Henry
Kissinger (sung by Richard Paul Fink), was a figure of
parody, whereas the others were treated more seriously.
In a piece by Max Frankel, published in *The New York
Times* a couple of days before the *Live in HD* airing, the
former editor of the *Times*—who was with Nixon in

China and won a Pulitzer Prize for covering the trip—squarely asked the question which the other reviewers only intimated:

> ...Why bother, as in *Nixon*, to lure us to a fictional enterprise with contemporary characters and scenes from an active memory bank? Why use actualities, or the manufactured actualities of our television screens and newspapers, to fuel the drama?

The answer, he feels, is "obvious but also treacherous," that the use of actual characters helps to "overcome the musty odor that inhabits many opera houses," drawing new audiences into the theater. But, Frankel continues, it brings other dangers with it:

> The danger is that despite the verisimilitudes of text, setting and costume, a viewer's grasp of events may not match the fabric being woven onstage. What the creators intend to be profundity may strike the knowing as parody.

Most of the reviewers agreed that the composer, writer, and director did give their figures a range of emotions, both serious and comic; and between acts, Winston Lord (of National Security) assured us that much of the talk between Nixon and Chairman Mao in the First Act was close to what actually was said in their meeting. But all also felt that the opera did move to a kind of parody in the Second Act performance of *The Red Detachment of Women*, in which Fink, the singer-actor who played Kissinger, also plays a lecherous, Simon Legree-like landowner who has stolen away a young maiden. Fink sings:

> She was so hot
> I was hard-put
> To be polite.
> When the first cut
> —Come on you slut!—
> Scored her brown skin
> I started in,
> Man upon hen!

Some characterized this scene as surreal and the last act as psychological, as if they were somehow different in tone from the more historicized events in the First Act.

If nothing else, there was a sense that *Nixon in China*, without a narrative arc, was a bit of a rocky ride. Certainly, at times, while always enjoying the shimmering glory of the music, I too felt that way while watching it. Yet now that I've pondered it for while, I believe I was mistaken; that, in fact, the opera is highly structured and fairly coherent in its tone and presentation

of characters.

First of all, John Adams and Peter Sellars are never going to present something that works as a Verdi opera might. Although all may work with a complex weaving of historical events, Verdi's sense of drama is highly embedded in narrative, while Adams and team, postmodern in their approach, eschew what we might call "story."

Nixon in China has "events," but they are presented in a series of tableaux, not unlike some medieval musical productions. Each character gets the chance to reveal his or herself. But what Alice Goodman, Adams, and Sellars are interested in is not so much the outer faces these figures present to the world, but what they are thinking and imagining within. And I think they would have to admit that every figure on their stage is, in one way or another, a bit unhinged; these are, after all—with the exception perhaps of Pat Nixon—people desperate for power. And all are on the edge of insanity.

Even before we meet any of the major characters, the people of China speak in a strange manner that we comprehend is not quite rational thought, as they sing from the text of "The Three Main Rules of Discipline and Eight Points of Attention":

> Prompt delivery directly to authorities of all items
>   confiscated from landlords.
> Do not damage crops.
> Do not take a single needle or piece of thread
>   from the masses.
> Pay for everything you damage.
> etc.

They chant, "The people are the heroes now," even if these "heroes" are highly manipulated and controlled.

Out of the sky drops the Nixons' Spirit of 76, and no sooner does the President descend the air-stair, shaking the hand of Premier Chou En-lai, than he begins inwardly calculating the great results of this journey. Cameramen catch him just in time for the evening news broadcasts in the USA, he hilariously singing out his fascination with his own acts: "News! News! News!

> News has a kind of mystery;
> When I shook hands with Chou En-lai
> On this bare field outside Peking
> Just now, the whole world was listening

James Maddalena, who has now sung this role in hundreds of performances, is an amazing actor who brings off those jowl-shaking absurdities quite brilliantly.

Nixon's and Kissinger's meeting with Premier Chou (Russell Braun) and Chairman Mao (Robert Brubaker) in the next scene is perhaps the most absurd of the entire opera, as the two powerful leaders speak in a series of alternating gnomic jokes, apothegms, and, in Nixon's case, simple American verbal blunders. As Mao becomes more and more incomprehensible ("Founders come first / Then profiteers") in sayings parroted by a wonderful trio of assistants, Nixon attempts his linguistic twists spun from what he believes the Chairman might be saying. It all reminded me, a bit, of the other Peter Sellers' performance as the totally innocent and ignorant Chance in the film *Being There*, where he spouts meaningless sentences interpreted by others to be full of profound significance.  Mao and Nixon, one a bit senile, the other humorless and often depressed, hit it off beautifully in their mindless chatter, while the more rational Kissinger claims to be unable to understand anything, and the Premier sits silently in sufferance.

What that meeting accomplished, an issue clearly of importance in this opera, is questionable. But surely we can feel, and, in Adams' delicious scoring, we can *hear*, the growing friendliness of all figures as they swill down Mai-tai after Mai-tai with toast upon toast. Again, non-drinker Kissinger misses out on all the glorious insanity of the evening.

In Act II we get a chance to see Pat Nixon at the edge. She begins the morning, in fact, downing a couple of needed pills. Like Premier Chou she is in sufferance, and, although excited by the whole trip, she is also exhausted and, we feel, not at all comfortable. The most American of this opera's figures, she flaunts a bright red coat. Flawlessly played by Janis Kelly, Pat comes off as a somewhat frail and slightly terrified being, as she is rushed through a glass factory (where the workers award her a green elephant) and classrooms in which the students have clearly been told what to say and how to behave, before stopping by the Gate of Longevity and Goodwill, where she sings her touching and slightly pathetic paean to the world she loves:

> This is prophetic! I foresee
> A time will come when luxury
> Dissolves into the atmosphere
> Like a perfume, and everywhere
> The simple virtues root and branch
> And leaf and flower. And on that bench
> There we'll relax and taste the fruit
> Of all our actions. Why regret
> Life which is so much like a dream?

Yet the homespun images she spins out of her sense of momentary joy—lit-up farm porches, families sitting around the dinner table, church steeples, etc.—are right out of Norman Rockwell paintings and are just as absurd of a vision as her husband's darker mumblings.

That evening's presentation of *The Red Detachment of Women* ballet, written by Chiang Ch'ing, Mao's wife—as she so shrilly reminds us later—is experienced by the now overwhelmed Nixons less as an objective performance—in reality the evening ended with enthusiastic praise by the President and First Lady—than as a psychological, inner viewpoint. It is clear that Nixon, as he suggests several times in the opera, admired Kissinger's mind, but he also mocked his ways and apparently disliked the man personally. Accordingly the Nixons both conjure up the evil landowner in their tired travelers' minds *to be*, or, at least, *to look*, like Kissinger.* Like many an innocent theatergoer, the Nixons become so involved in the story of poor girl who is saved and then destroyed by refusing to obey Communist doctrine that they confuse drama with reality, breaking into the action of the ballet itself to save and protect the young dancer.

Mark Morris, using some aspects of the original choreography, nicely stages his orderly squadrons of young military dancers against the chaos of the events. This is perhaps the most difficult part of the opera, and I am still not sure whether or not it truly succeeds, but it is crucial to our witnessing the truly mad person behind Chiang Ch'ing (Kathleen Kim)— who in real life may have been responsible for hundreds of deaths and had, herself, erratic nerves and

severe hypochondriasis—as she proclaims in the noted aria, "I am the wife of Mao Tse-tung," angrily declaring that all be determined by "the book." After Mao's death, we should recall, Chiang Ch'ing committed suicide.

After witnessing these six individuals' mental dramas—Richard Nixon, Mao Tse-tung, Chou En-lai, Pat Nixon, Henry Kissinger, and Chiang Ch'ing—we can only breathlessly watch as they slip into sleep. Kissinger shacks up with one of Mao's translators before disappearing into the bathroom. The Nixons share their disappointments, the President for being misinterpreted by the newspapers, Pat silently suffering, with tearful eyes, from her husband's inattention and having herself to attend yet again to what may be his ritual recounting of an attack he endured in World War II. Mao also finds relief in the hands of one of his translators before threatening his wife for having made political mistakes, until he falls with her into a lustful embrace upon their bed. Chou En-lai, clearly already in pain from the bladder cancer which would kill him four years later, awakens early to return to his never-ending work, drawing all the madness to a close with the most profound question of the opera: "Was there any point to any of it?" The "it" may refer, obviously, to the Nixons' visit, but it also suggests another possibility of meaning: "Was there any point to all their madness, to their desperate struggles to hold onto any power they might have over others?" All ended their lives in disgrace and shame, except for Pat; but even she almost disappeared from the public eye after the death of her husband, suffering a serious stroke the same year that Chou En-lai died.

In some respects, I now wonder, despite its occasional comic elements and always lush sonority of sound, if this is one of the darkest of operas. But then, aren't the young and the old—represented by the US and China—usually at the heart of the tragic, Romeo and Lear?

---

*Coincidentally, in my 1990 "opera for spoken voices," *The Walls Come True* (Los Angeles: Sun & Moon Press, 1995), I included Dr. Kissinger in my "Twelve Tyrants Between Acts: Mundane Moments and Insane Histories," based on the paranoia and ridiculous accusations he expressed in his *Years of Upheaval* (Boston: Little Brown, 1982) when, in 1973, he was in Hanoi attempting to negotiate the Paris Accords.

LOS ANGELES, FEBRUARY 19, 2011
Reprinted from *American Cultural Treasures* (March 2011).

Since I have quite obviously based my title of the above essay on the play Six Degrees *of Separation by John Guare, based on a theory by Hungarian writer Frigynes Karinthy that each human being is separated by only six oth-*

ers on earth, I should write that in the case of Nixon in China, *my companion Howard Fox and I are separated from three individuals involved in that work by no degrees!*

Our dear friend Betty Freeman (see My Year 2009*) originally commissioned the opera from John Adams, with John Adams playing parts of it and describing the work at one of her marvelous living-room salons in Beverly Hills. She once also invited Howard and me into her bedroom to hear a selection from the recording.*

*At the salon, we first met Peter Sellars, developing friendships that evolved over the years. Howard and Peter worked together, with numerous others, on the LA Festival of 1993 (unfortunately an unsuccessful festival, in part because of its far-flung venues), and I became a closer friend as I worked with him on the publication of Robert Auletta's play based on Æschylus' *The Persians*, directed by Peter at the The Mark Taper Forum in Los Angeles in 1993, a book for which Peter also wrote the Introduction. I attended many of the performances. The play, alas, was a failure, with numerous walk-outs each night.*

Howard once made Peter cry, while visiting his Venice, California home, by describing my love of theater as a young boy, when I purchased Broadway musical recordings—without owning a record player!

On a trip to Europe I encountered Peter as we were waiting to board the plane. He expressed great dismay since, as he described it, he knew "he was sure to be frisked and possibly led away for greater inspection" when he arrived in England, on account of his famously spiked red hair. "It happens every time," he declared!

Both Howard and I received especial pleasure, accordingly, upon seeing John Adams (who conducted his own score) and Peter (who directed both the opera and the Live in HD presentation of it) between acts of The Metropolitan Opera production.

LOS ANGELES, FEBRUARY 19, 2011

Details of the Experience

LUCHINO VISCONTI AND SUSO CECCHI D'AMICO
(SCREENPLAY, BASED ON THE NOVELLA BY CAMILLO
BOITO), CARLO ALIANELLO, GIORGIO BASSANI, AND
GIORGIO PROSPERI (DIALOGUE COLLABORATION),
TENNESSEE WILLIAMS AND PAUL BOWLES (ENGLISH-
LANGUAGE DIALOGUE VERSION), LUCHINO VISCONTI
(DIRECTOR) SENSO / 1954, USA 1968

BY AN ODD COINCIDENCE of Netflix timing, I saw this film, beautifully restored and recorded by Criterion, on the 145th anniversary, May 27, 2011, of the events that begin the film, a performance of Verdi's *Il Travatore* at La Fenice opera house in Venice. Wealthy and poor Venetians have gathered along with Austrian soldiers who control the city, as well as a few political provocateurs—relatives of the beautiful contessa Livia Serpieri—who shower leaflets demanding an end to Austrian rule and flowers in the color of the Italian flag upon the audience at the completion of Manrico's cry, "To arms! To arms!" As soldiers attempt to suppress the agitators,

 words break out between an Austrian soldier, Franz Mahler (Farley Granger), and the countess' cousin, Robert Ussoni (Massimo Girotti), who challenges Mahler to a duel.

Frightened for Ussoni's survival, the countess (Alida Valli) seeks a meeting with the Austrian in an attempt to dissuade him from the duel, and is assured by Mahler that the event will not occur. At the close of the meeting she requests her husband to take her home, since she is not feeling well.

The source of this ill feeling, we already suspect, are the sensations aroused by the appearance and bearing of Mahler, whom we have already been told is the talk of Venice women. And soon after the two meet again, with unexpected and truly shocking consequences, as the countess wanders the streets of the violent city with the soldier all night. Any respectable woman would not dare to be out after curfew and would not possibly allow herself to be seen, yet the countess even goes further a few days later, when she shows up at the barracks in search of Mahler.

Despite her political affiliations, it is clear that

Countess Serpieri will abandon almost all of her values in search of love. Before long, the two spend days together in a small hotel, using her personal maid as an agent in her deceit.

Mahler, a seasoned paramour, is clearly less than an avid soldier, and seduces the countess partly through his seeming passivity and joy in "the details of the experience of love-making," the quiet beat of the wings of a fly or a moth and other small sensations. The countess, in her first true romance, abandons herself, instead, to the passion, almost losing consciousness in the act, and that is her continual dilemma: she has lost all sense of who and what she was. She no longer has a past.

When Mahler fails to meet her the next day, she again appears at the barracks, and is ready to reveal all to her husband. But the young man to whom she rushes, when told by the maid that someone has visited her, turns out to be her cousin, returned from exile, not Mahler. Her husband, who has followed, is accordingly relieved to discover someone he knows within rather than a stranger, a possible lover.

Ussoni gives her a box containing all the partisans' funds for safekeeping, as war between the Austrians and the nationalists, led by Garibaldi, breaks out. Ussoni and others lead the fight in the north. The countess and her household, meanwhile, retire to their country manor for protection. But the war has reached that area as well, Franz Mahler showing up in her bedroom late one night.

At first, it appears that she has quelled her passion. "This is not Venice," she declares again and again, as if it were an incantation. Through trickery and deceit, however, Mahler wins her over, and before the end of the night has joined her in bed. The countess is now determined to hide Mahler in the granary, but when gunfire breaks out nearby, the men rush to see it better from the granary windows, the countess following in fear of her lover's discovery.

Mahler turns up again in her bedroom, having been served breakfast by her maid. We know the inevitable: to release him from the army and his need to leave her, the countess is willing to give up the partisans' treasure as a bribe for a willing doctor to declare Mahler unfit. The loss of those funds, indeed, ends with the Italians' defeat and her beloved cousin being shot.

Having now lost almost all self-worth, the Countess is utterly distressed when she hears, in a letter from Mahler, that she should not yet travel to Verona to see him. Determined to make the trip nonetheless, she chances death, arriving in the city exhausted and

covered with dirt. At Mahler's apartment, she discovers a drunken sensualist in bed with a prostitute instead of her former hero. Mahler recognizes himself now as a liar, a traitor, a cheat, and spits out his hate by calling attention to her blind abandonment of all and, most particularly, her loss of beauty.

Like a mad woman, she wanders the streets, finally reaching the Austrian army headquarters, where she reveals Mahler's deceit. The last images of Visconti's film show the former soldier, hands tied behind him, being shot by his comrades.

As many critics have agreed, *Senso* does not just begin as an opera, but truly becomes one—*sans* singing and without major heroes. Visconti's characters are grand failures, the husband being a political opportunist, the handsome soldier a petty cad, the countess a deluded woman of the upper class. None are commendable. The heroes of this piece, the Italian patriots, appear in the background and fail in their efforts as well. Yet through his lush camera work, the layers of color revealing both the splendor and decay of this world, Visconti allows us to take in the details of the experience, immersing us in the sensations of sexual lust. It is probably that fact which kept this film from US shores for 14 years after its making, even though redone in English with dialogue by the ardent writers of decadence of the day, Tennessee Williams and Paul Bowles.

LOS ANGELES, MAY 29, 2011
Reprinted from *World Cinema Review* (May 2011).

Out There

JOEL AND ETHAN COEN (WRITERS AND DIRECTORS, BASED ON A NOVEL BY CHARLES PORTIS) **TRUE GRIT** / 2010

IF I HAVE several times in these pages chided the Coen brothers for their sophomoric cynicism and exaggerated characterizations of the human species, I have also noted time and again their brilliant gifts as directors, particularly when they work, as they have here and as they did in *No Country for Old Men*, with pre-existing sources. In both cases the sensibilities of the authors nicely match the Coens' viewpoints. But the darkness of these films is far more profound than the shallow nose-thumbings that often occur in the Coens' more comic works.

Indeed, I believe *True Grit*—despite *Los Angeles Times* critic Betsy Sharkey's proclamation in today's paper that this film is far "nicer" than *No Country for Old Men*—is their most horrifying work to date. For in the earlier film, chaos and destruction were meted out by the evil villain; in last year's *A Serious Man*, the sufferings endured by the hero were obviously the "gift" of a wrathful God. But in *True Grit* it is the so-called "good people," as well as the villains, who kill.

 True, the evil Tom Chaney (Josh Brolin) begins it, killing Mattie Ross' father. But we soon recognize that in this Arkansas frontier world of an "eye for an eye" philosophy, death or, at least, its metaphoric representation, is something no one can escape. From the moment the grieving 14-year-old daughter enters the town to identify her father's body and send the corpse on its way back to her home, Mattie (excellently realized by Hailee Steinfeld) is faced with death. Having to pay almost everything she has for the embalming and shipping of the body, she is forced to sleep the first night, like Oliver Twist, in a coffin, beside three cadaverous criminals who, a few minutes after her arrival in town, were hung in the main square. When she finally does find other lodging, she must share the bed with an old woman whose dead sleep reveals that she is soon to become a corpse herself.

None of this, however, truly fazes this intense

moppet, and we soon discover that like most of those around her, when it comes to facing annihilation, she has a heart of stone. For Mattie is determined to get revenge, to track down the man who killed her father, presumed now to be in Indian Territory, the jurisdiction of federal marshals who are few in number and busy with larger crimes. Spouting the Gospel as if she were a child-preacher out of a Flannery O'Connor tale, Mattie doesn't even blink in her forward motion of righteous wrath. Unlike the 1969 movie version of *True Grit*, which significantly softened this figure's indignation, the Coens transform her into a pint-sized prophet utterly determined to accomplish what she believes she is destined to do.

When told that US Marshall Rooster Cogburn (played in the original by John Wayne, and here by Jeff Bridges) is the meanest of men she might choose to lead her on the chase, Mattie checks out a local trial wherein she hears testimony to his murderous ways. Cogburn, however, is not just a murderer—or, as some might prefer to describe him, a successful sheriff—but also a serious drunk (ridiculously euphemized by suggesting he likes to "pop a cork"), and Mattie has not only to get around his reluctance to the chase but his questionable ability to accomplish it. Part of the film's humor lies in her stubborn maneuvering of Cogburn and in his determination to keep her from attempting to join him in the task. Against her desire, Cogburn teams up with another man, LaBoeuf (hilariously played by Matt Damon), a roughly mustachioed and spur-jangling Texas Ranger who is after Chaney for a different murder and a large reward. Both men try to sneak away early in the morning before Mattie can join them, but she is soon hot on their trail and thoroughly demonstrates her "true grit" by fording the river on horseback.

In the Coens' telling, the three potential killers—who thoroughly reveal, as *The New York Times* critic Manhola Dargis pointed out, D. H. Lawrence's postulate that "the essential American soul is hard, isolate, stoic and a killer"—now come face to face with an even greater emblem of death, the vast "out there," the frontier itself. This is not the lush green or even picturesquely rocky landscape of most Westerns, but a bleached-out and barren world stripped of nearly everything, including the Indians. At the best the trio come across an occasional cabin or an eccentric loner such as Bear Man (Ed Corbin), a wilderness doctor cloaked in the entire pelt of a bear with head attached. In this world, death looms everywhere. And, as the two men—the grumpy and always woozy Cogburn, and the bragging, self-centered LaBoeuf—inevitably turn against one another, Mattie is put into the position of a scolding, cajoling guide, leading them, as much as they lead her, into harm's way.

I don't know how anyone might describe a film as being "nice" that shows a villain's fingers being cut off, the knife then thrust into his  heart, and presents a scene a few minutes later in which Cogburn shoots not only the robbers but LaBoeuf (it is debatable, given his obvious skill with a gun combined with his limited vision—he has only one eye—whether it was intentional or not). But the directors have gotten to the heart of Portis' fiction and come closer to the truth of the American West than most Westerns other than those by director Budd Boetticher. Without the controls of society, it is not a nice world, and Mattie, despite her determination and her own killer instincts—it is she who finally must face down her father's murderer and shoot him dead—ultimately learns that such an unforgiving world can only end in loss.

While both LaBoeuf and Cogburn take bullets, surviving nonetheless, Mattie, falling down into a sinkhole, must face nature itself, in the form of a true symbol of the evil of her and the others' acts, by being bitten by a poisonous snake. Even a mad rush across the starlit plane cannot entirely make her whole again; she loses her horse and one arm. We later discover that her strong-willed ways perhaps also led to a life of loneliness, for she never marries.

Although Mattie does not question her acts or attempt to justify her mad determination to gun down her father's killer, we must, at some point, judge her, just as the people of the city had judged Rooster Cogburn earlier in the film. And we realize that in her fanatical grittiness there is something heroic yet ridiculous, that she is a figure at once comic and tragic, similar to US history.

LOS ANGELES, NEW YEAR'S DAY, 2011
Reprinted from *World Cinema Review* (January 2011).

Drath and Muth

THE NAMES ALONE sound like something out of a strange detective story, "Drath and Muth," as if the legendary French Inspector Clouseau (Peter Sellers) were pronouncing "death and the moth," which wouldn't be far from the truth, given the essay I recently read about the death of German journalist Viola Drath through the hands of her younger husband Albrecht Muth.

Drath, a Washington, D.C. journalist of long renown, 44 years older than her young lover, was found dead in her Georgetown, Q Street house on August 12 of 2011, her reportedly violent husband, it appears, the perpetrator.

Franklin Foer's *The New York Times Magazine* essay recounted the horrifying story of their early meeting in 1982, before the death of her husband, Francis, the former deputy American military governor of Bavaria, "whom everyone called the Colonel." Drath had somehow insinuated herself into Washington, D.C. society, she and her husband throwing regular dinner parties

at their Georgetown house, and she writing essays for German language journals, as well as *Harper's* and *Commentary*. Her writing, filled with Teutonic-like pronouncements, once led a Hirshhorn Museum executive to react: "*Also sprach* Viola!"

Yet, Drath established herself as a significant figure in the D.C. world, befriending author Norman Mailer, who stayed in her house as he researched his fiction *Harlot's Ghost*. Working for the government, her husband commented, "When I speak German to Henry Kissinger, he talks like a little boy."

She and her husband, indeed, often entertained the German-speaking community in the capital city, dinners which included significant guests almost every weekend.

Upon the Colonel's death in 1986, Drath, lonely and distraught, began meeting with Muth quite often, and quickly became enamored with the young German-speaking "Muti," who matched her Teutonic memories, and with whom she argued, in German, deeply into the night.

Behaving, as Foer's essay relates, more like an intern than a companion, Muth slowly insinuated himself into Drath's life, reading the daily newspapers and reporting back, and, most importantly, assuming the domestic responsibilities including cooking and cleaning, for which Drath had no facility. After the later abandonment of Muth, Drath revealed to a friend that she did not even know how to cook breakfast.

As a couple, however, Drath and Muth achieved even greater recognition in the Washington, D.C. community than she had ever achieved with the Colonel. At regular dinner parties, attended by figures such as Pierre Salinger, Antonin Scalia, Dick Cheney, and numerous others, with Muth serving up dinner from their infamous yellow-tinged kitchen, D.C. insiders slowly grew to admire and respect Drath's new husband, who began to claim outrageously exaggerated relationships with Iraqi government officials. Gradually, as his lies spun literally out of control, he claimed a kind of double-spy involvement with the Iraqi community, using his supposed connections to reveal internal secrets to various governmental agencies, while simultaneously involving international figures from George Soros (who once quipped to the French Ambassador that Muth was the "the type of man who would have closed the oven door behind him at Auschwitz," a statement Muth saw as a testament to his worth) to Arun Gandhi, the grandson of Mahatma.

There is something almost touching about Foer's *New York Times* essay's description of Muti's madness, as he reveals Muth's strategies, wherein he contacted only the highest figures with whom he had access, ignoring the underlings, which only made the upper echelons, who believed that he had necessarily been vetted by their lower assistants, more vulnerable—and ignorant. Only a few bothered to check into his actual credentials, which eventually revealed that he was a complete fraud. Muth had it down perfectly; as he himself described it: "You meet someone of import, check him out, determine [if] he can be of use, you make him yours. At some point you must decide whether to run him as a useful idiot, he not catching on as to who you are and what you do."

By that time his connections with Drath had already established him within the political community; and the fact that Muth was also gay (one of his gay lovers actually lived in Drath's house), and, increasingly, a violent drunk, took ages apparently to reach the political consciousness. Muth, despite temporary escapes to Miami (during which he proclaimed he was in Iraq, working behind lines), contrived to be seen as a major government informant. Muth was even thanked for his fabulated email reports out of Iraq (written on Drath's Georgetown apartment computer) by higher-ups at the

State Department such as the seasoned Thomas Pickering. Only in 2011, the year of the murder of his wife, had Muth begun to be perceived by many in the higher levels of government as another fraud and even a mad man, in the manner of the great Washington, D.C. con-artists such as Edward von Kloberg III, Craig Spence, and Steven Martindale.

Certainly I was not surprised by this revelatory essay—although, I admit, I was completely entertained. After all, Howard and I had lived in the city for 14 years before moving to Los Angeles. If anything, the whole event sounded all too familiar.

Indeed, from the first statement of Foer's fascinating essay, "Dinners were served in the basement. Ambassadors, generals with many stars, senior White House officials and closely read columnists—all would  walk past the yellowing kitchen, which looked as if it hadn't been updated since the Ford administration, and down the dimly lighted dining room."

I suddenly became sickened with a kind of strange sense of déjà vu. I had been there! "Howard," I shouted out, "do you remember Viola Drath?"

After a slow pause of aging memory, Howard responded, "Yes, she was a German journalist."

"Didn't we attend a party at her house?"

Howard wasn't sure of the event.

"Read the article," I demanded! Suddenly everything came rushing back into my memory. I immediately recalled the dinner party we had attended, Howard invited, obviously, because he was a central curator at the Hirshhorn Museum and Sculpture Garden. I recall—and Howard eventually confirmed this—a great many significant figures crowding into the open living room of the large Georgetown house for cocktails. One man was draped with numerous metals—on his way to another party after. We descended that small staircase beside the yellowing kitchen down to the dining area, I following Viola, who said: "You're Swiss! The Swiss always make such good cooks!" Her comment entirely flummoxed me—was I suddenly in her mind a mad, gay chef? (Our acquaintances in that city often said such strange things that I sometimes felt I was living on another planet.) I remember the crowded dinner, but little of what occurred during our meal. I recall only my complete discomfort in having to endure the affair, typical of many a Washington, D.C evening for me in those tortured days. As we left the house, I whispered to Howard, "I feel like we've just descended into the heart of a Nazi enclave."

"Drath and Muth," of course! In those days of the early 1980s, however, I am confident the Colonel still stalked the halls, caring for his wife and daughters. I believe I never encountered the "moth," drawn to death's flame. But death was already in the air.

LOS ANGELES, JULY 18, 2012

End of the Road

TENNESSEE WILLIAMS **CAMINO REAL** / THE THE-
ATER AT BOSTON COURT, PASADENA, CALIFORNIA / THE
PERFORMANCE I SAW WAS ON MARCH 6, 2011

I HAVE ALWAYS greatly admired the works of Tennessee Williams, having even chosen to publish one of
his lesser—and undeservedly ignored—plays in Mac
Wellman's and my large drama anthology, *From the
Other Side of the Century II: A New American Drama
1960-1995*, of 1998. That play, *The Gnädiges Fraülein*
of 1966, is perhaps one of his most absurd works, but
worth a rereading. Recently, moreover, approaching
this centennial year of his birth, I have been fortunate
to see some of his earliest, far more romantically-in-
spired pieces, which has helped to me once again reassess this great dramatist.

After my own reinvestigation of *A Streetcar Named
Desire* in 2009, I was able to see a credible, if not entirely satisfying, revival of *The Glass Menagerie*, performed

in New York in 2009 and in Los Angeles in 2010; *Vieux Carré,* reconceived by the Wooster Group, a play begun early in Williams' career and finished late; and, now, the seldom produced *Camino Real* of 1953, in a delightful, if not perfect, production by The Theater at Boston Court, co-produced by the CalArts School of Theater, with most of the roles played by CalArts students.

The fact that this is primarily a "student" production should not make anyone wince; for years CalArts has produced some of the most interesting of productions presented in Los Angeles, and the school has spun off numerous younger groups, including the wonderfully inventive Poor Dog Group, whose 2010 production of *Brewsie and Willie* gets my nomination for the best LA-area play of that year!

Having said that, I can well understand why the 16 blocks (a one-act version contains only 10 blocks) of the full-length *Camino Real*—pronounced deliberately, with Williams' instructions, in the American way, Cámino Rēal, suggesting the real world as opposed to a fantastical one—is seldom revived. Williams' play is a series of fantastic and terrifying scenes that resemble nothing else in theatrical history. Without knowing that I was a critic (we did not speak at all before the first act of 90 minutes), the woman next to me said, in the intermission, "I hope you're going to tell me what this is all about." I assured her I would try.

But, of course, Williams' poetic expressionism cannot be that simply transformed into narrative explanation. A great part of this phantasmagoric world which enwraps the audience is better just being experienced instead of analyzed. There is no true comprehension for the conglomerate of lost souls trapped at the Royal Road, including a wild collection of individuals from time and space, most notably, Don Quixote (Lenny von Dohlen) (whose Sancho has abandoned him upon his entry into the plaza); Marguerite "Camille" Gautier (excellently realized by Marissa Chibas) (the famed courtesan who in Verdi's *La Traviata* and numerous other versions dies a horrible death of tuberculosis); Giacomo Girolamo Casanova de Seingalt (the noted nobleman lover, more commonly known simply as Casanova); George Gordon, Lord Byron (the romantic poet, lover of both Percy Shelly and his wife); Palamède de Guermantes (the Baron de Charlus of Proust's *Remembrance of Things Past*); and, most notably perhaps, Kilroy (the World War II legend who had been everywhere before all the others). Add to these the permanent denizens of this flophouse of a town: the near stage-manager Gutman (named after Sydney Greenstreet's character in *Casablanca*); a gypsy fortune-teller and her perpetually virgin daughter, Esmeralda; a pawnshop owner; Rosita the Whore; a blind mother; an effeminate waiter; the proprietor of the Ritz Men Only hotel; Abdullah; Tranny Streetperson (who is literally shot down in the street for fraternizing with others); and the horrifying, ever-present street cleaners, and you have an idea of the zoo-like atmosphere of the 16 scenes that reveal, little by little, the hell that is Camino Real. It is, obviously, a place of horror which will remind one of Tahirir Square, Tiananmen Square, or the streets of Tripoli—a place where authorities do not want one to gather.

Except perhaps for Kilroy, all of these individuals share outrageous exploits in love and larger-than-human lives. One might suggest they have all ended up here, from where there is no easy escape, simply because of their gargantuan lusts, their refusals to live life on any level of what might be described as normality. But even in Camino Real, in an endless now with no possibility of redemption, they refuse to give up. A large part of the relationship between Casanova and Camille concerns his insistence that they admit their deep love, and her refusal to give up her many drugs, including cocaine and kif, but also sex and outright infatuation.

Time and again, she is robbed, raped, and left for dead, but each time she rises to fall again, unable to stop the cycle of her dramatic spiral into death.

By the time Casanova (wonderfully played by Tim Cummings) has reached this dead end, he is too old to live up to his reputation, and too poor to even maintain his lifestyle—despite his attempt to keep up his appearance in a gold-embroidered coat. By curtain's end he has been thrown out of the best hotel (the Siete Mares run by Gutman) and is forced to take refuge in the cold, narrow bed of the Ritz Men Only, yet ready to share even that with the equally rejected Kilroy.

One by one we come to see that each character in

this god-forsaken place has been eaten up by life and circumstance. They are the grotesques of the world, hardly its heroes, people who, as in nearly every Williams play, have lived too much of their lives in dreams, and are now, like Blanche DuBois of *A Streetcar Named Desire*, forced to pay the piper.

Only three of the play's characters have any potential to escape or redeem themselves. The gypsy woman's daughter has at the least the symbolic possibility of regaining her humanity by performing a dance with each full moon that restores her virginity, after which everyone attempts to take it away from her again. But this time round she has chosen the American oaf Kilroy (capably played, in the production I saw, by a stand-in, Chris Chiquet) as her lover, the man, who, because of his big heart—"the size of the head of a baby"—has been advised to give up sex and cannot complete the act. And, in that sense, she is freed. She remains a virgin, at least temporarily, falling in love with the memory of his possible sincerity. Swept up into death by the street cleaners, Kilroy returns to her, but she can hear him only as a mewling cat.

The play begins with the arrival of the biggest dreamer of them all, Don Quixote, who like all the others is tired and lonely. Yet Quixote, as we all know, cannot be quelled, and after a good sleep lasting the length of the play, he arises to find a new replacement for San-

cho. That he should find the now "non-existent" (as he may have been always) Kilroy is perfect. For Kilroy has been throughout a bigger fool than even Quixote battling windmills as his enemy. Made to dress like a clown, Kilroy, a disturbingly innocent "patsy" who has lost his championship status, his lover, and, later, the mementos of that life, at least knows the difference between past, present, and future, changing the graffiti of "Kilroy Was Here," to "Kilroy Is Here," and back to past tense as he joins Quixote in his exit.

The only way to leave Camino Real in this production is to climb a small ladder into what appears to be a booth for camera snapshots, as if each has to face the reality of his image before he can escape. For these vain and lost individuals it is a frightening possibility that keeps them from attempting the unknown, fraught with all the perils of losing, on top of everything else, one's soul and sanity. But with Quixote's faith to support him, Kilroy takes the leap and, as Quixote declares, "the violets push through the rock."

Camino Real is not an easy play, either for its cast or the audience, but it is a beautifully poetic screed, like so many of Williams' work, for those who have lost their way through their endless attempts to live a full life, as well as a prayer that the sinful may not be forgotten by those who consider themselves as among the saintly.

LOS ANGELES, MARCH 7, 2011
Reprinted from *US Theater, Opera, and Performance* (March 2011).

Nell's Death

SAMUEL BECKETT **ENDGAME** / LOS ANGELES, SA-
CRED FOOLS THEATER / THE PERFORMANCE I SAW WAS
ON APRIL 15, 2011

> HAMM: We're not beginning to...to...mean
> something?
> CLOV: Mean something! You and I, mean some-
> thing! [*Brief laugh*] Ah that's a good one!
> HAMM: I wonder. [*Pause*] Imagine if a rational be-
> ing came back to earth, wouldn't he be liable
> to get ideas into his head if he observed us
> long enough.

BEWARE POOR VIEWER (or reader), Beckett seems to
warn of putting too many of your ideas into the often
quite meaningless actions of Clov and Hamm of the
playwright's marvelous *Endgame*. But of course Beckett is also suggesting, perhaps, that the play—carefully
looked at—*does* mean something, a great many things!
Beckett's equivocation about several issues are at the

heart of this play.

Seeing it again in this new performance at the Sacred Fools Theater in Los Angeles directed by Paul Plunkett, and reading it again soon after, set me to thinking and rediscovering all sorts of meanings, some new, some old, some likely chewed up by many of the hundreds of Beckett critics over the years—but perhaps most worth mentioning.

By accident I saw this play soon after seeing Benjamin Britten's setting of the medieval miracle play, *Noye's Fludd*, so that I recognized in *Endgame* this time round far more suggestions and references to Noah and his family.

One should never see *Endgame* (or any Beckett play for that matter), however, as a kind of metaphoric telling or allegorical story of something else. Rather Beckett riddles his play with references to Noah's ordeal, enfolding them within contemporary issues and other modernist concerns. This is not a play *about* Noah and his family, but certainly is a work that embraces the myths.

Noah's son Ham(m) (wonderfully played by Leon Russom)—shamed and cursed by his father to be the servant of his brothers for having seen him naked—is at the center of Beckett's work, enduring his seemingly endless life on earth. Noah lived 350 years *after* the flood, a total of 950 years according to the book of

Genesis. And each of the sons lived for hundreds of years also. So Hamm's crying out for death is obviously no small thing. In the post-holocaust world in which Hamm lives, where life has been completely blotted out—there are no tides, no waves, all is gray—the end is certainly to be longed for.

Hamm's father, living out his old, old age in an ashbin beside his equally displaced mother, Nell, is called in Beckett's play, Nagg, suggesting both his propensity to "nag" or scold (he, after all, has cursed his own son) and the fact, clearly, that like an old "nag," an old horse, he has been put out to pasture, so to speak, locked away in a covered ashbin. If one wanted to go further, and Beckett certainly does encourage this, one might play a game of anagrams, transforming Nagg into something like "Noah after God's grievance," or "Noah after God's gift," depending upon from which side of the coin one sees oneself. But this is, after all, only a game.

There is no question, however, of both Nagg's, Nell's, and Hamm's memories of rain, water, sails, fins, and other flood-like images, which Hamm insists that Clov inspect through the windows, high above normal placement, with a ladder and telescope in hand. It is as if they live still in the ark, attempting to spot signs of some vestiges of new life or survival. Nagg and Nell, moreover, remembering before  the flood, retell the story of how they almost drowned on Lake Como.

The only animals remaining, humorously, are a three-legged child's play-dog, a flea, a rat, and, possibly, some gulls and the fin of a passing shark. The animals, along with Noah's other family members, evidently have left long ago to be fruitful and multiply, while Hamm, his father, and his mother have remained behind, unable to witness that new green world the others might have discovered.

Clov (Barry Ford) seems the only misplaced figure in the play. Hamm treats him, occasionally like a son, but none of his Biblical sons, Cush, Mizraim, Put, and Canaan, suggest the name Clov. Perhaps he is the son of the old man of the fiction which Hamm retells day and after day, adding details as he goes along. Whoever he is, he serves, like Lucky in Beckett's *Waiting for Godot*, as an overburdened, maltreated slave to Hamm.

More likely, Clov is a manifestation of the cleaving process that daily occurs between the two, his name resembling the past tense of the cleavage which may or may not occur at *Endgame*'s close. But he is also the matching opposite of Hamm. Both are red-complexioned, but the blind Hamm can only sit while the thin Clov can only stand. Yet despite the abuse that Hamm heaps upon him, Clov has no choice, it appears, but to serve his master.

I think Beckett here is also playing with a wonderful pun, suggesting the perfect relationship of clove to ham, the two generally used in Easter dinners, one all plump asquat the platter with the other neatly studding it (one thinks of Clov's constant orderliness). In that sense, Beckett has moved away from the intricacies of Noah's story, but has brilliantly portrayed their lifetime relationship, and hinted at a new hope symbolized by an Easter dinner.

With no immediate possibility of death, trapped in a world beyond the end where, as Clov reminds us again and again, all they can see is "zero," it is no wonder that these two so suffer the pains of everyday life. Nearly everything around them has disappeared and provisions, including food and painkillers, are fast running out.

As many critics have agreed, theirs is a world of repetition, a day by day recitation of their sufferings that apparently has no end. As Hamm keeps suggesting, however, it will someday, *must* someday end, as

Nell's death—if it is truly a death—foretells. Like a bell announcing a funeral, or as in the knelling of a disaster, Nell's demise demonstrates that, despite the "game of dying" Nagg, Hamm, and Clov play each day, a real end is imminent, even if hundreds of years off. Clov's glimpse of a young boy (a potential Christ?)—which Hamm immediately describes as a possible "progenitor"—hints at a new world beyond the dead one in which they are trapped.

NEW YORK, MAY 6, 2011
Reprinted from *US Theater, Opera, and Performance* (May 2011).

Ash to Ash

MICHELANGELO FRAMMARTINO (WRITER AND
DIRECTOR) LE QUATTRO VOLTE (THE FOUR TIMES) /
2010, USA 2011

LE QUATTRO VOLTE has sometimes been spoken of—
quite mistakenly—as a documentary, or, at least, as a
quasi-documentary. While it has a bit of that feel, and
uses the locals of a small Calabrian village as its actors,
it is a very carefully constructed tale, and must be understood as a kind of ruminative fiction if it is to work
at all. As a documentary it would be merely coy in the
way that I previously described *The Story of the Weeping
Camel* (see *My Year 2003*). While many of the events
are natural occurrences in the town, others are clearly
staged and enacted only for the sake of the written and
plotted story.

Frammartino's "story" is a truly a simple one—so
simple that it is almost banal—about the cycles of life,
and, in his Italian neo-realist method, he trods a path

that is well worn. The film begins with a charcoal kiln, smoke pouring out from it into the land around, before focusing for a short period on the life of an elderly goat herder (Giuseppe Fuda), near death.

There is no recognizable speech in this film, no subtitles, and very little human talk. The sounds belong mostly to the animal world and nature, as we follow the herder and goats into the hills about the town, and return back to the old man's simple living space. The goat bells, church bells, dog barks, and the old man's cough, along with the occasional engine of a truck, quietly spoken words on a street corner, and the bleats of the goats, dominate the aural aspects of this film, which put together create a kind of profound music.

Similarly, the action is simple, the camera tracking the voyage back and forth into nature while revealing the glorious landscape and the stony isolation of the town in the distance. The old man believes that the cure for his cough is to drink water filled with ash, and he purchases ash swept up from the floors of the cathedral by a cleaning woman, who blesses them before carefully wrapping them up in paper.

On our second trip with the man and goats to the countryside, we observe him sitting (perhaps relieving himself) before he turns to take the goats home. The attentive viewer will notice that the packet of ashes has dropped from his pants. And when he returns home, after gathering up his snails which miraculously have escaped from their pot with the lid held down by a brick, he discovers his loss. A trip to the cathedral in the night proves fruitless, and by morning we see him lying, near death, in bed.

Meanwhile other villagers have gathered under his window to participate in a staged performance of Christ's journey to his execution upon the cross, many in costumes as Romans and Israelites. The old man's

 dog guards his territory, goats, and house, keeping several of the performers at bay, until a couple of costumed Roman soldiers attempt to chase him off. Returning to his post, the dog, almost as if in revenge, removes a rock that keeps a small parked truck from sliding down the hill. The truck, now freed, rolls across the street into the gate of the goat barn, freeing the animals, who soon can be found everywhere in the old man's house, including upon his table and chairs. As the goats congregate, the old man dies.

In the next scene, the old man is laid to rest in a crypt, Frammartino forcing us to witness the closing of the grave from within.

Suddenly we view a kid being born, dropping from its mother's uterus; and over the period of a few more scenes, we watch the new goat in its surroundings within an even larger congregation of goats led by a different goat herder. We follow him as well as he takes out the goats and returns, only to repeat the pattern, with the new baby goats included, the next day.

The small white kid, presumably a reincarnation of the old goat herder, becomes lost in the passage of the goats to a distant field, and after fiercely bleating as it searches for its mother, finally lies down exhausted at the foot of a great tree to die.

A huge storm rises, the wind blowing, the clouds roiling up, and when morning light appears, we see the whole valley covered with snow. The new kid surely would have been unable to survive.

A new "time" comes to the valley; the snow melted, spring has arrived. The tree is covered with ants and lichen.  Villagers come to cut the tree down, carrying it into town, where, with great effort, they stand it up in the square, with packages tied to its top. After celebrating, they let it fall again, several of the villagers scooping up the packages with pleasure.

The tree is chopped into pieces and transported to the location where the film began. Carefully and painstakingly the workers build up a kiln of logs and sticks, covering it over with straw and tar before lighting it up as they annually do to produce the charcoal which keeps the villagers warm. The ash pours out of the kiln over the entire valley, much of it obviously coming to rest once again on the cathedral's floor.

Frammartino's fable about the interconnectedness of peasant life is clearly sentimental, and, at times, I felt this film was unnecessarily manipulative. Yet the director presents these cyclic patterns with so much dignity and equal humor that ultimately his variations of human, animal, vegetable, and mineral interactions grow into something more meaningful. If nothing else, the film is a spectacularly beautiful, nearly surreal at moments, view into Calabrian life. The only professional used in the film, claims Frammartino, was the dog.

LOS ANGELES, APRIL 19, 2011
Reprinted from *World Cinema Review* (April 2011).

Another War

MOACYR SCLIAR **THE WAR IN BOM FIM**, TRANSLAT-
ED FROM THE PORTUGUESE BY DAVID WILLIAM FOSTER
(LUBBOCK, TEXAS: TEXAS TECH UNIVERSITY, 2010)

OFTEN DESCRIBED as the major Jewish author of Bra-
zil, Moacyr Scliar, who grew up in the south of the
country in Porto Alegre, died this year on February 27,
soon after Texas Tech University published his earliest
fiction, *The War in Bom Fim*, in English.

Originally published in 1972, this fiction appears,
at first, to be a kind of magical realist tale of the mostly
Jewish immigrant community of Bom Fim during
World War II. And in that context, the work, at times,
might remind one of a mix between Sholom Aleichem
and Neil Simon, as the story weaves in and out of descriptions of the poor Jewish citizens and their lives.
It involves two young boys, their father Samuel, their
fearless mother Shendl, Samuel's lovable and somewhat
resistant mare Malke Tube, and magical events that de-

fine this Yiddish-speaking society, including the omni-
presence of Chagall and his "floating violinists," whom
the narrator transports to the streets of Porto Alegre,
along with the possibility of Kafka living nearby. On
the other side of this somewhat nostalgic vision exist
the games of the young brothers, Joel and Nathan, as
they and their neighborhood friends imaginatively
fight a war against the Nazis, who, unknown to the
adults, have invaded a nearby beach. With Joel as their
leader, Nathan as a flying savior, and every child and
beast at their side, the city of Porto Alegre is amazingly
saved again and again, even when, at the end of the war,

Hitler attempts to hide out in a nearby mansion.

This part of the story, which takes up a larger portion of the book, presents a sort of wonderfully and innocently benign picture of the dying Jewish community; but as the boys begin to grow up, and the older parents begin to leave the neighborhood, things gradually turn grimmer, finally collapsing into a series of absolute horrors that demonstrates that, despite their primarily symbolic battles with hatred, this community is affected as well by anti-Semitism and the abandonment of social and religious values.

From the earliest pages of the book, moreover, there are clues that not everything in Bom Fim is right. The local dog, Melâmpio, hates Jews, and barks on winter nights to point the way to their houses for Stukas and Messerschmitts. The author's insistence on mentioning—every time he describes the large tree-lined Redenção Park in the middle of town—the benches of waiting pederasts seems almost homophobic; and, ultimately, one of the children, Alberto, is described as letting "himself be buggered." Rosa, a young girl, is raped in the park and leaves home. With the end of the war, new shops and high-rise apartments come to Bom Fim, making it more and more difficult for Samuel to sell his meager wares from his cart.

But these are only the rumblings of far more terrifying events that bring down the curtain on Scliar's seemingly rhapsodic recollections. The younger, frailer brother, Nathan, suddenly dies. Joel's mother goes insane and is locked away in an institution. His father, Samuel, is grotesquely trapped under his beloved mare, and must disembowel the beast to escape. Joel, himself, leaves Bom Fim, as he becomes increasingly assimilated into a non-Jewish world, and ends up selling jewelry. One by one the poor homes of Bom Fim are torn down to be replaced by newer and larger structures.

Near to where old Samuel now lives is a German bartender, who, trying to keep a low profile, endures the occasional tirades of Samuel and other Jewish customers. For his birthday, however, his two reprehensible sons capture Samuel, hoping to show him off to their father, as they threaten to burn him as in the Nazi death camps. The terrified old man attempts to run off, but falls, hitting his head, and dies. To hide the crime, the sons cut up the body into pieces at the very moment that their mulatto mother returns home from a night of sexual pleasures, and, witnessing the pieces of meat before them, is insistent that they continue with what she perceives to be a barbecue. Inviting several other friends, she and the speechless, now sickened brothers sit down to a cannibal feast.

In another part of the city, Joel attempts to entice a wealthy young girl to have sex. Ultimately, realizing that any relationship with her will be impossible, he steals a car and, with a strong sense of nostalgia and self-pity, determines to visit his father to talk in Yiddish with him about the old times. So ends Scliar's memorial to his Jewish past, none of which now appears to be salvageable or to represent any possible salvation.

Joel's ending realization that "the war is over" may also signify his inability to perceive that another war—a war to win back his heritage and meaning—has just begun.

LOS ANGELES, MAY 23, 2011
Reprinted from *Rain Taxi* (Summer 2011).

The Traveling Table

ARISTÍDES VARGAS (WRITER AND DIRECTOR) **LA RAZÓN BLINDADA (ARMORED REASON)** / LOS ANGELES, THE 24TH STREET THEATRE / THE PERFORMANCE I SAW WAS ON OCTOBER 24, 2010

TWO MEN SIT at a table, quietly talking, occasionally—at moments more and more often—breaking out into long poetic or narrative passages, then, with an explosion of terror, suddenly growing quiet, facing one another as if they had nothing to say. It is the world of an Argentine prison during that country's "Dirty War," where men are allowed only one hour each Sunday to interact with their fellow prisoners, a life-saving time when they come together to escape their growing mad-

ness, acting out stories and dramas of life, most of them vaguely based on *Don Quixote*, through which they can embrace both the impossibilities, the dreams, and the absurdities of their lives.

Author Vargas created this play from events that occurred to his brother during that brutal military regime in the 1970s until 1983, where the only line between madness and memory was the enactments of these amateur performers. Since the prisoners were not allowed to stand or move about, the drama is one of the imagination, a salvation of words only. In the dramatic presentation of this Kafkaesque, sometimes Beckettian reality, the actors—symbolized by two players, Jesús

Castaños-Chima as de la Mancha and Arturo Díaz de Sandy as a sometimes reluctant Panza—play out their recreated versions of the Cervantes classic. Both are brilliant, encapsulating their imaginative voyages by moving chairs and table, which roll across the floors of the small 24th Street Theatre in South Central Los Angeles in conjunction with leaps of creativity and dismal pauses as they briefly lose all hope.

The production, presented in Spanish with English-language subtitles, is difficult to follow for the non-Spanish-speaking visitor. I longed for an English-language version of this complex text which I could crib to help comprehend the dense poetic complexity of the original. Yet anyone with an iota of theatrical experience might be able to imagine the wonder of actors, forced to remain basically frozen across from one another, creating a literary forum in which they explore some of the most poetic and profound of dialogues that deal with their foes, real and imaginary, as they hallucinate a reality outside of their internment. The fact that even these flights of imagination are constantly interrupted by guards who invisibly return again and again to

check on the prisoners' behavior only accentuates the prisoners' intellectual courage.

Throughout this intense drama, in which action is permitted only through the rolling furniture, the characters often grow despondent; like Beckett figures, unable to go on. Yet time and again, they do go on: they talk, dream, imagine, speak, shout, scream, cry out, and go dumb in an attempt to bring meaning into their empty and often absurd lives, in what one critic of this play correctly describes as "an oblique strategy for survival."

LOS ANGELES, JANUARY 11, 2011
Reprinted from *US Theater, Opera, and Performance* (January 2011).

THE KOREAN WAY

At the Edge of the Continent

KO UN, A READING FROM HIS POETRY, UNIVERSITY
OF CALIFORNIA, LOS ANGELES, APRIL 22, 2010
A COCKTAIL PARTY AND READING BY KO UN AND
DOUGLAS MESSERLI AT THE HOME OF HYON CHOUGH
IN LOS ANGELES, APRIL 22, 2010
KO UN, A READING FROM HIS POETRY, KOREAN
CULTURAL CENTER, LOS ANGELES, APRIL 23, 2010

IN APRIL OF 2010 I had the opportunity to host the noted Korean poet Ko Un and his wife Lee Shang-wha. After a reading at Smith College in Northampton, Massachusetts, the couple flew to Los Angeles, where I picked them up on April 21st at the Los Angeles International Airport, driving them to the JJ Grand Hotel in the vast area of the city we call Koreatown. In part because Ko does not speak English, and the hotel contains a fine Korean restaurant, I thought it would be more comfortable for them to stay in that part of the city, which is also not terribly far from our house.

Clearly they were tired by the time we reached the hotel, so we didn't speak much that evening, and I quickly checked them in and departed. The next morning, however, would begin early and include great deal of speaking and socializing.

At 9:00 I met them at the hotel, where I had arranged a press reception in the hotel restaurant. Two different reporters from Korean newspapers were in attendance, and soon were interviewing Ko Un, snapping his photograph and sharing experiences. A woman from the Korean Consulate also arrived and spoke to Ko Un and Lee Shang-wha. My role consisted primarily of greeting the journalists and introducing them to the poet. Typical of their disinterest in international activities in their city, the *Los Angeles Times* sent no one, even though the event had beforehand been mentioned in the Korean papers. My cleaners told me they had read that Ko Un was in town for a reading when I mentioned his name the week before.

Meanwhile Lee Shang-wha, always the manager of Ko's activities, selected the poems he would be reading later in the day, and handed me copies of them in Eng-

lish, I having previously told her that I would be reading the poems in translation.

Soon my companion Howard joined me and, together, we drove them to the University of California, Los Angeles, where I had arranged a reading in the Korean Department. The faculty, in turn, had planned a pleasant lunch at the Faculty Club. The professors and staff, perhaps all a little in awe of Ko Un, were somewhat uncomfortably quiet, but Howard and I peppered Ko with questions, and finally the faculty began to speak up.

After a short tour of the Korean Department offices, they took us to a large classroom in Royce Hall where the reading was to be held. Seated at a table we faced a filled room, including my wonderful intern / now typesetter, Pablo Capra, who I'd hired for a couple of days to sell books and take photographs.

Ko is a wonderful reader, a true spellbinder, and I tried to keep up with his obvious sense of drama and humor. We had both been given glasses of wine, so when reading one poem about a drunk he began with a sip, so too did I, reading it in English a few minutes after. The room burst into spontaneous laughter, and Ko beamed with approval.

The reading ended with a few questions and a gift from one woman of a Korean-style painting. We sold a substantial amount of books.

We then drove on Mulholland Drive to the beautiful home of businesswoman Hyon Chough, whose stunning glass house overlooks both sides of the city, south to the Stone Canyon Reservoir and, in the distance, the ocean, and north to the San Fernando Valley. Before entering the house we walked the grounds, Ko standing at the very summit to look south, so close to the edge that I, who suffer some vertigo, grew frightened. "Come back, further back," I begged him, but he remained at the very edge of the cliff, almost as if he were some pioneer standing at the edge of the continent looking off into the distance. I was terrified: what if he fell? Would I be the indirect cause of his death?

Fortunately, he eventually turned back, joining us in the gloriously lit house.

Hyon and I had invited a large contingent of the art community, Korean friends, and several poets (including Dennis Phillips and Martin Nakell), who all dined splendidly on the dozens of different dishes of Japanese and California cuisine. We also did a reading in the vast living room, but my voice was beginning to give out, as I began to develop what would become laryngitis, so we cut it short.

As we left the place I asked Ko and Lee what they had thought of the house. He, a Buddhist monk, quietly said, "I prefer my simple house." We all laughed.

Having kept them very busy the day before, on Friday I allowed them the entire morning alone, during which time Ko Un, so Lee later reported, had taken a long walk, seeing much of the Korean part of the city, an area that used to be somewhat devastated, but is now almost entirely rebuilt and quite stylish, with new highrises, apartments, and stores.

About 4:00 we picked up the pair again, and this time took them to an excellent Japanese restaurant at the edge of Beverly Hills. The head of the Japanese Department at the Los Angeles County Museum, Rob Singer, had given me a card of the restaurant's owner and handwritten, in Japanese, a message to him. Accordingly, we were served a number of special dishes, in course after course.

We then drove to the Korean Cultural Center near our home where the fairly large theater was packed, new chairs having been placed in front of the permanent seating. The crowd was almost entirely Korean, save a few friends of ours, again Dennis, Martin, and also Rebecca Goodman, Deborah Meadows and Thérèse Bachand. By this time I had nearly lost my voice, and it crackled when I spoke. Yet I valiantly carried on, explaining my problem to the audience, but still getting across the spirit of the poems as much as I could in English. Pablo sold hundreds of copies of both of our Ko Un titles. Others drove Ko and his wife home, and we returned tired but pleased.

The next morning we picked up Ko Un and Lee Shang-wha and took them to the airport, sad to see them go. Throughout it all, Ko (then 78) appeared full of energy and not in the least bit tired. By Saturday I had completely lost my voice and was coming down with a terrible cold. But what fun it had been.

LOS ANGELES, MARCH 12, 2010
Reprinted from *Green Integer Blog* (March 2011).

Incheon City

AFTER THE LONG 13-hour air trip from Los Angeles to Korea, over oceans I watched every time that the clouds briefly opened up a view, I arrived at the Incheon Airport.

I had been told that I would be met by my translator, who would whisk me off to my Seoul hotel.

Although it took me a while to move through passport control and to receive my small bag, I rolled out of the entry doors with a feeling of being on time, ready to greet the person holding a sign bearing my name. No such sign appeared. No signs appeared save discreet hotel announcements: "Meet your Hilton Hotel representative at gate 15, meet your Marriott Hotel guide at gate 21."

I stood still in bewilderment, then turned back to look at the billboard over my head regarding the flight announcements. So many were listed that I couldn't quickly find my flight number. But I knew I had exited from the door closest to our baggage carousel. What

could I do? I had been given, despite several queries, no name of a hotel, no name of a contact. It had been repeated and repeated in emails that *someone* would be there to meet me.

But after a half-hour, I had to admit to myself that there was no one. Perhaps he/she was late; was I early? No, I was on time. She/he was late. I walked back and forth across the waiting area, attempting to strongly convey to those waiting for others that I was seeking someone. No one responded in the least. I was not for whom they were waiting.

I even dared to walk out of the waiting area for a few moments, perceiving that there were several such entry gates; but I quickly determined that they were inappropriate spots, containing mostly domestic flights, and returned to my original location. No one even looked in my direction.

So here I am, I thought to myself, at Incheon International Airport without a clue what to do, even if I were to reach Seoul.

I was tired; I had not slept during the flight, and it was now 2:00 a.m. in California time, hours after I usually retired to bed. Well, I sighed to myself, I am a seasoned traveler. I'll take a taxi into Seoul to a major hotel; certainly I can find a single room!

Still—in all meanings of that word—I remained, feeling somehow guilty, that I was at fault. My translator had simply missed me; she/he had gone to the wrong gate or failed to recognize my face, had been delayed in heavy traffic. Fortunately, I'd never witnessed the Seoul traffic jams, or I would have perhaps never strayed.

I walked away. I came back. Walked on. Clearly, no one was going to come for me.

Out of nowhere appeared a kindly Korean man. "You are obviously lost," he began in English.

"Yes," I quickly responded, "I was to be met by a man or woman to take me to a hotel in Seoul."

"Do you have the number of the hotel or the number of the person who was to have met you?" he inquired.

"No, that's just the problem. I have *no* telephone numbers whatsoever except for those who planned the event I'm to attend."

"You know," he slowly offered up the facts, "there

are four or five major gates. Are you sure this is the one at which you were expected?"

"Yes, it has to be this gate," I insisted, looking again at the overhead listings of flights. My flight was no longer on the board.

"Do you have anyone's telephone number?" he continued, as if speaking to a very small child, which I felt I had become.

"Well, I do," I admitted, "but these are only university numbers and, surely, on a Saturday evening, they would not be there!"

"Let us try," he attempted to reassure me, taking out his cell phone and dialing up the numbers I displayed. He rang each number three times without result.

"Thank you so very much for your kindness," I finally cut off his good Samaritan attempts. "No one can be in their offices tonight. I'll just get a taxi into Seoul."

But where in Seoul? I pondered to myself.

At the information desk I described my situation and had my own name paged, hoping that if someone were waiting for me they would come to the desk. No one arrived at the desk, and I was not even sure that I heard the announcement.

"Across the way," she blithely pointed, "is a woman who can help you get a hotel." I looked across the way, but no one was there. "She will be back soon."

When her colleague finally returned, I encountered a friendly, good-looking woman, seemingly happy to serve me.

I told her my story, hoping she might help me find a hotel in Seoul.

I suddenly remembered my father's absurd way of obtaining hotels during our family travels across Europe in 1965. At each airport in which we arrived—Copenhagen, Paris, Zürich—my father simply approached just such a woman as she who stood before me, and fearlessly obtained quite pleasant accommodations.

In Copenhagen, for example, we stayed at one of the major hotels (I cannot identify the hotel in today's listings on the internet). I believe it had to be, however, a four-star hotel, since the series of events that occurred there would not have taken place at a hotel of lesser quality.

My brother David and I shared one room, while my father and mother slept in another. My brother quickly drifted off to sleep, but all night long I was kept awake by rumbling and roaring noises, as if a crowd of angry protesters were stationed just a few blocks away.

My parents, so they reported the next morning, had also been kept awake. Dave had heard nothing.

While we spoke at the breakfast table near the lobby, loud screams of young women suddenly silenced our conversation. Across the lobby, in full view of our table, marched a group of musicians, led by two men I immediately recognized as Mick Jagger and Keith Richards. It was June 26, 1965, the day on which The Rolling Stones began their famed first Scandinavian tour.

I had heard their new record, "Satisfaction," just a month before in my Norway dorm room on the English off-shore Radio Caroline. No one else in my family knew who they were or why people might be screaming at them.

"Rockers!" the head waiter contemptuously declared.

In Paris, my father found us, again at the information desk, a wonderful hotel just across from the offices of *Paris Match*, with high-ceilinged rooms and a small elevator that reminds me of the one in the movie *Charade*. I loved the hotel, although my mother complained vociferously, as she did about any hotel or motel in which we stayed. It was in that hotel room, when I argued for staying in Norway, that my father broke into tears as he entreated me to return home, the purpose, I suddenly perceived, of our little Grand Tour. I had just turned 17, an age when a father's tears still had an enormous impact, and, accordingly, I acquiesced, despite my desire to stay on for the rest of the summer.

In Zürich, once again through the airport information booth, my father procured a lovely *pension*, in which my brother and I were perfectly happy, despite my mother's distress on account of heat and noise.

Now, here in Incheon, 45 years later, I knew things had changed. Before this trip I had always planned everything out, arranging for rooms long in advance. I would never have trusted to luck. Yet, in memory of those halcyon days, I felt that certainly I could find a single room available in a city with a population of over 12 million inhabitants.

"Do you have a reservation?" she innocently asked.

"No. As I told you, I don't know the name of the hotel in which I was to have stayed tonight."

She smiled sympathetically at my predicament, while reporting, nonetheless, with a complete sense of authority, that there was not a single hotel room to be found in the entire city of Seoul!

I was dumbfounded. "How could that be in a city with hundreds of hotels? There clearly has to be something available."

"It *is*," she paused, "Saturday, the beginning of the weekend!" as if that explained everything—or anything.

I laughed. "You're not telling me, surely, that not a single room can't be found in the city. There must be some place to sleep."

"Nothing," she politely and emphatically declared.

"Perhaps, if I catch a taxi to the Hilton, they might have a room for me."

"Not without reservations," she proclaimed. "There

might be something near the airport."

"But I don't want to stay out here," I declared. "My business is in the city." Little did I know that Seoul was situated more than an hour away.

"I'll call the Airport Hilton."

After only a few words, she hung up. "Nothing available there."

"I have to have some place to sleep tonight."

"You don't remember the name of the hotel in which they booked you?" she scolded.

"I enquired, but they never told me. Someone was to meet me here and take me there."

A slightly disgusted look crossed her face, the kind of expression one might save for an itinerant gypsy. I was perspiring out of simple fear and frustration.

"There may be one room left in a nearby tourist hotel, the Eulwang Hotel, not far from here. Here's a brochure." She suddenly waved it before me as if she had produced it out of thin air. "I'll check."

The brochure displayed a white-painted, concrete structure in the Korean palace style. The rooms looked somewhat pleasant, in a rustic manner with polished

redwood.

She came back to me with an open smile. "They have one room left."

Although I inwardly rolled my eyes in disbelief, I outwardly responded enthusiastically. "Then let us book it," I caved in, like a rube just off the bus. Clearly she was taking in a healthy under-the-table income as that hotel's agent. But what choice did I have? "And what's the price?"

"It's reasonable. Only 85,000 Won."

I gasped, trying to convert that into dollars. "That seems like a lot."

"About $75," she responded.

Now I *was* afraid: at that price it might be a dump.

"A driver will be here to pick you up in 10 minutes. Gate 33," she summarily dismissed me, handing me a slip of paper announcing my reservation. I looked up to discover that I was at Gate 3.

Somewhat relieved, if nothing else, I walked to that far gate and went out onto the sidewalk. There were several large buses arriving at regular intervals, dozens of them, each sweeping away huge crowds. I waited for a long while, but no hotel shuttle bus arrived.

One large bus, so its sign announced, was headed to Dankook University, the host of the conference I was attending. For a second I fancied riding out to the University, except that I knew no one would be there to greet me, and perhaps the events might not be happening there. I waited for a longer while. No hotel bus showed up.

In the very next lane I could see a lineup of taxis. Perhaps I was waiting in the wrong lane? My luggage cart and I rolled out into the next circle of hell, where I attempted to ask a taxi driver if the bus to the hotel might be arriving at this location—presenting him with my small slip of passage.

After much scrutiny of my paper, he brought out a pair of reading glasses and studied it anew. He pointed back to where I had come from. And I retreated, waiting for a longer period.

I was tired. I had had no sleep now for over 17 hours. I was anxious to reach the hotel, email my hosts, and crawl into bed. No bus arrived.

With grim determination, I returned to Gate 3 in order to complain. My friendly guide was waiting upon other suckers, and I had no patience left. I grabbed the brochure which she had previously offered, and marched out to the waiting taxi line: "Can you take me here?" I asked.

He too brought out his glasses to study the brochure. Fortunately, the flier contained a small map of the area. And after a brief survey of the thing, he walked me forward to his cab. Finally, I was on the move, I thought to myself.

"All right," I attempted to calm myself. "When I get to the hotel, I'll take a shower. I'll email Hae Yisoo, the General Secretary of the International Creative Writing Center." He had been my line of communication throughout the months before my arrival. "Perhaps they will meet me tomorrow morning at the airport. Or I'll take a taxi into Seoul, after they tell me where to go. I've traveled a great deal. This is no big thing. It's important to get a good night's sleep."

Looking out the window of the taxi, I noted that we had just passed the Airport Hilton. Many rooms looked empty, but I knew there was no turning back.

We drove down a road on which nothing else seemed to exist, but I realized that much of this land, so close to the ocean, must be marshland that I couldn't make out in the dark.

We took another turn and drove down an equally empty road, and then another, and another. Where was this driver taking me? At another turn there were a few of what appeared to be roadside stands selling fireworks, all lit up by colored firefly lights. A few larger buildings were also lit up by strings of outdoor light bulbs, some with red-neon depictions of women in supine positions, which I presumed represented the existence of sex-bars or -hotels.

"Where are we going?" I quietly asked.

"This is where," the taxi cab driver mumbled in

Beckettese.

"Where what?" I wondered to myself.

Long stretches of empty highways followed, replaced with a few more brightly-lit roadside stands and
bars or hotels with sometimes unidentifiable symbols.

"This seems to be awfully far from the airport," I
spoke up. "The agent who arranged for my room told
me that it was 'airport adjacent.'" I mumbled to myself.

"This is the way. Very popular," spoke the sibyl in
the front seat.

We drove on and on into the night.

"Where are you taking me?" I repeated with some
alarm.

"This is where," he repeated.

I wanted to laugh, but couldn't quite get up the
energy.

There was another stretch of sexual institutions,
another series of what appeared to be fruit stands surrounded by what looked like Christmas lights.

It reminded me, a bit, of the Thai countryside and
small villages depicted in Apichatpong's films, which
I'd recently been viewing.

Finally, a few higher structures appeared, and
the driver took a turn into a narrow side-street, what
seemed to be a dirt alley. He drove halfway up the alley, before backing down and turning at a fork into
an equally dark lane. A few yards off lay what looked

somewhat like the Eulwang Hotel of my brochure.

"Here, arrival!" proudly announced the driver.

I looked around in some small distress, but felt happy to have arrived at any destination.

"Thank you. I'm sorry I doubted you," I apologized, paying him something like 20,000 Won, which seemed like a ransom instead of a fee.

He helped me carry my bags to the lobby, filled, it appeared, with about 100 people lined up at the front desk. But I soldiered on, suddenly perceiving that these tourists had already checked in and were awaiting their room assignments from the tour guide. Accordingly, I walked straight to the desk.

The young clerk quickly checked me in and, after a shower (in mid-bathroom with a hose), I returned to the lobby to use my computer, since there was no access in the rooms.

I sent messages to both Hae Yisoo (who uses the nickname Heysoo) and Ko Un's translator, Brother Anthony—fortunately, because the next day I discovered that Heysoo, exhausted by all the festival preparations, had not checked his email; at 11:00 p.m., Brother Anthony called him, and at midnight, Heysoo called the hotel with a message for me: he would be there to pick me up the next morning.

Despite the shouting voices one could discern in the nearby streets, along with the occasional explosion

of fireworks, I was fast asleep by the time Heysoo called, and slept comfortably all night.

The morning light sent me downstairs for a 5:00 a.m. breakfast, which an even younger clerk described as an "American brunch," consisting of fried eggs, bacon, and French fries. I laughed at the combination as I bit into a slice of toast, as did the Korean-American couple from Atlanta seated at the next table. There is something surreal about beginning one's day with fries.

As I began to explore the underdone yolk of my egg, the clerk announced that I had received a telephone message, reporting that someone would be here to drive me into Seoul at 10:00 a.m.

I finished as much of my "American brunch" as I dared to consume, and determined to take a short walk. Who made up these noisy night crowds? I wondered. And what were they doing in this outpost?

A block away was a huge arch, a marquee, apparently, to mark off one's entrance into what at evening must be an array of small shops selling trinkets, food, and other unidentifiable objects. There were also small motels, which, when I looked into their long halls, appeared to be made up of rooms the size of the windowed booths of the red-light district in Amsterdam. This center, clearly a city of quick and sud-den thrills nestled against a nearby beach, was what one might describe as a kind of boardwalk, just as rundown and ragtag as the so-called boardwalk of Venice in Los Angeles.

No one was here this early in the morning, although it was already partially lit, as if primping itself for its nightly show. I walked to the end of the street and stared across a small park abutting it. There, spread out in front, was the subject of the conference—the sea, in all its splendor! This was the Yellow Sea, beyond which lay China.

I returned to my "tourist hotel" to observe several buses, which the tourists from the night before had gathered around, as if waiting for someone to tell them to climb aboard. It was a desolate spot where Heysoo would find me a few hours later. I was equally embarrassed that he had felt the necessity to "save face" by coming out to rescue me himself. He might have easily sent the translator or just the driver, I counseled.

"Please don't worry about me. I was fine. I slept

well. The sea, even though I didn't know it was close by, must have comforted me, as it always does, by its rhythms."

When we had finished apologizing and thanking one another, I concluded, "There's no problem; here I am!"

"Here you are," he laughed.

We quickly became friends. The fact that, despite his unbelievably hectic schedule for the day ahead, he had come so far to retrieve me would envelope him forever in my heart. And I was secretly delighted in having witnessed another view of the Korean landscape.

SEOUL, OCTOBER 8, 2010
Reprinted from *Green Integer Blog* (October 2010).

Although I had never heard of Incheon City before I stayed there, it now is very much in the news, particularly after the late November 2010 North Korean attack on the island city of Yeonpyeong. The missiles the North Koreans lobbed at the city destroyed many of the buildings and did damage to almost every building on the island. A large majority of the island's citizens packed the daily ferry boat to Incheon City, where they were put up in temporary buildings.

As part of my visit to Korea, we were asked to select two literary works we had written and to present a paper on the conference's central topic, "The Poetic Spirit of the Sea." Since I had just published an English translation of the great 19th-century French naturalist and writer Jules Michelet, talking about some of the very concerns suggested by the overriding topic, I determined to deliver a paper on that book, The Sea. Because other papers had gone over the time constraints, I was asked to delimit my comments, and I only summarized the paper, although it had been published in full in the conference catalogue.

The Ocean's Voice

JULES MICHELET **THE SEA**, TRANSLATED FROM THE FRENCH BY KATIA SAINSON (LOS ANGELES: GREEN INTEGER, 2012)

UPON REFLECTION, it seems a little odd that I, born in the landlocked state of Iowa in the US—a state which has but a few small lakes—should be standing here in Korea speaking of "The Poetic Spirit of the Sea." For a while as a child, I lived with my parents on one of those tiny lakes, Clear Lake (which today, I am told, is overgrown with algae, being anything but "clear"); and one day my mother gasped and rushed from the house to save me as I was being led to the end of the pier by a slightly older child. I am sure I would not have jumped in, for I was afraid of water throughout most of my childhood, and only learned to swim in college.

Nevertheless, I have spent most of my life since age 16 near the seas, living my senior year of high school in a small Norwegian town on the Oslo fjord, and shifting a few years later to New York, Washington, D.C. and Philadelphia, before settling—now for some 25 years—in Los Angeles, which is the largest seaport, incidentally, in the US.

Perhaps it was in restitution for my long dry childhood that I drifted to the Atlantic and Pacific shores. And so too I discovered during my adult years how very much I enjoy traveling by any water-going vessel, being attracted to everything from large ships to sizeable ferries (by which I traveled a few years ago from Oslo to Copenhagen and commuted several times from Naples to Ischia and back) and even small row boats, by which I traveled from Praiano to Positano on the Amalfi Coast one dark midnight, and recently floated, for an afternoon along the canals of Ghent. I have never been seasick during the obvious sufferings of some of those around me.

Despite all of this love of water, however, I must

admit that I am not the beach-going type. My doctor has long ago warned me of sitting in the sun for more than five minutes, and I have never enjoyed the grate of sand and rock upon the surface of my body. The light, moreover, is usually far too intense, so that even my favorite activity, reading, becomes difficult. If I were to live directly on the ocean I suspect I would prefer the coast of Brittany in France or Maine in the USA on a winter day, when large storms toss about the ocean's tumultuous waves. I would love to be inside a well-protected sea-side cottage on those days!

This is, of course, a Romantic conception of the sea. Today we need only to look to the oil-slicked tides in the once pristine Gulf of Mexico or remind ourselves of Hurricane Katrina's 2005 devastation of New Orleans to perceive that the sea is quickly being transformed by man into something that is dangerous to live near or even traverse. In a few decades from now the lovely and fascinating cities and beaches of Venice, Santa Monica, and Malibu near my home may no longer exist, having been flooded over by the rising oceans.

I've not come here, however, to lecture on the obvious: the fears we all share for those waters that sustain and connect our shores. Instead of abandoning that "Romantic" concept of the sea, I thought I might return to it in the guise of the great French naturalist and historian of the 19th century, Jules Michelet, who

wrote on everything from women, birds, and insects, to religion, education, and the history of the French Revolution. One of his most important books, moreover, was titled *The Sea* (1861)—a book which, coincidentally, my publishing house, Green Integer, has just published—which I thought might be appropriate to share with you in this conference dedicated to that very subject. Michelet treats the great oceans less like a scientist than a devoted lover; perhaps the latter is what we most need today, a wise admirer who will help us all realize the beauty and importance of the matter that covers most of the earth and, as the ice caps melt, may roll over even more of our planet's surface.

Michelet begins his book, surprisingly, by relating stories from the shore, beaches, and cliffs of the powerful forces and fearful behavior of the ocean waters. Like me at the edge of that childhood pier, he seems, at first, so terrified of even looking at the great roll of waves, that it appears he will never jump in.

Throughout his highly poetic recounting Michelet gives the sea voices, but the first of these voices presents "her" (and for Michelet the sea is not just linguistically but psychologically a feminine force) as having a most "formidable" character:

> ...we feel or we believe that we feel the vibrant intonations of life. In fact, at high tide when one wave—immense and electric—rises above another, the sound of shells and of thousands of diverse creatures brought in with the tide mixes with the stormy rumble of the waters....
>
> And the sea has still other voices! When she is emotional, the sea's moans and deep sighs contrast with the silence of the mournful shore. In fact, the shore seems to be quietly meditating, in order to better hear the threats coming from the one who just yesterday was flattering it with a caressing wave. What will the sea be telling to the shore next? I don't want to predict. I do not want to speak here of the frightful concerts that the sea may give, of her duets with the rocks, of the basses and the muffled thunder that she produces deep inside the caves, nor the astonishing cries in which one thinks one hears: "Rescue me!"

Even witnessing the sea from atop a cliff or other promontory can be a dangerous act:

> At the highest point of the Mont-Saint-Michel, one can see a platform called the Madman's Terrace. I know of no place more apt to drive some-

one crazy than this vertiginous structure. Imagine being surrounded by a vast secluded plain of what looks like white ash—dubious sand whose misleading smoothness is its most dangerous trap. It is land and yet it's not. It is the sea and yet again, not. It's not fresh water either although beneath the sands rivers constantly burrow through the ground. Rarely, and only for a few short amounts of time, a boat will venture forth. And, if passing by when the water is receding, you are likely to be swallowed up. I speak from experience. I myself was almost engulfed.

By the time he gets to the great storms, quoting seafaring explorers such as James Cook, François Péron, and Jules Dumont d'Urville, we are nearly overwhelmed by the power of this dreadful force:

> ...At the shore of the Aiguilles Banks also known as the d'Urville Banks, the waves reached heights of eighty to one hundred feet. I had never seen such a monstrous sea.... At times the sailors on deck were submerged. There was awful chaos that lasted no less than four hours that evening...a century that was enough to turn your hair white!...—This is what southern storms are like, so horrible that even on land the natives that can sense their arrival are horrified by them in advance and hide in their caves.

One particular storm of 1859 on the western coast of France was witnessed by Michelet himself, and his recounting of that event, with its "shifting and bizarre winds," is perhaps one of the best written descriptions of the fierceness of ocean storms.

It is no wonder that, in a later chapter, the author writes what seems almost like an ode to lighthouses, beacons that call out to the frightened sailor: "Persist! One more try!...if the wind and the sea are against you, you are not alone. Mankind is there watching out for you." The naturalist is understandably proud of France's "ring of these powerful flares," each armed with the Fresnel lens (invented by the French physicist Augustin-Jean Fresnel, and first used at the Cordouan lighthouse in 1823).

If the drama of the sea is what the reader seeks, Michelet does not disappoint either in his sections on storms nor in his recountings of various sea-creatures, particularly the giant octopus (which, he admits, no longer exists), and his tales of whales and sharks. Jules Verne used the giant octopus as a major figure in his *Twenty Thousand Leagues Under the Sea* and Lautré-amont parodied the author in his *Les Chants de Maldoror*. In short, Michelet is determined to engage his readers with numerous exciting adventures regarding his subject.

However, the author warns us early on, despite all this seeming fury, the sea itself "is quite innocent."

> Moreover, one cannot be fooled by the tremendous illusions she creates, by the immensity of her wonders or by what on the surface appear to be moments of fury that are often in fact acts of kindness.

And it is already here, in the second chapter of the book, that Michelet takes up one of his major themes, which elevates this text to stand as a significant work even today. After describing the terrible landscape around Mont-Saint-Michel, the naturalist ponders:

> Is it the sea's fault if this beach is so treacherous? Not at all. The sea arrives there, as she does elsewhere, noisy and strong but loyal. The true fault lies with the land whose cunning immobility always seems so innocent, and who, below the beach, is filtering stream water—a sugary and whitish mixture that undermines solidity. *It is especially man's fault, because of his ignorance and neglect* [italics mine]. During the long barbarian ages, while he thought only of legends and establishing this great place of pilgrimage dedicated to the archangel, who had vanquished the devil, the devil took possession of that neglected plain.... Far from doing harm, this madwoman carries in her menacing waves a trea-

sure of fertile salt. Superior to the Nile's silt, it enriches the area's cultivated fields and is the source of the charming beauty of Dol's former marshlands, which today have been transformed into gardens.

This culpability of man is at the heart of Michelet's plea for the survival of things relating to the oceans. First, he establishes the oceans as the source of life itself by noting the great fecundity of the sea, which he describes as "the sea of milk," a kind of gelatinized water. A single drop of water, he insists, carries thousands of infusoria, "moving about and vibrating," coming together to create links of maidenhair. "This is not fable," he argues, "it is natural history. This hair with its dual nature—plant and animal—is life's eldest child."

Importantly, Michelet goes on to establish the international patterns of the sea's movements, and the shifts in the oceans' currents, from hot to cold, around the globe. It is, accordingly, only by seeing the sea globally that we can truly comprehend its importance. Describing different sea-life throughout the planet, Michelet gracefully incorporates his admiration of his favorite explorer, Vasco da Gama (he dismisses Columbus' journey as a mere repetition of what the Normans and Icelanders had done long before). And in doing so he gradually makes us fascinated with the abundance in our oceans.

By the time Michelet comes round to talking about whales, he quite clearly anthropomorphizes his subject:

> Because such a life form is inherently shaped like a ship, the mother's waist is narrow and this means that she cannot have the profuse waist of a woman—that adorable miracle of life on land, that stable and harmonic life, where everything disappears into tenderness. No matter how tender the whale—that great woman of the sea—is, she still must make everything dependent on her battle against the waves. Moreover, her organism is the same under this strange mask—the shape, the same sensitivity. Fish on the surface, woman beneath it. [This analogy continues for a few more paragraphs]

By doing this, however, Michelet has created a true link between the nursing whale and his readers that can only shock when, a few pages later, he decries what have become of these wonderful leviathans:

> The strongest of the strong, the ingenious one, the active one, the cruel king the world has finally arrived. My book is flooded with light. But what will it show? And how many sad things do I now have to bring into this light?
>
> This creator, this tyrannical God was able to produce a second nature within nature. But what

did he do to the other one, the original one, his wet-nurse and his mother? With the teeth that she gave him, he bit her breast....

The freest of beings, who formerly brought joy to the sea, those good-hearted seals, the gentle whales, the peace-loving pride and joy of the Ocean, all have fled to the polar seas and to the awful world of the ice floe. But they cannot bear such a difficult life, and soon, they will completely disappear.

Soon after, the author introduces a chapter on "The Harpoon," and moves forward to the discovery of the three oceans. And it is now, in the newly discovered world, that he truly cries out against the barbaric acts of mankind. After describing the conquerors' treatment of the native populations, Michelet continues:

It is obvious that if Man has treated Man in this way, he was no more merciful, no kinder to the animals. He carried out a horrific slaughter of the gentlest species. He made them savage and barbaric forever more...

In the New South Shetland Islands, Dumont d'Urville says, the English and the Americans exterminated all the seals in four years. In a blind rage, they would slit the throats of the newborns, and would kill the pregnant females. Often they killed for the skins alone and wasted enormous amounts of oil that could have been used.

"The water gushes forth with the red droplets..." the naturalist ends his description of the "drunken butchery" of tuna by men and women alike on a European shore.

As a solution to some of this mad abuse, Michelet proposes, along with other writers, a new bill, a "Declaration of the Rights of the Sea" to change regulations on the periods of coastal fishing, to create more humane ways of killing, and to ban fishing entirely during the season when each species reproduces. "As for the precious species that are on the verge of disappearing, especially the whale, the world's largest and creation's richest life form, we need absolute peace for a half-century," concluded Michelet in 1861.

Not only does Michelet argue for these prescient measures of conservation, what he describes as a *Truce of God*, he more importantly recognizes in the ocean's many voices a kind of international (perhaps even universal) community that will bring world harmony. I quote this powerful passage at length:

There is one extremely big difference between these two elements—land is silent and the Ocean speaks. The Ocean is a voice that speaks to distant stars and responds to their movement in its deep and solemn language. It speaks to the land and the shore, conversing with their echoes in poignant tones. In turn plaintive and threatening it rumbles or sighs. Above all, it speaks to man. Since the Ocean is the fertile crucible in which creating began and within whose strength it continues, it possesses creation's animated eloquence. This is life speaking to life. The beings, which are born from the Ocean in the millions and billions, are its words. It speaks, even before the white and foaming sea of milk—from which they emerge—with its fertile marine jelly, is organized. All this, combined together is the great voice of the Ocean.

What does it say? It speaks of life, the eternal metamorphosis. It speaks of a fluctuating existence. It puts the petrified ambitions of terrestrial life to shame.

What does it say? Immortality. An indomitable force of life can be found in the lowest rungs of nature. And yet, theirs are so much more superior!

What does it say? Solidarity. Let's accept the rapid exchange, which occurs between the different parts of an individual. Let's accept the superior law that unites the living members of a single entity: humanity. And beyond that, let's accept the supreme law that means that we cooperate and create, with the great South, that we are associated (to the best of our ability) with this world's loving

Harmony and that we show solidarity with the life
God has created.

Romantic? Yes. A few of Michelet's topics may
even appear, in retrospect, a bit silly (his discussion of
the restorative powers of the ocean are outdated and
somewhat quaint, to say the least). But when it comes
to describing that vast and troubled lake that surrounds
all our continents, I can best hear his voice—the voice
he has given to our oceans.

LOS ANGELES, JULY 10, 2010
This essay was first read to a Korean audience on the occasion of the
2010 World Writers' Festival, "The Poetic Spirit of the Sea," hosted
by Dankook University in Seoul, Jukjeon, and Cheonan, Korea on
October 5, 2010. It was published in both Korean and English in
the programme for that event, *From the Sea of Discovery to the Sea of
Communication* (Seoul/Jukjeon: Dankook University, 2010).

The comments in the pages below are based on just a week's stay on my visit to Seoul, Korea in 2010. Accordingly, my observations are meant neither as representations of nor criticisms of Korean culture, but rather are written out of humorous observations of quickly perceived differences as I encountered this complex society in a near virginal euphoria. A Korean might as easily have noted similar differences—perceived oddities in a newly encountered culture—upon first visiting the USA. At no point do I intend my comments as applying to the society at large, which I highly admire and have just begun to explore. These jottings represent just what they suggest by their collective title: things briefly noted and observed—and, I should add, for the most part joyfully experienced.

Noticed and Overheard in South Korea

FOR FINGERS ONLY

IT APPEARS TO ME that Koreans are stingy with towels, cloth, or paper. Western-sized towels are likely available in the larger hotels (they were available at the

Hotel Seoul KyoYuk MunHwa Hoekwan, where we writers invited to the 2010 World Writers' Festival stayed). But in  smaller hotels, certainly in the tourist hotel where I stayed the first evening, the towels provided were the size of very small American hand-towels, insufficient to properly dry Western-sized bodies. The more rustic Seoul Art Space, where I stayed the final few nights, expected their guests to bring their own towels, and we had each to insist that we be provided with one; somehow I received two very small towels, but gave one up to my neighbor, Antonio Colinas, who had not so insisted. To be fair, the Art Space may tell its regular guests beforehand what to expect; we were sudden and unexpected visitors.

This lack of towels, however, extended also to many public facilities. In a number of public bathrooms I found a sink and even soap, but nothing with which to dry one's hands. Even in Dankook University there were no towels to be found, which does tend make one a bit shy about washing one's hands in the first place, and certainly makes for an unsanitary experience. A few of these public bathrooms did offer hand-driers (which I abhor, but will use if necessary), but the majority offered nothing.

Table napkins are even smaller, more for the fingers than mouths or hands, and are as thin as facial tissues.

THE DECLARATION OF THE ROOF

It was fascinating to me that most of the high-rise apartments in Seoul, of which there are hundreds, are aligned perpendicularly to the streets and highways, their vast rectangles of concrete, each marked with a number, possibly in a sequence from left to right or vice-versa: 102, 103, 104, etc.

Whereas most Western apartment buildings, influenced obviously by Bauhaus architecture and modernism in general, are topped off by a flat surface as if to emphasize their sleekness, many such buildings in Seoul, when they are not built as spectacular architectural statements, bear mansard-like roofs or, even more often, are topped by a small model of a house (presumably containing the equipment that runs the elevator),

themselves crowned by a traditional roof in the manner of the American Red Roof Inn motels. Accordingly, it is as if each architect has placed

atop his or her construction a little cap or a tri-cornered hat, influenced, quite obviously, by the roofs of the great Korean palaces. Indeed, sometimes the arcs of the palace roof is itself imitated.

These decorative elements atop what are otherwise simple rectangular boxes have the effect of rendering the buildings, at least to Western eyes, as slightly *kitsch*, as if there has been some attempt to prettify a form that so shouts out its utilitarian function: a number of stacked floors containing variously sized cubicles in which humans are housed. This may be your home, but it is definitely not a palace—despite the declaration of the roof.

Although there are different "waves" or "phases" of Korean meals, there is no sense of different "courses" as there is in the West. Except for rice and the Korean version of udon, all dishes, consisting of small plates of various cabbages (kimchi), meats, fish, fried foods, salad, etc., are placed upon the tables in restaurants all at once and are shared by one's table-mates. Each of the low tables, requiring sitting upon the floor, have from four to six settings, around which these small platters are placed. There is no order in the selection; one simply takes up the small, pointed metal chopsticks and selects a bit of what one desires, placing it upon the diminutive plate or bowl before one. If a platter is out of reach, another diner will help with the serving. One never pours one's own drinks; one must pour for others and they, in turn, will pour for you. My 21-year-old translator and her friends reported, however, that that tradition—since it had been essentially the task of the

 woman, a role Korean Feminism now frowns upon—is beginning to disappear, yet at every lunch and dinner I shared with others the tradition

was maintained.

This communality of eating, accordingly, helps to involve everyone, and contributes to the sustenance of conver-  sation, while still allowing for individual tastes. As the different dishes begin to be eaten up and are quickly cleared away, the next "phase" is served, and often afterwards a third, sweeter "wave," at which time the waitresses also serve tea.

Although I had eaten several times in Los Angeles' Korean restaurants before my travels, I discovered several new Korean dishes, some of which I preferred to others, and by the end of my visit, I had begun to make determined choices in what I ate. With the abundance of different alternatives, however, I certainly never went hungry. The Koreans seem to be hearty eaters.

A SLIPPER FETISH

Koreans, like those of other Asian cultures, have what might be described as a shoe fetish, or more correctly, a "slipper fetish." It is one thing to take off one's shoes before entering a house—Howard and I do that in our own home, although we do not require it of others;

and at a recent party at the home of Michael Ovitz, the founder of Creative Artists Agency and former president of the Walt Disney Company, guests were asked to remove their shoes and put on slippers before entering. But it is quite another thing to require, as they did at the Art Space, that one differentiate between a slipper to wear in the rooms and hall, a slipper to wear in the outdoors, and a slipper to wear in the bath.

The latter is necessary since many homes and hotels do not have a shower stall in their "bathrooms," and one bathes, accordingly, by holding a shower hose over one's head in the middle of the room, the water eventually running to a floor drain, usually located under the sink. Depending upon how often one showers, the bathroom floor remains wet throughout the day and into the night, and returning to it is a bit like entering a wading pool. The floors of many Korean homes and hotels, consisting of highly polished wood, moreover, does not wed well with the tracks of wet feet. Plastic slippers, kept just inside the bathroom, facing the direction of one's feet, are the perfect solution!

Leaving a restaurant, particularly with a large group, involves the discovery and reckoning of one's footwear, usually stowed upon entering in large cabinets or stacked upon shelves. The deep bend of each guest to fit and tie up his shoes has a feel almost of a ritualistic act. Fortunately, I wear loafers.

I should add that the so-called "Ripper Slippers" found in Korean-American hair salons, patronized by neighborhood women, have become popular with both black gang members and gays in Los Angeles.

THE TENTH SAINT

In the Itaweon neighborhood of Seoul I lunched at a French bistro titled Le Saint-Ex, one of the first of the higher-class restaurants opened when the area was still a red-light district and off-limits to most Koreans not working in the sex industry. The restaurant is run by Benjamin Joinau, who has since become a noted figure in the Itaweon community.

Their Steak Poirve is truly excellent, and while en-

joying it, along with a good bottle of Merlot, and an hour-long nursing of a gin and tonic beforehand, I produced much of the writing in this piece.

I puzzled, however, over the name of the place. Did it mean to suggest just *any* saint, a saint without a name, the tenth saint—whoever that might be—or was it suggesting that we should just cross the saintly off our list?

My editor Pablo Capra argues that it refers to St. Francis Xavier, one of the first Catholic missionaries in Asia.

AT THE EDGE OF THE CLIFF

At the Cheonan Campus of Dankook University, I met In-Ho Cho, Vice President in charge of the Chenon Campus. He spoke English and had studied dentistry at UCLA in Los Angeles. As we moved from his offices to the theater for our readings and lectures, we were stopped by a photographer to have our picture taken.

There, to the left of where we stood, was a sign that Ko Un's translator Brother Anthony pointed out, warning that a cliff began just beyond the barrier which stood behind us. DANGER, it shouted out

in both Korean and Kor-English: HEED-FALL. We laughed, explaining to Mr. In-Ho that there was no such word in English, but that it was such

473

a wonderful creation it should perhaps be introduced into the language. Certainly there was no way to translate it properly!

THE IMPORTANCE OF LANGUAGE

At the 3 Alley Pub in the same small street where I had lunch, the bartender spoke endlessly with the American military personnel from  the nearby Yongsan Garrison who gather there. "Even when I lived clear out in the country," he proclaimed, "I made the long journey into Seoul and Itaweon to come here. It's important in Korea to have a place where the bartender speaks English!"

MISS PAK AND MR. FRITZ

I had come to the 3 Alley Pub precisely for what it offered, a chance to write while overhearing the local news and gossip. What I most like about any city is trying to comprehend how people live in it, what they do, etc. Since I did not understand Korean, however, I could not "overhear" things the way I do in some other cities. I needed a place where the bartender and customers spoke English.

Accordingly, my comprehension of Korean life is a bit far-fetched, since it is based mostly on hearsay from Americans living in the midst of the most international and sexually open section of Seoul. Yet no tour guide could have offered up a more delightful mix of conversations than the ones I assimilated at the 3 Alley Pub.

Somehow the discussions turned to the neighborhood characters. The bartender described how one night he was visited by the very famous Miss Pak. Miss Pak, evidently, is quite ancient, without teeth, and with cheeks that have gradually caved in over the years—yet she is a legend in Seoul. Her name is Dakju Pak, but she is known only as Miss Pak, a whore who haunts the streets of Itaweon. She has been at her job for nearly 60 or even 70 years, they all agree. Although greatly loved, just for the absurdity of her situation, she is also quite dangerous to some. Apparently, she has crushes on some soldier boys, even if they have had nothing to do with her, and shouts at them in the streets, sometimes at inopportune moments such as when they might be out walking with a military superior: "I love you best, Ralphie!" Miss Pak screams. Ralph blushes of course, but even if innocent, he is forever suspect.

They attempted to calculate—forgive me dear reader for the coarseness of these soldiers' imaginations—how much cock she must have had, given her age and averaging two medium-sized customers six days a week (they gave her a day off, even if she didn't take it), and summarized that it might reach—if you took it south—clear to Busan!

The denizens of this bar followed up with a brief mention of Mr. Fritz, another neighborhood figure, who goes about dressed only in his pajamas, pointing his umbrella at desired individuals as if to say, "Take this!"—with all sexual implications included, I presume.

MOTHER KOREA

Oh, that reassuring, yet commandeering voice of the Korean mother! In Seoul she exists everywhere: at streetlights she tells you when to cross and when to stop; in elevators she announces what floor you have reached, "Please exit now." Taxis could never reach their destinations without her navigational skills. She seems to be everywhere, that wise, bossy, scolding, slightly sexy, and utterly terrifying woman, informing everyone—particularly the Korean male—of when, what, and why he should act. Often she sneaks up on you. On the escalator down she commanded me in Korean to "step off immediately." Yet to my knowledge she said nothing on the way up!

Even as we sped to the Incheon airport, Mother Korea took the time to tell us, as we drove through the toll booth on the freeway, that "You need to buy a new ticket" or "Your ticket remains in good stead," I couldn't determine which. For her ever-vigilant helpfulness she makes very large demands.

TAXIS TO SOMEWHERE ELSE

Most of the taxicab drivers I encountered in Seoul were in their late 40s and 50s, few of them comprehending more than a dozen words of English, unless it had to do with a financial transaction.

Whenever I handed the driver a card with the address to which I wanted to be taken, he had first to put on his glasses before squinting at the business card as if he had never seen such a thing or was attempting to interpret the strange characters displayed upon it (although it was written in Korean). Five out of six times, the driver seemed utterly perplexed until I suggested he check out his navigational system.

The drivers' mastery of this system, however, was another problem. In four trips to the "lost paradise" hilltop Seoul Art Space, three of them ended in a place I could not recognize, once very late at night, where the drivers were ready to "dump" me, despite my complaints. At one point, I tried to tell the driver to take me back to where he had picked me up—I would pay for the whole trip in order to be in a place where I would know where I was. Fortunately, he asked a passerby who was able to explain the Art Space's nearby location.

The other two times that I arrived at the wrong destination ended in something like a shouting match as I proclaimed my lack of recognition while the drivers pointed with assurance at their navigational system's map. After all, Mother Korea had told them they had arrived at their destination. My refusal to leave the cab, accordingly, resulted in something like a standoff, until I handed the card to them again, beseeching them to call the Art Space's office. The helpful staff explained each time to the drivers their errors and how to reach their goal.

Although all of these trips ended on a friendly note, I entered each vehicle with a sense of trepidation, never knowing where I might end up. And there was always the chance that Mother Korea would win out over me, leaving me high in the hills at an unknown doorway.

When I expressed these fears—without adding any of the details above—on a visit to Brother Anthony, he reassured me in his delightful Cornwallish accent: "Not to worry. The taxicab driver will take out his glasses, study your little card, and take you straight to gate."

I could only wonder that all taxicab drivers in

Seoul must suffer the same affliction of far-sightedness. Perhaps it was merely a trick of the trade, a way of assuring the customer that they were seriously attending to his destination.

SIGNATURES AND PHOTOGRAPHS

I have never signed more programmes, documents, and objects than here in Korea. It was very sweet for 15 high school girls, dressed all in red, to want our autographs. I signed each one, dedicating it with the name of she who requested it. It was also very nice to sign the large banners bearing my intensely smiling face on the opening night. I also was asked to sign a large placard, which was difficult to do with a permanent marker, given my small handwriting.

At Dankook University we were all asked to put some words and our signatures upon a large ceramic vessel waiting to be kilned. Later, we were asked to affix our signatures to a plate.

At the Seoul Art Space we again signed placards. Everywhere people begged for signatures above our photographs.

My hand hurts. It is the

mentality of "Kilroy was Here," the sign as symbol of being and event.

Another Korean (and pan-Asian) infatuation is the photograph. I have never been shy with the camera, myself, and for years have stubbornly documented my friends and acquaintances in the US, Europe, and South America, so I am quite in sympathy with this activity. Yet, I admit it, I cannot match the obsession with photo-documentation of this trip.

There has hardly been a moment during our tour in which we and are audiences were not being filmed or photographed. At every venue, both before and after, we have been gathered together for group photo shoots, most of them exposing my fat belly along with my over friendly smile (my translator, Soo Min, overheard children at the Changdekyung Palace describing me as Santa Claus).

I have never in my life felt so exposed, so *over*exposed. Posters of our faces hang on street lamps, across the sides of buildings, in every theater in which we have performed, are pasted even on the sides of the buses which carry us about.

Beyond all this, each of the writers and translators gleefully snap the others' pictures, and filmmakers following us take pictures of us taking pictures. News photographers even get into the act, snapping up pictures of our documenters taking pictures of us taking

pictures of ourselves!

Surely among these hundreds and hundreds of images there must be one photograph worth retrieving—the one that makes me look like someone else or, at least, a better me! I invite all of you who captured my image to return them to me before my image of myself is forever lost!

Although one can easily find beer in the Incheon Seoul Airport, in the concourse from which my plane left there was only one tiny bar, with the unlikely name of Fizz & Jazz, which served vodka (no tonic), Jack Daniels, Chevas, Hennessey, and Bicardi—nothing else. Four beers: Heineken, Asai, Corona, and Budweiser. There was also no music while I was there, so, in short, they had neither jazz nor fizz!

Indeed, even in the major hotel in which I stayed, they had balked at serving me a vodka and tonic and claimed to have no gin. What was this absence of certain popular spirits all about?

I spoke to the young woman who bartended this small space. She reported that, although her girlfriends loved gin and tonics, her boss wouldn't stock the place with either. "Why?" I queried.

"No one in the older generation would drink them. They drink beer. They drink soju [a slightly sweeter drink like vodka, but with a low liquor content, that is drunk "straight"]. They don't drink vodka, never tonic."

"But don't tourists want gin and vodka? At home we drink it all the time."

I knew, in part, the answer to the question. Brother Anthony had explained that when the American soldiers gathered in Seoul after the war, the Koreans dis-

covered them to all be whiskey drinkers. No "effeminate" mixed drinks for them. They wanted the real "stuff."

Consequently, the contemporary American tourist must suffer for this 60-year-old misconception. And now I comprehend why Fizz and Jazz is where it is! May I suggest Sprite?

THE KOREAN WAY

Representing a culture of consensus, Korean restaurateurs, shopkeepers, waiters, and other service people can be very strict when it comes to rules and regulations.

At the Hotel Seoul KyoYuk MunHwa Hoekwan one morning, I awoke quite early at 5:00 a.m. After answering my emails, shaving, showering, and brushing my teeth, I determined to write for a while. My room, however, was poorly lit and the sun had yet to fully shine. So, I determined to go down to sit in the lobby waiting room, a commodious, inviting place with numerous tables and chairs next to the restaurant, which opened at 7:30. When I arrived, however, the room was dark. The restaurant, preparing for service, on the other

hand, was brightly lit, and I saw only a few young servers laying out the foods for the buffet.

Quite carefully, I moved back the table setting and sat, writing peacefully for several hours—including the sketch you are now reading. No one bothered with me in the least. As time moved on, however, and it got closer to 7:30, the maitre'd suddenly appeared, his eyes growing large with horror as he moved toward me. Half in Korean and half in English he informed me that I was not allowed to sit there, that the restaurant would not be open for another half-hour. I attempted to explain to him that I would put everything back, and that I had chosen this place only because the lobby was dark, pointing to the room beside us. To my surprise, the lobby was now fully lit, and I readily agreed to move.

"7:30! 7:30," he adamantly repeated.

"Yes, I know. It opens at 7:30," I spoke as I rose, carefully placing the mat and silverwear as I had found them.

"Go!" he exhorted.

I stubbornly remained in place until I had returned everything to perfect order before retreating to the lobby where I continued to write.

At precisely 7:30 he came to me in the lobby, inviting me back into the restaurant. I thanked him but continued where I was for at least another hour. No one arrived in the restaurant until 8:00.

I did understand that I had intruded upon the perfect order of his world, that I had been "out of place." Yet, he perceived a slight exception to that order as a disaster.

An even funnier event like this occurred one afternoon as we paused for lunch at a restaurant near Deoksugung Royal Palace. Here we sat as usual on the floor, awaiting service, which was brought to us over a period of some time, the waitresses bringing out dishes one by one and placing them in various spots around the tables. Each time something was put near my publisher and poet-friend Jerzy Illg, however, he would compulsively move it. A rebel from Poland, a man who grew up under the Communist rule, he could not, I surmised, resist putting the dish in a place of his own choosing.

After he had done this several times, the waitress scolded him, explaining (through his translator) that he should not move the dishes since she was working hard to find room for the numerous platters which she would serve us.

Yet the next time she set down a platter within his reach, without thinking he pulled it again in his direction. This time she had no patience, and quickly bending down, gently slapped the back of his hand. We all laughed, and Jerzy resisted touching anything else until all was set into position.

Another day, visiting the Manila Bar in Itaweon, in which I was the first and lone customer, I sat on the balcony, only to be told by a Korean waitress quickly scurrying to my side that I must not sit without first ordering. "I'd like to order a San Miguel then," I responded.

"No, you must order and pay," she replied.

"Don't you trust your customers?" I laughed in mild defiance.

"Over there," she pointed, "over there."

"But I intend to order several beers," I pushed back. "Must I get up and pay over there every single time?"

She looked at me disconcertedly, as if I were a simple child unable to comprehend: "It is our way," she insisted.

Despite my aching legs, due to my arthritis, I stood, walked down the few stairs, and went to the counter to order through another Korean woman what I already had requested. I paid and returned to my balcony seat.

With a satisfied flourish of recognition of my obedience, the first waitress served it up with a bowl of peanuts. I did not desire another round. And besides, it was now the time when most of the restaurants opened up for lunch.

I am certain such behavior occurs thousands of times each day in the USA, but my guess is that it would not occur so readily in Japan or Malaysia, this slightly surly insistence of the right way of doing things. It emanates, surely, from a culture that has too often been dominated by outsiders; perhaps even American soldiers during the Korean War influenced this insistence upon the Korean way of doing things.

SEOUL, OCTOBER 6-8, 2010
These pieces are reprinted from *Green Integer Blog* (October 2010).

Two Publishers

ALTHOUGH MANY fellow writers think of me primarily as a publisher, I think of myself as a poet, fiction writer, critic, and memoirist who is also a publisher. I love publishing, to which the 400-some books I have published to date attest. But my heart is in the art of writing, not in the process of publishing; indeed if I had a great amount of money (or even *any* money to spend on publishing), I would pay someone else to do everything except make the initial selection.

These feelings were reinforced when I was invited as an *author* to the 2010 World Writers' Festival in Seoul, Korea. Similarly, Polish publisher Jerzy Illg, whose Znak press publishes much of the writing of Czesław Milosz and Joseph Brodsky, felt delighted to be there as a poet—even though he had published just one thin book of poetry.

We both recognized that we (and perhaps some of the other writers as well) were there only because of Ko Un's suggestion. Both of us publish Ko Un. But that

didn't diminish the joy of being featured so prominently in banners and placards throughout the city and on the campuses of Dankook University. And I think we both admired each other's essay more than the writings of some of the prominent international writers and critics included in the event.

Both of us also shared a sense of humor about the conference, whose seriousness was, in some small way, subverted by the "continually reincarnated" boygenius, who we both agreed Ko Un is, a man with the force and energy of eternal youth, accompanied by the attendant freshness of thought. Despite their roots in traditional Korean writing and their relationships with Western narrative, Ko Un's poems are full of an energetic spirit that breaks out impulsively with dissociative images and sounds. He is, consequently, both a traditionalist and an experimenter, in the Modernist sense of that word.

Although Jerzy seemed to take himself less seriously than I as a poet, we both shared a kind of mad passion for literature, and, consequently, for much of our lives we felt driven to become publishers. Despite the fact that Jerzy worked for a much larger and financially sounder publishing house, I felt, in the fact that for many years he had suffered under the Soviet oppression (a much harsher environment than my penniless one), that as an independent publisher he was one the few people I had met in a long time who could truly comprehend just how lonely and difficult (logically *impossible*) it was to publish all the books I have. Talking with Jerzy I suddenly felt very old and tired, but perhaps it was just the beer we were drinking that made me feel that way. Both of us enjoyed drinking, and were delighted to find the small bar where we chatted for several hours.

There we discovered, through those shared "difficulties," that in some profound sense we understood each other—not that we felt sorry for ourselves; we had both chosen, even if by accident, our roles. And both of us expressed our love and pride in our endeavors. We agreed we still love what we do—at least *most* days! Each of us, in our own different way, has lived a remarkable life, he as a close friend and ally to Miłosz, Brodsky, and others (he is the Polish publisher, for example, of Mario Vargas Llosa, who won the Nobel Prize for Literature while we were visiting Seoul), I with a whole array of very different figures described in these pages. Accordingly, we felt a deep rapport.

Hearing Jerzy's descriptions of his youth when he joined an atelier in a Polish industrial town with no connections to culture, and where several evenings each week a woman sat reading the German texts of Hermann Hesse, studies of Eastern religion, and numerous other writings, translating them into Polish as she read—texts, totally unavailable in Polish, that revealed completely new worlds to him—brought tears to my eyes.

"When I first traveled to the West, to England," Jerzy continued, "I went into a bookstore and found, to my amazement, row upon row, in many editions, of my now beloved texts. I was astounded. There they were, in all their glory, waiting on the shelf for a people who no longer needed to care for them, while for me they stood upon those shelves as sacred artifacts. My wife was furious with me because I could not bring myself to leave that spot."

"How disappointed I was," continued Jerzy, "when I met Lawrence Ferlinghetti. I was attending an editors seminar at Stanford University—an excellent series of courses—and called Ferlinghetti, out of my love of Ginsberg and the Beats, to ask if I could meet him. Finally, he agreed, and I went quite expectantly to the famous City Lights bookstore.

"After I introduced myself, he growled out, 'What are you doing at a dreadful place like Stanford?' I tried to explain the wonderful things I was learning, but he waved it away.

"I switched topics, attempting to ask him about the important events surrounding Ginsberg's *Howl*, its censorship, and the trial.

"'That's old business,' he grumped. 'Let's talk about something more contemporary and *important*!'

"'What do you think is more important?' I innocently asked.

"'I've just gotten back from San Salvador,' he pronounced, 'where the rebels are successfully overtaking the government....'

"'I'm sorry,' I responded, 'but I've lived years under Communist oppression, and I do not sympathize with this.'

"He called me a Rightist.

"'Tell me,' I came back, 'has there ever been a Communist or Marxist government that has lived up to its utopian claims? Look at Cuba or North Korea, etc.'

"Needless to say, there was no more conversation between us. I feel saddened that one of my former heroes, who fought against government censorship, was now promoting governments that surely would not allow a Ginsberg, a Miłosz, a Brodsky, or any other poet I loved."

I have my own problems with Stanford, given what I know of the English Department and its abysmal treatment of Gilbert Sorrentino and Marjorie Perloff, and when Jerzy began to praise the Hoover Institute, I reminded him that it had once been the home of Condoleezza Rice. But I comprehended Jerzy's outrage and his dismissals of "correct" thinking. His perspective was simply more profound than Ferlinghetti's, an outsider's interpretation of reality. All of which reminded me that when it comes to international issues, an ignorance in world affairs is shared by both the right and the left. In order to understand another culture, one has to begin with humility, accepting one's stupidity along with any supposed insights.

Perhaps that's why, despite our vast aesthetic differences, Jerzy and I got on so well. I don't know how he felt, but I found in him a new friend.

SEOUL, SOUTH KOREA, OCTOBER 7, 2010

Two Poets

AFTER MY RESCUE from the city of Incheon in South
Korea, the very first thing I did was to meet with mem-
bers of the steering committee for the 2010 World
Writers' Festival in the Hotel Seoul KyoYuk MunHwa
Hoekwan. I don't believe the entire committee was
there, but there were four or five individuals, Kim Hye-
won, Park Duk-kyu, Lee Si-young, Kim Soo-Bok, and
Hae Yisoo (my rescuer) among them.

I was asked to sign some documents, and paid, in
the traditional way—in American dollars—the amount
promised for the lecture I was asked to present.

My inability to remember names is quite notorious among my friends, with whom in conversation I
sometimes must make two or three associations before
anyone comprehends of whom I am speaking. In Korea, because of the popularity of the names Kim, Lee,
and Park, it was even more difficult to remember the
names of those who were entertaining us. Moreover,
other than Hae Yisoo, few of our hosts spoke English,

 and, accordingly, conversations were held through my wonderful translator. Fortunately, I would whisper to her, from time to time, to tell me to whom I was speaking, and by the third day, I finally was able to develop relationships that involved their individual identities.

The two poets of the committee, Kim Soo-Bok and Lee Si-young, particularly interested me. I encountered Kim's poetry in the festival catalogue, where just a few lines fascinated me:

> The sea surging at the the tip of your toes, from the tip of your toes, to your knees, from the knees, to the thighs, to the stomach, to the heart, and as you breathe, hearing your, your, your free breathing, we cross your meandering stream, bearing our shadows on our heads.

I asked my translator to check the original to see if the repetitions I so loved, and felt were so appropriate in this breathless action of the poem, were in the Korean as well, fearing it might have been only a typo in the English. Yes, she assured, they were there!

Upon a break in sessions, I asked my Ko Un translator, Brother Anthony, whether there had

Kim Soo-bok

been any other English-language translations of Kim's poetry. He had translated some other poems, he assured me, but not many. "However," he continued, "I have translated a substantial amount of Mr. Lee's poetry in my Cornell East Asian Series book, *Variations: Three Korean Poets.*

The next morning he brought me a copy of that book, and I read several of Mr. Lee's poems, which also seemed excellent, although perhaps a bit more conventional or, at least, traditionally Korean in tone and subject matter. But there were wonderful narrative moments in the work, particularly in poems such as "Chong-im," about a young girl of his youth, now long vanished. I could see the possibility of publishing small books by both poets, particularly if I could get some aid from the Literature Translation Institute of Korea. That afternoon I mentioned my idea. Both po-

ets beamed with excitement.

It was about that time that the relationship between me and the poets began to alter, as they became more and more attentive to me. I had asked if I might be able to stay on after the Festival in Seoul for two days to better see the city. But they explained that I would have to pay for my expenses—which I had offered to do—and find my own hotel, since the one in which I was staying was only for special groups and events such as the Festival.

Accordingly, I had asked my translator, Soo Min, to help me find a hotel, and she had done so, in the Cheongdam-dong district. The price seemed right, and the hotel, when I looked it up, seemed pleasant. But at our last big dinner, both poets decided that I would be unhappy there, and arranged for me and a couple of others who were extending their visits to stay at an artists retreat, Seoul Art Space, at a much more isolated distance from the areas that I wanted to visit. Yet, since the offer meant that we would not be paying, I could hardly turn it down.

Soon after, Mr. Lee suggested that we go on a tour of the city the following day, and Mr. Kim invited me to a southern island where he and his wife had a condominium in the woods. In Korea, as in many Asian countries, it is considered rude to leave guests alone for long periods of time, but I had to decline their graciousness, explaining to Mr. Lee that I love walking around cities, discovering things for myself as I alternate between wandering and resting in cafes and bars. I told Mr. Kim that I truly appreciated his offer, but would never forgive myself if I returned home without seeing any of the city in which I had stayed.

Mr. Lee later introduced me to his girlfriend, who spoke English and explained that she would love to be my guide the following morning. Again, I had to demur.

The Art Space location, although quite lovely, was somewhat distant from the shopping areas I had planned to visit, and far more rustic than would have been any hotel. I took a long taxi ride to the Itaweon

district of Seoul, enjoying, as I mention elsewhere in these South Korean memories, the day all to myself.

But on the last day, both poets again insisted on touring me through Myeong-dong and elsewhere via auto, Kim's daughter serving as translator. There was no way I could possibly reject their offer. They took me to a wonderful Chinese lunch, and Mr. Kim drove me the long distance to the airport—kindnesses that, although truly heart-felt, seemed somewhat more forthcoming because of my role as a potential publisher. In any event, I was truly appreciative. And my friendship with both poets will hopefully continue in the years to come.

In late 2011 I met with Mr. Lee in my own city of Los Angeles, and had a very enjoyable lunch with him, his wife, and a friend of theirs in Koreatown. In 2015, I met with Mr. Kim in Los Angeles, again sharing a pleasant lunch in Koreatown.

LOS ANGELES, MARCH 9, 2011, 2015
Reprinted from *Green Integer Blog* (March 2011).

In 2014, my Green Integer press published Patterns, *a collection of poems by Lee Si-young, translated by Brother Anthony and Yoo Hui-Sok. In January 2016, my press published Kim Soo-Bok's* Beating on Iron, *also translated by Brother Anthony.*

While ordering up a copy of Jonathan Demme's film Vanya of 42nd Street *on Netflix, I was also referred to Michael Cacoyannis' 1999 filming of Chekhov's* The Cherry Orchard, *a play I had inexplicably never seen. It was time, I thought to myself, to fill in this missing link in my never-ending education. Cacoyannis' film, unlike the André Gregory-Wallace Shawn production, also appeared to (and actually did) present a more traditional version than had* Vanya, *about which I had criticisms for that very fact.*

During this same period in 2017, I was correcting and indexing the pages for My Year 2011, *and, after seeing the second film and doing some research, discovered what I had forgotten, that the Greek Cypriot director of this film and his more famous work,* Zorba the Greek, *had died that same year,* The Cherry Orchard *representing his last film.* The Cherry Orchard, *moreover, was very much about a house in which no one was any longer at home, and which soon would be destroyed, with no other place for its former denizens to go. It seemed perfect, accordingly, for the 2011 volume of my cultural memoirs, and, after cutting out another, less interesting piece, I included it therein.*

A Place Not Really Theirs

MICHAEL CACOYANNIS (DIRECTOR AND WRITER,
BASED ON THE PLAY BY ANTON CHEKHOV) **THE CHERRY
ORCHARD** / 1999

UNLIKE THE STAGE VERSION of *The Cherry Orchard*,
Michael Cacoyannis' 1999 film version of the great
Chekhov play begins in France, where Anya (Tushka
Bergen), along with her eccentric governess, Charlotte Ivanovna (the wonderfully comic Frances de la
Tour), has traveled to bring her mother, the beautiful
Ranyevskaya (Charlotte Rampling), home. They find
her in the small, grungy apartment, after she has run
away from her Russian home because of the drowning
death of her son, taken up with an unnamed lover, and
recently attempted suicide.

By beginning the work far away from their provincial Russian home, Cacoyannis establishes from the
very outset of this tragicomedy that the house's owner
has already abandoned it. And, although the story will

take a while to unwind in describing the entire series of events, it is clear from the mother's condition of near-poverty (having already had to sell her villa) that despite her returning to the nest, so to speak, she, her brother Gayev (Alan Bates), and the entire family have already lost their estate.

One can almost sit back, accordingly, for the rest of the film and watch the often comic and sad machinations of the family and its servants that demonstrate their downfall.

Bates plays Gayev as a kind of madman, addicted to billiards the way, it is hinted, that Ranyevskaya is to—is it snuff or cocaine? Or, perhaps the way Ivanovna's dog is addicted to nuts.

Yet the true marvel of this film is that Ranyevskaya is not played, as she often is, as a kind of frail early version of O'Neill's Mary Tyrone, a woman  with no head for money or facts, but rather as a woman who intentionally resists what she knows is the truth: the fact that, as Lopahin (Owen Teale) reminds her again and again, she must sell the lovely cherry orchard to create expensive subplots for the growing rich in order to pay off the estate's debts. Rampling portrays Ranyevskaya, rather, as a woman who *will* not act precisely because she believes that, having sinned so deeply, she and her slave-owning family of the past deserve their fates.

Certainly there are moments when, caught up in her loving memories of life at the estate, of life beside a lake that also contains one of the largest cherry orchards in Russia, she appears to be living in a dream. Yet, we often catch a glint in her eyes of steely determination, perceive a quiver about the lips of terror, making it quite clear that the woman everyone else perceives as frail has a heart, perhaps, of rock. In Rampling's deeply moving portrait, Ranyevskaya has already died, and her only real role is to help her beloved daughters, Anya and

Varya (Katrin Cartlidge), her brother, and her servants realize that they too will soon be homeless, if not dead themselves. If only she could marry off her daughters, perhaps they, at least, might be saved.

Perhaps for that very reason, Lopahin, in this film version, is not portrayed as the utter villain he has been, as critics have pointed out, in many stage productions. Here, despite his inability to comprehend the family's adoration of the house and land which surely represent their sacrificial pyre, he attempts, again and again, to help and save them. Yet the one thing that he might do to redeem any of them, to marry Varya, he simply cannot accomplish. Besides, he is already married—to his money and to his determination to rectify his own past. For a moment, this far more gentle Lopahin, at least during the estate auction, might, we can for a moment imagine, not be fighting for his own gain, but on behalf of the family he has attempted to warn. Yet, in the end, he is still a kind of monster, unable to even allow them a few more moments of peace before the hack of axe put to the cherry trees can be heard in the distance (here actually visualized).

The only one who truly might have escaped is Anya, particularly after she meets up again with the former family tutor, Trofimov (Andrew Howard), the eternal student who attempts to educate her about what the future will soon bring, a complete transformation of cultural order. And, for a moment, she seems to perceive the truth: that all the beauty about them, the rambling house and its orchards, has never been "theirs" (the wealthy and elite), but was created by the serfs. As she puts it, "the place has not really been 'theirs' for a very long time."

But, of course, Trofimov has no money, and can offer her no protection from what is soon to occur, even if they survive the complete destruction of their kind.

There are some problems with Cacoyannis' telling. At times, in his attempt to let the story tell itself, the director's script is simply too oblique. It is hard, for example, to quite know what the role of Yasha (Gerald Butler) is all about. How, precisely, has he somehow attached himself to Ranyevskaya, and how, later, does he fall in—although it makes perfect sense—with Lopahin? And it is hard to comprehend why Trofimov, given his current values, has even bothered to return, except perhaps for his sublimated love of both Anya and her mother. And, except as comic relief, why does the German-educated Ivanovna even exist? Obviously these are problems in Chekhov's original as well.

Overall, however, Cacoyannis does a quite splendid job of portraying both the humor—which I might have put a little more in the foreground—and the sadness of events in this grand melodrama of the end of 19th century Russia. Yes, these folk, like those in *Vanya*, are all quite tired and, at times, boring. But here, there are indications of the joyous folk they once were. And Rampling as Ranyevskaya makes such a remarkably astounding ghost.

LOS ANGELES, MAY 12, 2017
Reprinted from *World Cinema Review* (May 2017).

Talking in Circles

CHARLES BERNSTEIN **ATTACK OF THE DIFFICULT POEMS** (CHICAGO: UNIVERSITY OF CHICAGO PRESS, 2011)

> "I'm not joking, and if I seem to talk in circles, it just seems that way."
> —Raymond Chandler, *The Big Sleep,* as quoted in Charles Bernstein's *Attack of the Difficult Poems*

I MENTIONED TO my friend Howard the other morning that, except for conservatively close-minded, humorless poets and readers, I could not imagine anyone not enjoying and agreeing with Charles Bernstein in his

wonderful new critical collection, *Attack of the Difficult Poems*. No matter what kind of poetry one reads or writes, readers will find Bernstein's book to be a call for multiplicities of approaches, rereadings, *mis*readings, poems entirely removed from the page, or emphatically spilling over the page in alphabetic abandon. His methods are often humorous and, at times, even silly as he seeks out meaning—never a rote summary or simple answer. He enjoys discovering poets where one might never have looked, from the songs of early black jazz singers, to the humorous Yiddish *shtick* of Fanny Brice and early lyrics by Irving Berlin; from the recreated Scots of Hugh MacDiarmid, to the Broadway songs of Cole Porter and Oscar Hammerstein II.

That is not to say that Bernstein has no prejudices, that he posits no values behind the diversity of poetic approaches he discusses; it's simply that his way of argument is inclusive rather than confrontational. As the author himself writes in the addendum to his essay "Is Art Criticism Fifty Years Behind Poetry?":

> I am as partial and partisan as anyone. Preference and selection are a necessary part of aesthetic judgment. Yet, my radar might be the exact map of another person's exclusions, just as another's exclusions might be a map to my paradise. The relation of these two ideas (conviction in one's aesthetic judgment and its inevitable limitations) is not irreconcilable but dialectical.

For Bernstein, the dialogical approach is everything. Disagree with me, and we have something to talk about, Bernstein repeats time and again throughout these pages. In short, he is a nice guy who believes in poetry with the devotion of a devout rabbi or priest.

But then, I forget that Bernstein has often shaken up institutional organizations and angered noted individuals in and outside the poetry communities. As Marjorie Perloff begins a short conversation with the poet, published in this book,

> Charles, almost twenty years have gone by since that fateful MLA [Modern Language Association] meeting when you delivered the lecture "The Academy in Peril: William Carlos Williams Meets the MLA" (1983). I still remember what a tempest you caused and how furious the old timers like M. L. Rosenthal were at your demolition job. You were, in those days, a great fighter against "official verse culture."

I myself recall a dinner party where I had invited several poets of what might be described as the "second generation" of the New York School, who furiously chastised me for my publishing of Charles' work, proclaiming, as Bernstein himself discusses in *Attack of the Difficult Poems*, that he was a theorist instead of a poet. Apparently poets can't talk and tie their shoes at the same time, as Bernstein might quip.

But it is still difficult for me to comprehend why anyone in love with poetry would not want to embrace a work that so humorously and passionately offers ways for readers to enter the texts and speaks for the importance of poetic endeavor.

Bernstein's work sets itself up in the first essay, "The Difficult Poem," as deflating the fears readers may have approaching a work that appears to have a vocabulary and syntax that is difficult to understand or that makes one feel "inadequate or stupid"... in short, a poem that requires a struggle to appreciate and find meaning. Like a friendly dentist, Bernstein—employing the comic gestures of a science-fiction film—reassures readers that the "problem" is not theirs alone, and requires just a little painless effort to turn the reading experience into a joyful discovery.

Soon, however, things turn more serious, as Bernstein seeks ways to help students everywhere deal with poetry. In "A Blow Is Like an Instrument: The Poetic Imaginary and Curricular Practices," the author takes the reader through his own experiences in the classroom as he proffers a "radically democratic" approach to teaching, encouraging students to read diverse works that raise more questions than answers. For Bernstein this begins at the door of the university or college, where he makes a plea for "enriched content, especially aesthetic and conceptual content, over a streamlined vocational goal orientation."

Along the way, Bernstein takes on issues of university tenure (he thoroughly supports it as a way to protect the whole thinking-questioning process), academic standards, and numerous other issues. A short quote will have to summarize Bernstein's intelligent criticisms of current academic values:

> And what of academic standards? Aren't these the dikes that protect us from the flood of unregulated thought? Or are they like the narrow Chinese shoe that deforms our thinking to fit its image of rigor? When I examine the formats and implied standards for peer-reviewed journals and academic conferences, they suggest to me a preference for a lifeless prose, bloated with the compulsory repetitive explanation of what every other "important" piece on the subject has said. Of course, many professors will insist that they do not subscribe to this, but the point is not what any one of us does, but the institutional culture we accept.

That these clear-minded queries about college and university policies come from a professor who has published in nearly all the major academic journals, as well as in hundreds of smaller literary publications, speaks volumes, and helps to convince us of his protests.

Throughout *Attack of the Difficult Poems*, moreover, Bernstein gives specific examples, not only of how to structure a program that will better allow students to think and question poetic art, but of specific classroom tactics to encourage their explorations. I suggest that any young (older too) teacher of poetry might find Bernstein's suggestions useful for the classroom, and helpful in showing how to approach texts that may at first seem beyond the students' grasp (although it is, just as often, the other way around, I am afraid).

Bernstein goes much further, discussing the whole history of language and poetry, comparing, for example, the early use of the written poem in Homer's day (when it served less as a finished text than as a reminder of the oral performance) to the current alphabetic text that is a thing in itself.

Along the way, in various essays, the author considers the effects of the computer and digitalization of poetry (many aspects of which he refreshingly embraces), and in a brilliant discussion of "Making Audio Visible," helps readers to understand the importance of hearing poetry (read by the poet or a performer; Bernstein argues for the value of numerous hearings). His and his students' creation of PENNSOUND, a large audio archive available online, has been, perhaps, one of the most important acts in preserving poetry as an oral force in our time.

My favorite essay in the book is "Objectivist Blues: Scoring Speech in Second Wave Modernist Poetry and Lyrics," in which Bernstein considers a wide range of poetic voices from Zukofsky and other Objectivists to American folk music and popular black lyricists such as poet James Weldon Johnson. His inquiring mind takes us from Oscar Hammerstein II's lyrics for "Ol' Man River" to the altered lyrics in the performances of singer, political activist Paul Robeson. By the end of the essay, I found myself spending hours in tracking down various online recordings and performances, as well as rereading song lyrics of this period (I had already published a volume of American song lyrics of the 19th century), all of which I found fascinating and illuminating for comprehending the more "difficult" works of Zukofsky, Oppen, Eliot, and others.

In later essays in the book, Bernstein explores poetry's relationship with art, and forms of poetry that are as much at home in the art gallery or museum as in a poetry anthology. His brilliant analysis of poetic frauds that were played out in presses and poetic publications by figures such as Alan Sokal, Max Harris, Yasusada (Kent Johnson), and others is filled with the tension between the desire to satirize or mock social and political poetic strictures and the failure to live up to the sacred trust of the reader, publisher, and author, to say nothing of the larger community.

Along the way are other mischievous and funny inventions that pepper the more erudite conversations, and, just as Bernstein has promised, sweep up the reader (at least this reader) into the arms of poetic euphoria.

The author ends this phantasmagoria with a very funny, but also somewhat frightening, satire: a Galileo-like recanting of all the ideas he has promulgated throughout. As the recantings of Bernstein's "Recantorium" build up in pace and absurdity, the recantings themselves grow into recants, so that by work's end no one can possibly determine whether the poet is recanting his own ideas or his recanting of his ideas, or, possibly, his recanting of the recants ("And for this I recant my cant, cant and recant"). But there is a dangerous double-edged sword to this silly performance that seems to suggest that the reader still may hold with the nonsensical viewpoints that the author is now purportedly embracing. And if that is so...well then Bernstein's brilliant arguments have had no effect, a possibility that at least this reader simply cannot imagine.

LOS ANGELES, JULY 15, 2011
Reprinted in *Los Angeles Review of Books* (July 2011).

Fractures of Self

DAVID ANTIN **RADICAL COHERENCY: SELECTED ESSAYS ON ART AND LITERATURE, 1966 TO 2005** (CHICAGO: UNIVERSITY OF CHICAGO PRESS, 2011)

ONE OF THE FIRST THINGS anyone approaching David Antin's marvelous new collection of essays on art and literature will notice is the striking image on the book's cover, a photograph that depicts David Antin, looking perhaps a bit more Buddha-like than he does in real life, walking toward another image of himself. There is something arresting about this image, even a bit eerie, but I made little of it when I first saw it, except to register that it represented an image of the author, symbolically speaking, from 1966 coming towards his current self. A few friends, however, found that image quite disturbing, one suggesting he had to keep the book face down on his coffee table. Perhaps it was just the oddity of having a photograph, which we associate with the real world, representing something that we

516

know cannot truly happen, one aspect of self meeting up with the other.

Yet, if we read on in Antin's book, particularly in his essay "The Beggar and the King," we recognize that this transaction between two aspects of the self is precisely what the author projects as being behind the narrative genre he has created in the "talk poem." Speaking of his early work, generated by a kind of collage sensibility, Antin observes:

> ...I started out in the 1950s like many young experimental artists with a strong commitment to most of the received ideas of early-twentieth-century modernism, the most important of which for an artist was the idea of the exhaustion, experimental and aesthetic, of the representation in all its forms. For a language artist this mostly meant the uselessness of narrative.

Antin goes on to suggest that over the years, as he recognized the exhaustion "of nearly all the modes of experimental communication," he began to reexamine narrative, exploring worlds of folklorists and ethnographers (the Grimm brothers, Afansiev, etc.), as well as V. Propp's structural study *The Morphology of the Folktale*, and others as far-reaching as Zuni Tales and Bernardino de Sahagun's definitions compiled from survivors of the Aztec culture. What Antin finally determined is that some narratives are not stories, and some stories have no narrative, coming eventually to articulate a definition of narrative:

> ...a narrative requires a sense of something at stake for somebody in some particular subject position, which is what characterizes the stake. It is this sense of stake that should be taken as the center of narrative.

Like dreams, Antin argues, narratives build bridges across change.

> The act of reconnecting subject positions across the gulf of change is what constitutes the formation of self. All self is built over the threat of change. There can be no self until there is an awareness of one's subject position, which can only be created by the threat of change or the memory of change. Every change creates a fracture between successive subject states, that narrative attempts and fails to heal. The self is formed over these cracks. Every self is multiply fractured, and narrative traversal

of these fracture planes defines the self. Narrative
is the traditional and indispensable instrument of
self creation.

It is this definition of narrative and Antin's own exploration of that genre in his "talk poems" that came
eventually to define his art. One must understand the
picture on the cover, accordingly, not just as an encounter of an older Antin with a newer one, but as one kind
of self facing the spectre of another and redefining that
vision of self in the process. And in that sense, the image on the cover *is* a slightly disturbing vision of these
two selves coming together almost to duke it out over
the changes that have obviously occurred in the writer's
own life: one might say, another kind of "radical coherency."

Yet I was struck in these revelatory essays, at how
much continuity Antin demonstrates in a writing that
bridges 39 years. There are only four works that actually
fit the format of what the author describes as "talk poems" ("the existential allegory of the rothko chapel," the
title piece, "radical coherency," "the death of the hired
man," and "john cage uncaged is still cagey," although
Antin tells me that "Fine Furs" was originally written
in the form, but later transformed into an essay), but I
would argue that all of the pieces in this volume have
the same Antin inflections of voice and structural pat-

terns as his later works. Antin's is a voice filled with pauses, not always at the place one might suspect, but as in Stein, always there as part of the syntax itself. These caesuras are a product of Antin's whole process, which is so different from most critical writing that it is sometimes difficult to think of Antin setting out to write an "essay." For Antin does not "answer" anything, but poses of each artist, poet, or groups of these questions which he then ponders and pauses over in sentence after sentence, wandering and wondering aloud, in astoundingly profound ways, how and why certain things are being said or done. Occasionally, for Antin is a true wit, these can be somewhat whimsical—in "Warhol: The Silver Tenement," for example, Antin's major summary is that in order for Warhol's beautiful creations to succeed, they must necessarily develop "scuffs," transforming his paintings, films, novels, soap operas, and even his planned "silver tenement" into a kind of "precisely pinpointed defectiveness," a kind of tawdry version of glamour—but by and large, no matter what his own position about the quality or purposefulness of the various art and poetic endeavors upon which he focuses, Antin asks serious questions, challenges set notions, and makes us rethink our assumptions.

In order to cover a large range of territory, Antin has clearly winnowed down what was to have been a far bigger book (sometimes with essays on the same artist at different periods in his or her career) into a whole that explores various aspects of the art scene from the mid-1960s through today. From Pop art, Antin moves on to the new representational work of artists like Alex Katz, taking out time in a wonderfully, slightly daffy piece to consider the work of machine-builders such as Jean Tinguely, before turning his attention to a "Pollution Show" in Oakland, California, consisting of photographs, drawings, kinetic junk sculpture, funk, discreet piles of rubbish, and even a dead seagull.

From these "earthwork" pieces, the author turns his attention to different kinds and traditions of constructivism and the issues of flatness in contemporary art, moving through Sol Lewitt, Robert Irwin, Michael Asher, Carl Andre, and others. This is followed by a bruising criticism of the famed "Art and Technology" show, organized by Maurice Tuchman at the Los Angeles County Museum of Art in 1971. Later essays include discussions of video art, a hilarious consideration—using the example of artist Robert Morris—of how one might comprehend the "proprietary rights" of an artist, followed by a sensitive evaluation of the color fields of Rothko's art in Houston's Rothko Chapel, often viewed under the light of clouded skies, and ending with a reevaluation of performance artist Allan Kaprow. In short, Antin's writing serves almost as a textbook, without textbook-like presentations and conclusions, of what art meant throughout the 1960s and 1970s.

I should add that not only can I hear Antin's voice in all these pieces but I perceive his various viewpoints as splendidly *personal* appreciations or disparagements. Reading Antin on art is as if one were accompanying a lively friend or uncle on trips to the museums and galleries throughout the country over a period of several years.

Miraculously Antin does the same thing for literature, beginning with a substantial 1972 essay exploring issues of modernism and postmodernism in American poetry long before anyone else had thoroughly considered these issues in depth. I remember sitting in Marjorie Perloff's class—Marjorie being one of Antin's first major critical supporters—four years later, where we still hadn't accepted the idea of there being a "postmodern" poetry. Antin was there first! His "Some Questions about Modernism" bravely explores, again long before it had been done by others, notions of different kinds of modernism, opening itself up to all kinds of literary texts that move away from the Pound-Williams-Eliot-Stevens kind of poetic genealogy.

"Radical Coherency" humorously discusses its central concept through a visit to a large shopping mall store where he attempts to help his elderly mother pick out some undergarments, priced at the amount she has been used to paying for years. That metaphor, of bargain shops within large clothing sections, striated by aisles and aisles of other ready-to-purchase goods, helps to explain what we might mean by a coherent thing that has radically exploded to contain all sorts of strange categories and subdivisions to meet the needs of contemporary culture.

Essays like "The Stranger at the Door," the already-discussed "The Beggar and the King," and "Fine Furs" open up the whole notion of what a poem is or might be understood to be. In one of the funniest works of the entire book, "the death of the hired hand," Antin deconstructs some of the poetry of Robert Frost (and, incidentally, of my artist acquaintance Siah Armajani's poetry room, in which Antin was speaking). Antin's discussion of the kind of dishonesty—a "wearing of hats" as he terms it—of Frost's diction and poetic positioning will forever change, I can assure you, the way you see this plain carpenter of imitative New England poetic dialogues.

The penultimate essay is a brilliant reconsideration of Wittgenstein's work in the context of some critics' contentions that his philosophical studies are also works of poetry. Antin dares to ask and attempts to explain just what that poetry might consist of, and how, sometimes rather strangely, it functions as such. In the last essay, "john cage uncaged is still cagey," Antin takes on work that has perhaps been very influential to his own writing, suggesting how the performances of this "cagey" composer, collector of mushrooms, and sometimes unofficial manager of Merce Cunningham's dance company function as poetic events.

I have a few minor quibbles with Antin's book, namely concerning the lack of information the author provides about some of the artists and events on which writes. It would be useful to know the names and places of the shows he reviewed; in one case in particular, Antin, a close friend of the artist, does not ever mention Allan (Kaprow's) last name! It occurs only in a footnote. But these are small matters that might have been ameliorated by more editorial involvement.

The book as a whole is a stunning summary (although there are dozens of other works by Antin remaining to be republished) of one of our most engaging and challenging intellects. *Radical Coherency* is filled with the goods you can enjoy again and again.

LOS ANGELES, MAY 17, 2011
Reprinted from *Jacket 2* / Charles Bernstein Blog (May 2011).

Exploratory Fiction

EXPLORATORY FICTION, at least in the United States, is arguably near death. Determinedly mediocre American publishing aligned with tepidly written and rapidly disappearing critical commentary have left us instead with a seemingly endless series of dispirited personal narratives, flat-footed fantasies, and sentimentalized social statements.

By *exploratory* writing I do not merely mean "experimental writing," but works that in their language and structures challenge our thinking, surprising and sometimes even mystifying readers, who are left not with simple comprehension but with wonderment. When I first began publishing in the mid-1970s there were a substantial number of writers of such fictions (Walter Abish, Tom Ahern, David Antin, Paul Auster, Russell Banks, Michael Brownstein, Robert Coover, Guy Davenport, Lydia Davis, Jaimy Gordon, Marianne Hauser, John Hawkes, Spencer Holst, Fanny Howe, Steve Katz, Tom La Farge, Nathaniel Mackey, Clar-

ence Major, Harry Matthews, Mark Mirsky, Toby Olson, James Purdy, Gilbert Sorrentino, Johnny Stanton, Robert Steiner, Ronald Sukenick, Rosmarie Waldrop, Wendy Walker, Lewis Warsh, Curtis White, and Dallas Wiebe, to name just a few). Indeed, my Sun & Moon Press published several of these figures. But since that time, many of these writers have died or ceased writing, and only a handful of younger writers have joined those still active. Accordingly, the great tradition of US writing, from Gertrude Stein to William Faulkner, from Flannery O'Connor to Vladimir Nabokov, is in danger of disappearing. What to do?

One person or perhaps even a small group cannot resolve the situation. But I can, as I have attempted to do in my activities as a publisher, present and reveal such writing. *EXPLORING*fictions, my new online magazine devoted to narrative writing, is another such attempt. Perhaps by simply standing in the path of the dart [see photograph above] I can deflect those whose attention is centered only on a single point in time and space, and help to refocus their vision upon the wide world about them.

Clearly such a publication will be strongly dependent upon my own contributions, but I hope the entire literary community interested in fiction will join me in presenting (living and dead, US and international) writers, reviews, short essays, interviews, news, and other related commentaries.

I must emphasize that the title of this publication is purposely plural, and will be edited with the recognition that fiction is not merely a Gemini (the novel or short story), but is a many-headed beast made up of numerous forms including epistolary writing, picaresques, anatomies, fables, pastorals, encyclopedias, and other such structures.

*EXPLORING*fictions will be published daily or weekly, depending upon when I write or receive appropriate new works. Perhaps, if it functions as I hope, Green Integer will collect each year into a single paperbound volume.

LOS ANGELES, MAY 24, 2009
Reprinted from *EXPLORING*fictions (May 24, 2009).

Synchronic Fictions

DOUGLAS MESSERLI **CONTEMPORARY AMERICAN FICTION** (COLLEGE PARK, MARYLAND: SUN & MOON PRESS, 1983)

ATTEMPTING TO DESCRIBE the state of contemporary fiction, one finds oneself in much the same position as the ancient sailors must have felt, tracing the routes laid down by the geographers, of the day, who, Plutarch observed, "crowd[ed] into the edges of their maps parts of the world they [did] not know, adding notes in the margins to the effect that beyond [lay] nothing but sand deserts full of wild beasts and unapproachable bogs." After even a casual reading of current fiction criticism, one suspects that some of today's literary cartographers not only map parts of the terrain "they do not know," but—taking the methods of the early geographers one step further into the absurd—define the unknown less by what they suppose it to be than by what they imagine it is not. Increasingly over the past two decades,

contemporary American fiction—plotted by many critics as lying in the deep seas of Postmodernism—has come to be depicted as a sort of *terra incognita*, an unknowable and frightening region that stands apart and against the familiar shores of Modernism, mimesis, the symbol, experimentation, interpretation, moral value, and even itself.[1] And there is just enough of an atmosphere of parody and nostalgia in the present-day environment to have convinced some of its explorers—most notably, John Barth—that they have strayed into a world of fiction in which the old cannot subsist.[2]

Other critics—Robert Alter, Philip Stevick, and Alan Wilde, among many—argue, more convincingly, that what seems to be an island, if I may extend my metaphor a bit further, is actually a peninsula, linked to literary tradition; that contemporary American fiction basically is a restoration and amplification of pre-realist modes and genres of fiction (Alter and Stevick) or a new episode in an evolving and reactive patter of fictional irony (Wilde).[3] Still others, portray the contemporary scene as a vast archipelago, a topographic

free-for-all in which self-reflexive, experimental, paro-
distic, and more classically-structured works coexist
with Modernist fiction in a pluralist Eden, so to speak.[4]

In short, where once our literary guides focused
their energies on describing specific aspects of the landscapes of current fiction, it now appears that they feel
a necessity to map the shape of new fiction in relation
to this and other centuries. It is as if suddenly critics of
fiction have grown fearful that readers may lose their
footing in the morass of contemporary culture; as if
they must assure themselves and their fellow readers
that new fiction is either "dangerous" or "safe."

This moral imperative, in part, has to do with the
fact that many contemporary fictions do not seem to
require or reveal much of significance through thematic interpretation; and with the end of that formalist
function, several critics have abandoned the study of
individual authors and works in preference of investiga-
tions of various critical methodologies themselves. For
those who continue to write on contemporary fiction
it often seems that there is little choice but to turn to
literary history in order to establish contexts in which
to understand and evaluate new writing. But there is
an obvious danger in this, for what begins as an outline
has a strange way of becoming the border; what may be
understood as charting the course can ultimately work
toward the establishment of a canon as inflexible as that

of the formalists. For, surely, whatever else might be said about contemporary fiction, "it" is not an "it"—is not a thing to be mapped—but rather the process itself. How can one "locate" or "define"—as either friend or foe—a literature that has neither been assimilated by the culture nor finished being written? To speak of contemporary fiction, even a part of it, as a *body* that stands "against," "for," or "post" anything is merely conjecture, is to imagine its completion, its death.

Ironically, if the contemporary writers, of this collection at least, share anything in common, it is an opposition to these very attempts to historify and exclude or canonize their works. In their baroque embellishment of genre, authors such as Mel Freilicher, Michael Andre, Gilbert Sorrentino, John Ashbery, Tom Ahern, Harrison Fisher, Jeff Weinstein, and Michael Brownstein challenge concepts of cultural necessity and literary destiny. Through the superimposition of numerous traditional and popular forms (drama, catalogue, dialogue, romance, autobiography, literary history, political satire, and textbook, to name only a few), a fiction such as Freilicher's *Genre Studies* implicitly advocates a non-linear, synchronist approach to literature, asserting a structure which permits the contemporary writer to be less anxiety-ridden (to borrow Harold Bloom's expressive description of the condition of today's authors) than enthusiastic about the influence of writers present and past.

Behind this exploitation of genres, no doubt, is the desire to parody formalist fiction techniques.[5] But this same synchronist sensibility also permits a genuine recovery of the Gogolian comic fable in Ahern's "Chenken and Nartzarzen in Several Days on the Town"; a rediscovery and infusion of new energy into the genre of the masque in Ashbery's "Description of a Masque"; and a transformation from a travesty of the academy in Sorrentino's "The Gala Cocktail Party" to a dazzling linguistic anatomy of names and types. This same fascination with structural simultaneity, moreover, is the force behind Leslie Scalapino's and Norma Jean Deak's experimentations with the performative possibilities of fiction that put it beyond text. Indeed, despite the notoriety of explicit parodists such as John Barth, Donald Barthelme, Kurt Vonnegut, and Robert Coover, one is struck by the seriousness of purpose with which many contemporary fiction writers explore the potentials of simultaneous structures and styles.

Particularly in the past couple of years, storytellers have begun to re-incorporate chronological narrative, the objective point of view, and even realist characters into their works. To label this as a "return" to Modernist or realist modes of fiction, however, is precisely the kind of misreading fostered by the attempt to *locate* fiction in a particular time and place. Pointing to this misapprehension, Alan Wilde perceptively describes several of these parable-like works as mid-fictions, fictions in which the world is perceived "as neither objectively knowable nor as totally opaque...."[6] But by placing such fiction between "the indicative and subjunctive, realism and reflexivity," Wilde, himself, is caught up in the metaphor of the map. Perhaps these works do not lie *between* two extremes as they make use of both. For, like their peers in this anthology, Walter Abish, Richard Padget, Russell Banks, Mark Sacharoff, Toby Olson, Steve Katz, Donald Olson, John Perreault, Joe Ashby Porter, Paul Witherington, Roberta Allen, Corinne Robins, and Laura Ferguson are engaged, in part, in an attempt to reveal parallel and antipathetic realities.

Walter Abish's "Alphabet of Revelations," for example, is, on one level, a fairly straightforward satire of suburban life; its small-minded characters, their gossip, extramarital affairs, divorces, and meager revelations might equally be at home in a novel by John Cheever or John Updike. But even the incompetent reader cannot help recognizing that there is something "rotten" on Sustain Drive. For the "reality" that Abish presents is something like that of an old maid schoolmarm's who has watched too many soap operas over summer vacation. The alphabetization of the characters' names (Arlo, Bud, Clem, Donna, Erna, Faye) deflates them from rounded figures with whom the reader might empathize to flat signs that emblematize contemporary society in general. The surprising revelation at story's end, accordingly, belongs less to the characters than to the author, who—turning the tables, so to speak—suggests to the reader that these characters and, by extension, the society are more complex than what meets the eye. Through a combination of conventional and inventive structures and techniques, in other words, Abish undermines what David Antin describes as the "normative-realist" notion of fiction in order to build anew a more complex fictional reality for the reader and himself. By engaging with the reader's expectations, Abish not only parodies the values of middle-class society, but challenges the ways in which it sustains those values in its fictions, in its conceptions of itself.

The fictions by which we define our lives are also the focus of John Perreault's "The Catalogue." Described in painfully objective detail, the sole character of this tale is the consummate consumer, a creature of the Victorian culture confronted with the superabundance of 20th-century artifacts. One by one, her dreams and desires are revealed—in what must be the most extreme use of the objective correlative in all of fiction—by the objects she procures through her mail-order catalogue. The story itself, in fact, becomes a kind of catalogue, not only of this woman's wants and purchases, but of the products by which her culture defines itself. Despite the story's near-absolute objectivism, no reader can miss the irony that Katherine's culture is our culture as well; thus, as the author implies, his character's fate is the fate of all who passively accept the artifacts of society rather than engage in their creation. Ultimately, Perreault's fiction is less a study of an Iowa recluse than it is a guidebook to cultural icons, a kind of dictionary of the culture's dead fictions.

Similarly, Toby Olson's "The Game"—a chapter from his novel *Seaview*—presents a series of scenes which function in terms of realist plot while simultaneously serving as *tableaux vivants*, which reveal to both characters and readers their psychological and metaphysical conditions. Not since the final chapelhouse scene of Djuna Barnes' *Nightwood* has an American fiction used such theatrical trappings. Olson's broken-down miniature golf course, replete with dolphin, sea, moon, bird, and snake, is a virtual diorama in which a confrontation between good and evil is enacted.

A more secular struggle between sin and salvation is the subject of Donald Olson's "Objects in Mirror are Closer Than They Appear." In this work the battle is waged between two sisters against the backdrop of a paranoic dystopia. In fact, in several of the stories of this collection, the authors imply that only those whom the society sees as abnormal recognize that good and evil are forces with which to be reckoned. In "Keeper,"

Steve Katz leaves the salvation of the race to a man who is convinced that the souls of all human beings are about to be stolen by bats with whom he shares his bedroom. The narrator of Richard Padget's Kafkaesque tale, "A Brief Guide to the Fall Repertory," wakes one morning to find his paranoia confirmed by a cannon aimed at his bedroom window. In short, as Noni Hubner, of Russell Banks' "What Noni Hubner Did Not Tell the Police About Jesus," recognizes, in today's society it is often dangerous to reveal one's visions.

Behind the "real" worlds presented in these tales, in short, there is authorial acknowledgment of other realities, which in their very inexplicability are alluring and perilous both. The flat-footed realist, like Mark Sacharoff's plainclothes cop, can never comprehend the world around him, will never be able to answer the questions with which he is obsessed: "Why is everybody behavin' so queer?" "What's happenin'?" Only those who go beyond what they see, beyond the bounds of socialized normalcy, these authors suggest, will experience through the synchronicity of time and space a revelation.

Certainly such thematics are not original in the history of 20th-century fiction (one thinks immediately of the search for transcendence in the works of William Faulkner, E. M. Forster, Virginia Woolf, and Eudora Welty); but, then, neither have these concerns been previously expressed in these new ways. And that, in brief, is my argument. Despite the assertions of literary critics and historians, I suspect most contemporary writers do not write because they have something to say but because something cannot be said. And it is that effort to express an ineffable "something" that energizes these works. The reader of this editor's *Contemporary American Fiction* may have to forego the search for implicit or explicit statements revealing the author's *position* in order to participate in the creation of a world not on any map. For it is only as a participant, as an attentive, empathetic, and inquisitive listener, that the reader of these tales—like the character who listens to Fletcher's chillingly mad story in Katz's "Keeper"—can find a way to share the author's perceptions of simultaneity, a mind-expanding sensation described by Katz as taking "seventeen steps away from the tower, twenty-six steps away from the moon."

These stories, accordingly, are not indicative of all the varieties of contemporary fiction. Rather, they are 24 of the most exhilarating and inenarrable experiences the editor has participated in during the recent past.

———

1 Among the most vehement of critics of contemporary fiction are Gerald Graff and John Gardner. Graff's *Literature Against Itself: Literary Ideas in Modern Society* (Chicago: The University

of Chicago Press, 1979) and Gardner's *On Moral Fiction* (New York: Basic Books, 1978) are particularly virulent attacks on contemporary literature, viewed from the postmodern perspective.

2 John Barth, "The Literature of Exhaustion," *Atlantic Monthly*, August 1967, p. 29.

3 I must confess that, despite my avocation of a more experiential approach to contemporary fiction, my own criticism might generally fall into this category. At their best, these critics less "map" the contemporary scene than they "trace" certain of its patterns; and when they succeed at this, I have little criticism of their methods.

Robert Alter, "The Inexhaustible Genre," *Partial Magic: The Novel as a Self-Conscious Genre* (Berkeley: University of California Press, 1975); Philip Stevick, *Alternative Pleasures: Post-realist Fiction and the Tradition* (Urbana: University of Illinois, 1981); Alan Wilde, *Horizons of Assent: Modernism, Postmodernism, and the Ironic Imagination* (Baltimore: The Johns Hopkins University Press, 1981).

4 See Ihab Hassan's *The Dismemberment of Orpheus: Toward a Postmodern Literature* (New York: Oxford University Press, 1971), Jerome Klinkowitz's *Literary Disruptions: The Makings of a Post-Contemporary Fiction* (Urbana: University of Illinois Press, 1975), and Larry McCaffery's *The Metafictional Muse: The Works of Robert Coover, Donald Barthelme, and William H. Gass* (Pittsburgh: University of Pittsburgh Press, 1982). In the latter work, McCaffery argues that the contemporary scene in general might be characterized as having a "metasensibility"

5 A list of other explicit parodists might include Tom Veitch, Steve Katz (in a work such as *The Exaggerations of Peter Prince*), Russell Banks (in *Family Life*), and Jaimy Gordon. What is interesting is that, except for Veitch, the lesser-known group of writers might all have been said to have shifted to fictions that rely less

on parody alone.

6 Wilde, "Strange Displacements of the Ordinary': Apple, Elkin, Barthelme, and the Problem of the Excluded Middle," *Boundary 2*, 10 (Winter 1982), p. 182.

TEMPLE UNIVERSITY, PHILADELPHIA, 1983
Reprinted from *Contemporary Fictions* (College Park, Maryland: Sun & Moon Press, 1983).

Horse Sense

JAIMY GORDON **LORD OF MISRULE** (KINGSTON, NEW YORK: MCPHERSON & COMPANY, 2010)

THE DARK HORSE WINNER of the 2010 National Book Awards, Jaimy Gordon's sixth book of fiction, *Lord of Misrule*, is, like most of her others, a brilliant piece of writing. One can only wonder how Gordon, a professor at Western Michigan University in Kalamazoo, has come up with so much information about the dirty world of cheap horse racing—where horses on their last legs are not just raced but may be claimed by others for a small price—that we totally believe in her credibility and her having captured these small-time gamblers' and mobsters' voices.

The very list of characters, Medicine Ed, Kidstuff, Lady "Gyp" Deucey Gifford, Suitcase Smithers, Two-Tie, and Joe Dale Bigg, sounds right out of Damon Runyon. Yet, while Runyon's figures, all obvious stereotypes of street-smart hipsters, seem bigger than life, Gordon's

characters seem relatively "real," and, in that respect, involve us emotionally. I felt real caring for the aging Medicine Ed, and was almost shocked at Two-Tie's murder, when he dies gently stroking his dog Elizabeth's fur. In part, it is Gordon's ability to capture the rhythms and patterns of their speech. Consider, for example, a paragraph from one of the numerous chapters written from the voice of Medicine Ed:

> The way Medicine Ed hear it, Joe Dale Bigg run the horse off and so he was Deucey's but he wasn't Deucey's, wasn't nobody's horse right now. A Speculation grandson and looking for a home! Jesus put me wise. Now, what was the name of this boy? Medicine Ed couldn't recall. For all his fancy blood he had an ankle almost as big as he was, but that wasn't what cause him to lose his home. It was Bigg, Joe Dale Bigg's boy, one day when Biggy was helping Fletcher the dentist in the back of the horse's stall and the horse pinned and about killed him. Biggy what you call simple, a gorilla-size child-for-life, and now he was back from the industrial school from Pruntytown. Joe Dale Big thought he better be shed of the animal before something go down.

It's all there in the Gertrude Stein-like reversals of logic ("he was Deucey's but he wasn't Deucey's"), the localisms ("Jesus put me wise"), the exaggerated metaphors ("he had an ankle almost as big as he was"), and the colloquialisms ("before something go down"): real horse sense. Medicine Ed speaks like a true human being might in an original language (although I do keep hearing Walter Brennan behind my back) that Gordon has perfectly rendered.

Into this dark underside of the gambling world come two relatively bright young figures, Tommy Hansel, an ex-car salesman, and his new girl, Maggie Koderer, who previously wrote on food for a small city newspaper. Neither seems to have much experience with horses, but Hansel, who has somehow gotten his hands on several horses, intends to enter them each in races, win quickly, and get out before anyone has dreamed of claiming them. On the surface the animals look worn out and not worth much, but Hansel, in a slow descent into horse-racing madness, truly believes in luck. He is convincing enough that Maggie has gone along for the ride, intensely caring for the horses, mucking out their stalls, brushing, feeding, taping, and sleeping with them as if she has done it all her life. She's also a quick learner, and easily picks up methods from Medicine Ed and others on how to better care for them.

The Lord of Misrule is organized around four races, each named after one of the central horses: Mr. Boll Weevil, Little Spinoza, Pelter, and Lord of Misrule. Some win, some lose, some even tragically die, but the real heart of the fiction concerns how Maggie becomes increasingly woven into the lives of everyone around her. A frank and openly sexual woman, Maggie—the sister of Ursie, the central character in Gordon's previous work, *Bogeywoman*—discovers, both comically and somewhat tragically, that the individuals with whom she now shares her life embody simple humanity, comic stupidity, hate, madness, and finally murderous passions that stir up a tornado of emotions while proving to the reader that Maggie has more courage and pluck than anyone else.

Although, by book's end, Maggie returns to her absurd job of writing *Menus by Margaret* for the *Winchester Mail*, she remains in nearly everyone's memory; certainly she will never leave mine. Medicine Ed, perhaps Gordon's most memorable male figure in this fiction, again quietly sums it up:

> Now that she was gone and out of his bidness, he had to give this much to the frizzly hair girl, she must had did something right with all that modern science she use to make it up as she go along. Damn if Medicine Ed be caught petting and nursering

an animal like that, but he had taken sometimes to rubbing Pelter up with cloths after he worked, like a young horse. Couldn't hurt, and they had the time. The horse gone good for fifteen hundred, and sometimes when they walking the shedrow like now eye-balling each other like now, he was careful to remember into the horse that the Mound has claimers at 1250 too. It's still another place left for them two to go, even if it is down.

LOS ANGELES, MARCH 3, 2011
Reprinted from *Rain Taxi*, Vol. 20, no. 2 (Summer 2011).

Frictions of Desperate Severity

STACEY LEVINE **THE GIRL WITH BROWN FUR: TALES & STORIES** (BUFFALO, NEW YORK: STARCHE-RONE, 2011)

STACEY LEVINE has subtitled her new collection of stories "tales & stories," as if there were a significant difference between the two. I'm not sure that I could make a case for a genre separation, unless the one, "tales," suggests a looser and less formalized structure than the other. What it does hint is that the author herself recognizes these works to be, at times, ephemeral, a kind of literary potpourri of narrative. And indeed some of these works seem more like the beginnings or ends of dreams and fantasies than coherent stories. Nearly all of Levine's short works—true of the first volume, *My Horse and Other Stories* (published by my own Sun & Moon Press), as well as these new works—might be said to be closer to fragments than to organized fictions.

But anything coming from the fertile imagination

of Levine is worth attending to, and, although for some readers I am certain that the inconclusiveness of her tales may seem irritating, for the adventurous reader it is the dream-like web upon which she weaves her works that makes them so very intriguing. The first piece in this volume encapsulates some of these very  issues, pushing Levine's startling images from the concrete into abstraction. In "Uppsala" a family is speeding to a winter vacation home, but rather than suggesting retreat and pleasure, their journey reveals a complete breakdown of family life and communication. The mother "is terrible," a kind of monster who screams at the appearance of a flea, at her forgetfulness to bring a loaf of bread, and numerous other events. "Father resembles a hassock." Brother and sister retreat to the bathroom where he, in an inarticulate babble, "speaks his own language," creating a world different from their cold one, filled with "people who adore the sun."

It is Levine's "friction of desperate severity" that might describe one of the author's central themes. In the title story, in the book called simply "The Girl," the subject, a child-like girl kept by her parents on a leash, becomes to the narrator not only someone whom she recognizes she will steal, but the force behind the dream-tale she is telling.

> Of course this dream was less about the girl (surely
> she was older than her body) than about the way
> I always had looked for something to raise me up,
> following the part of the story in which I had fallen.

Levine continues, "The girl was about being poor and I was about the luxury of being able to choose...." The telling of the story and the consequent actions, accordingly, become confused with the narrational imagination, as we gradually recognize the dreamer in the process of dreaming. In a way that you seldom encounter except in stories by Kafka or Borges, Levine's "tales" reveal, in the way they are being told, how and why a writer writes. By the end of this work, as the girl finally bites the narrator and, refusing the leash, escapes from a taxi, we discover that the child-like human is easily transformed into the metaphor behind the images, a cat who, when the narrator sees it, "was old and cast off, with a bad eye." And we perceive the author as a kind of shape-shifter moving from sign to metaphor to symbol within the span of a few pages.

Among the most "story"-like works in this volume is the hilarious "The Danas," about a family that carries such a deep sense of family life and all that it might entail—"family home-cooked, sweetened milk in jars"—that they come to isolate themselves from the world outside, the eldest brother and sister, Mike and Tina, marrying one another and moving to an apartment three blocks away.

The gossipy and intrusive neighbors closely watching the family's activities, are both disgusted and envious of their condition. As the neighbor, Mrs. Beck's companion, puts it, "Well, I suppose the Danas just love each other so much that they cannot bear new people, or new situations, besides their own." But the effects of this intense family loving unhinge several of their neighbors in ways that ultimately lead to a mother slapping her own beloved child, as if punishing him for what she recognizes will someday be their separation.

So many of these works intrigue and startle the imagination that it is hard to know which of the 26 pieces to write about. But certainly one of the most noteworthy is "Believing It was George Harrison," in which, in a suburb north of Caracas, a group of people have come together in a condo to celebrate. At first the party seems to be a typical embassy gathering, from which the narrator, newer to the city than the others, feels slightly estranged. Yet the conversation concerning how to cook different dishes, how the narrator is "settling in," and other mundane topics appears to project this work on a realist track until—

Across the room, on the far side of the archway, I saw George Harrison pouring water into a glass from a carafe. Floating orange slices and ice slid in the stream, yet the bubbling water moved slowly enough to look like a gel. The sad dance music beat through the rooms. Harrison glanced around a moment, neutral faces, and then greeted another guest, a Caraqueño, certainly, and most likely a pensioner. Harrison mock admonished the man with something like, "Hey, old timer!" and the two embraced and settled into a conversation.

Other guests noticed Harrison, too, exchanging looks, but no one said a word.

Here is Levine's writing in its typical brilliance. The fact that the narrator spots a dead man at a party in Venezuela is abruptly "washed over" as the author watches an orange slice slip through the water, and the dance music intrudes. The very natural behavior of this "ghost" seems to contradict the remarkableness of the event. Indeed the inane party conversations continue as the guests, one by one, spot the celebrity, until a young woman, Saundra, breaks the complacency of her elders by screaming out, "Don't patronize me.... The man is *dead*. How can he be here?"

Yet even this refuses to budge the rational defenses of the guests, as the conversation turns upon metaphysical and philosophical issues, beginning with the comment, "Maybe we're *all* dead," which shifts the conversation to the role of the dead, and to ludicrous speculations about what each of them might do if they returned after they died, ending in obvious conspiracy theories about Harrison's disappearance. By tale's end, Harrison simply admits that once he had existed, then stopped, but somehow, having returned, it "meant that he now could continue to exist." Yet even this miraculous event is converted into banality as the young girl blurts out, "We missed you."

In Levine's world the banal and the extraordinary are eternally mixed; hysteria is interfused with cool logic, fear counteracted with absolute daring—all emanating from a viewpoint of the world that seems to recognize that despite all the horrors and dangers of living, issues often put front and center in her work, people are determined to and must necessarily go on living in the most ordinary ways. The last piece in this book, "The Water," a kind of environmental prose poem, reiterates this, as the author turns her attention to water and its disappearance—for example, in Florida, where an ordinary Tallahasseean, Gale, has watched Florida lose its lakes, "while the lizards died papery in grass."

> The lakes' deaths were a shame, Gale said, resting in his chair, and Mother [his wife] wrote a blaming

letter to a magazine. Gale liked chicken. His children would soon retire. The water will be algae-oily and never consciously suffer.

We might reach an arm toward a dark surface someday, gasping alongside the rowboats and birds, alongside this incomprehension of water and the way those living at the top always rule. Gale knew it. Still and all, he was glad he lived. He said to mother, Hi, Koo-koo. Aren't you glad you lived too?

LOS ANGELES, AUGUST 29, 2011
Reprinted from *EXPLORINGfictions* (August 2011).

Language Writhing Machines

TOM LA FARGE 13 WRITHING MACHINES NO. 1: ADMINISTRATIVE ASSEMBLAGES (BROOKLYN: PROTEO-TYPES, 2008)

TOM LA FARGE 13 WRITHING MACHINES NO. 2: HO-MOMORPHIC CONVERTERS (BROOKLYN, PROTEOTYPES / PROTEUS GOWANUS, 2009)

TOM LA FARGE 13 WRITHING MACHINES, NO. 3: ECHO ALTERNATORS (BROOKLYN: PROTEOTYPES, 2010)

THE FIRST VOLUME of Tom La Farge's promised 13-volume series on structures for writing describes it as "writhing," "writing with a difference," as if the activity were something accomplished with a coiling snake in hand or through a discharge of electrical energy. Certainly the kind of "writhing" La Farge speaks of—writing with constraints, arbitrary rules "imposed upon composition that drive you to say what you had not thought of saying in ways you would not have chosen to say it"—in its formal and often comical Oulipian

twists, bends, and folds requires a mastery of language and an artistry that allows one to give oneself up to the possibilities and accidents produced through the form itself.

In *Administrative Assemblages* La Farge explores several larger systems of arrangement: "Lists and Catalogs," "Memory Arrangements," "Full Disclosure," "Invisible Libraries," "Classifications," "Timelines," "Map & Gazetteer," and "The Composite Portrait," and suggests some methods of composing in each of these categories. These systems, based primarily on methods attempted by members of the Oulipo writers, offer up new possibilities of how to write; and La Farge's clear and concise descriptions, along with his list of methods, if nothing else, should well serve creative writing classrooms from here to eternity, particularly when he has completed all 13 volumes (forthcoming pamphlets will consider *Dictionary Drives, Permutants & Recombinants, Visual/Verbal Hybridizers, Decryptions & Reëncryptions,* and *Homomorphic Converters*).

That is not to say that every form will appeal equally to all. While I am a born list maker, I find the kinds of listings La Farge mentions—shopping lists, the lists of Walt Whitman, and even the lists of the American Oulipo-influenced author Gilbert Sorrentino—to be mindless narratives that demonstrate a lack of connection and complexity, which are the things I seek in fiction. Similarly, although the "Memory Arrangements" of books such as Joe Brainard's *I Remember* are often charming to read, I think of them as literature "lite."

More interesting, it seems to me, are the formulations of Marcel Bénabou's patterns of "Perhaps you... Not me," or "Me too."

> Perhaps you like the records of Lawrence Welk.
> Not me.

And of even more interest are the constraints of "Formal Disclosure," which often use official-seeming forms as guides to creative composition. La Farge points to the works of J. G. Ballard, who "uses physical structures that assemble a social reality in order to shape his fictions." For example, Ballard's 1975 *High-Rise* "uses the stratified sociology of an apartment building as the basis for a story of class war in a disaster scenario prompted by the failure of the complex systems on which such buildings rely." In my own condominium building it would be fascinating, I suspect, to explore the radical differences between the numerous older

Jewish couples, the younger Korean families, and new Russian immigrants, along with the several gay couples that make up the majority of units.

My companion Howard would adore La Farge's "Invisible Libraries" systems, in which, for example, he suggests amalgam-books such as *Crime and Prejudice* or *The Bleak Doll's Heartbreak House*. Howard is always spouting such titles as *Death of a Venice Salesman* and *The Color of Purple Summer*.

Of equal interest is La Farge's discussion of "Classifications," works which deal with issues of classification such as "kinship systems" or "inheritance patterns." In Jorge Luis Borges' "The Analytical Language of John Wilkins," the author explores that British Royal Society founder's attempt to create an ideal language by dividing the universe into 40 classes, a systemization that quickly falls into a kind of absurdity that is ridiculously poetic.

Whenever I think of "Timelines" I am reminded of Harry Mathews' brilliant experiment in *My Life in the CIA*, where, pretending to be a travel guide, he lectures on a possible trip through the USSR using several systematic rules: 1) They should only take trains and buses whose departure times read the same right to left as they did left to right; 2) For every departure, a return must be assured that strictly obeys rule one.

In "Map and Gazetteer," forms more directly in-

volve the visual artist by presenting various allegorical travel routes and comic maps based upon the outlines of countries coinciding with what La Farge describes as "an agglomeration of national caricatures." But, of course, there are verbal gazetteers, an example of which was recently presented in *The New York Times* as a map of Britain showing only towns with profane sounding names such as Crapstone, Penistone, East Breast, Pratts Bottom, Titty Ho, Crotch Crescent, etc.

Similarly, visual artists are at the center of La Farge's discussion of "The Composite Portrait," particularly the painter Nicolas de Larmessin, who created portraits representing human figures made up of the things with which they were associated, such as his "Librarian," a man made up of books, or his "Musician," a man wearing various musical instruments. I once created just such a portrait of individuals in my fiction *Letters from Hanusse*, using 19th-century phrenological systems that depended upon the bumps and fissures in the skull to determine the moral condition of the people of my mythical country Hanusse.

In short, La Farge's *13 Writhing Machines*, given the contents of this first volume, promises not only

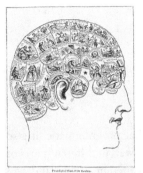

to be an utterly entertaining presentation of various formal systems of literary writing, but an illustrative example of how to get writers, young and old, to experiment with new and empowering systems outside the scope of realist psychological narrative. We have long needed such a thorough discussion of such systems, and perhaps in the 21st century our younger authors can go forward from these examples with an exciting energy of new possibilities.

LOS ANGELES, JANUARY 27, 2009
Reprinted from *Green Integer Blog* (April 2009).

THE SECOND INSTALLMENT of Tom La Farge's grand effort to name and describe literary constraints to writing—what he describes as "an arbitrary rule imposed upon composition that drives you to say what you had not thought of saying in ways you would not have chosen to say it"—is devoted to more complex systems than those outlined in volume one.

"Homovocalism," for example, is a system where

one takes from an-
other text, beginning
with as little as a sen-
tence, and replaces all
the consonants, keep-
ing the vowel-sounds
from the original. But
although this may sound rather programmatic, it also
depends on how you speak, vowels in different parts of
the country sounding quite different in England and
its dialects and in various American dialects. The *u* in
"buy," for instance, in Los Angeles would be a very different sound than in Minnesota or Wisconsin, where
it would sound more like the *y* in "bye" or "by," and
throughout the Midwest the *a* in "Mary" would sound
more like the *e* in "merry." In the West, as La Farge mentions, "Get" often becomes "git."

Accordingly, "homovocalism" is far more difficult
than it first sounds and, as Harry Mathews writes of
the procedure, "Its interest will probably remain that of
an exercise." But the wonderful example that La Farge
quotes from Gilbert Sorrentino's "Generative Devices
in Imaginative Writing" course at Stanford reveals its
possibilities: "...there was no horse to be had, no horse,"
transformed into, "For once no noise. Cruelly black
those morns."

"Homoconsonantism" is similar except that it

uses the consonants in the original order while replacing the vowels, without reusing the original words of another text. His example is again revealing: "Thanks, these tough shoots need a lot of watering, my chore of choice," becoming, "Then kiss those two oafish Tucson delete-vow touring macho ear-vetches." A further constraint would be to match the word-units of the original sentence.

"Homosyntaxism," a variation of the above, so La Farge tells us, is a better system for longer texts. From the original text, all words are replaced but the syntax stays the same, so that nouns are replaced by other nouns, adverbs by adverbs, etc. This exercise, it seems to me, would be a brilliant way for high school grammar teachers to be certain that their students had comprehended the many sentence diagrams performed upon the blackboard (do grammar teachers still diagram sentences?).

The "Chimera" is a truly complex replacement of texts where you choose a passage A. Then the nouns, verbs, and adjectives/adverbs of that passage are replaced by those selected from a different writer B, parodying or imitating A while attempting to keep the "phrasing, rhythm, rhetorical formations." The vocabulary can be from B or from the author himself C. Various other constraints can also be applied, creating a truly mixed beast like the Chimera, a mix of lion, goat, and snake.

In "Homosemantic Translation," instead of changing a set of words from one language into another while attempting to keep the meaning, the author, working within the same language, is required to change the words while keeping the sense. Here's my brief attempt using a random selection from one of La Farge's own fictions (*A Hundred Doors: The Crimson Bears, Part II*):

> They presently found a handle, set low in the wall. Edgar worried that a door built to cat-scale might not let them pass in the machine.

> Soon after they discovered a haft, lying close to the floor. Edgar was troubled that an entrance constructed to the size of a small dog would discontinue their progression into the dynamo.

Not a brilliant example, but it will do.

"Anglish," a variant of homosemantism, is a method in which the substituted words are fairly analogous in meaning to the original, but are taken from very different contexts, for example, replacing a text of primarily Latinate word choices with those of Anglo-Saxon phrases, etc. This is obviously a test of any student's true understanding of the English language, and would be best undertaken, it seems to me, with an *Oxford English*

Dictionary by one's side.

"Homoradicalism," created by Michèle Métail, creates statements only from words which share the same root, so that the various uses of a word such as clean (noun, adverb, adjective, and all of its other variations) define the text: "Cleanish cleaner, clean clean clean."

"Allosyntaxism" reuses the words of an original text but employs a different sentence structure, "Beauty is truth, truth beauty, that is all / Ye know on earth, and all ye need to know," becoming, "Beauty is earth, ye know? Beauty is need, ye know? On to truth, truth and all that!"

Finally, "Homoikonism" represents an application of the visual into writing. One kind of homoikonism, for example, is the famous "duck-rabbit" which can be read in two different ways, depending upon the shift of one's eyes from right to left. Other forms are an interplay of images and letters, which lends a kind of calligraphic quality to writing. Throughout La Farge's text he has

used Amadine Allessandra's alphabetic/ ideographic symbols, forms (chairs, tables, etc.) that appear to us as letters of the alphabet; Lisa Rienermann's alphabet, formed by patches of sky shot between buildings in Barcelona; and Monica Alisse's "Human Alphabet," which uses positions of the body to create letters.

As in his first volume, La Farge also includes a section devoted to "Suggestions for Writhing Exercises," which once again demonstrates the usefulness of his pamphlets for the classroom.

LOS ANGELES, NOVEMBER 15, 2009
Reprinted from *EXPLORINGfictions* (November 2009).

LA FARGE BEGINS his third volume of "13 Writing Machines," the beautiful pamphlets on various Oulipian and other devices to create formal constraints that liberate the writing of fiction and poetry, with the following words:

> Rhyme—the echo, shadow, twin, mirror-image—
> fascinates me. In a world of differences, identity, or
> similarity pushed close to identity, seems to suggest
> less chaos, or a different chaos, than we're aware of.
> Rhyme is used in magic. Rhyme is also a composi-
> tional constraint for writers.

La Farge, however, is not talking here only of standard end rhyme, but of numerous poetic devices, games, and challenges which echo or mirror the words and ideas of creative texts. I will name a few of the author's suggestions, while readily admitting that I am not sure that every one of them would work for me to create an interesting text.

Certainly La Farge demonstrates, through several of his own examples, that he is not only a skilled fiction writer—he is the author of three works of fiction—but also a skilled poet. For years he and his writer wife, Wendy Walker, have made the argument that excellent narrativists and fiction writers *must* also be—or, at least, should be—skilled poets, connoisseurs of language.

La Farge begins with "Homophonism," a process whereby an author takes a larger text (he takes his example from the back of a cable company's bill) and, rhyming with the same sequence of syllables, creates a new text. It is a difficult process, and La Farge points out that, in his example, liberties were taken. Here's my example, a somewhat literal rhyming of the first 13 lines of a longer poem, "A Lecture upon the Shadow" by John Donne:

"A Vector of the Straddle"

Sandhill & lye still need the sea.
Conjecture, dove, above theosophy.
    Trees, the flower at bee, salve scent

Stalking dear through meadow's dent
A song, mythos: hitched knee, lower calves seduced
Put low the one his lust loved t'ward bed.
    (See-through clothes addle thread).
    Man to save Eros falls, sings arias to soothe
Though guiles sour & pant above his bow.
The skies have hid, land rattles, grows
Dumb, blustering, tears; glut rots bliss' grotto.

Fat plovers at the rotted grain fly free
O'er ditches, rills indigent, best mothers be.*

Although there are a few variations from the original in the above ("That love hath," for example, becomes, in my version, "Fat plovers") these are minor examples of *clinamen*, what La Farge defines for the reader as "a swerving," which is essential to much Oulipian writing. As the author points out, the *clinamen* often allows for greater aesthetic possibilities than do the "consequences of a restriction."

La Farge's discussion of the differences between polysyllabic rhymes ("*rime riche*")—often used in French but sounding clumsy and, at times, absolutely silly in English (he points to the example of the operettas of W. S. Gilbert)—is elucidating. While in French the alexandrine form is still possible, in English we tend to rhyme in one or two syllables at most. But he does suggest an interesting or difficult experiment that English writers might attempt, the holorhyme, a series of identical sequences of letters that do not necessarily parallel the sound. His example from Howard Bergerson is interesting:

> Flamingo: pale, scenting a latent shark!
> Flaming, opalescent in gala tents—hark!

One of the most wonderful things about La Farge's "Writhing Machines" series is his recountings of historical figures and texts. For any serious reader of Oulipian-like writing, it is crucial to know the works of Raymond Roussel, which in eight pages of this small text La Farge describes, sharing some of the various devices and their relationships with other texts of Roussel's novels *Impressions of Africa* (1910) and *Locus Solus* (1914). This short disquisition alone is worth the publication of volume three, and reiterates how useful these books would be in the classroom. More and more I feel these texts should be used in every creative writing class across the country. Who better to take poets and fiction writers, young or old, through various and sundry literary forms such as "the Rebus," "Echo Poems," "Punkwatrain," "The Strasbourg Tramway," "La GuaGua," "the Brazzle," "Pig-Language," "Anguish Languish," "Literary Homophonic translations," the "Zukofskan Translation," and even the absurd "Poems for Dogs?"

The Punkwatrain—what Robert Rapilly calls a *katrainbour* (a cross between a quatrain and a *calembour*, the French word for pun)—is a particularly fascinating form, wherein one takes a noun (La Farge uses "Gowanus Canal") and translates it into a homophonic equivalent (La Farge's is "Go on askin', Al"). Then one takes the new phrase as the "moral" of a short fable or riddle in a verse quatrain which obliquely makes reference to the original phrase. The rhyme scheme and meter are left up to the poet. La Farge's hilarious, and quite excellent, example is:

> Gore takes the global view: "Go Green!"
> Well, carry on, but there's a spot
> Of brown in Brooklyn Al's not seen.
> A waterway it's not.
>
> Go on askin', Al.
> (Gowanus Canal)

What fun! I can't wait for the next volume.

*Reprinted from Douglas Messerli, *Maxims from My Mother's Milk* (Los Angeles: Sun & Moon Press, 1988). The first 13 lines of the original John Donne poem are:

"A Lecture upon the Shadow"

Stand still, and I will read to thee
A Lecture, love, in Loves philosophy.
    These three houres that we have spent,
    Walking here, Two shadowes went
Along with us, which we our selves produc'd;
But, now the Sunne is just above our head,
    We doe those shadowes tread;
    And to brave clearness all things are reduc'd.
So whilst our infant loves did grow,
Disguises did, and shadowes, flow,
From us, and our cares; but, now 'tis not so.

That love hath not attain'd the high'st degree,
Which is still diligent lest others see.

LOS ANGELES, MAY 24, 2011
Reprinted from *EXPLORINGfictions* (May 2011).

Index

Stay

Douglas Messerli

GREEN INTEGER 218

Stay (2018)
[978-1-55713-447-9], $12.95

"My poetry, highly disjunctive and following its own associative course, interweaves word pairings and bits of lines from others, weaving and unweaving their originals, creating, like Odysseus' Penelope, through a bit a chicanery, an attempt to delay a parting and to keep by me the deep relationships I have with these artists."

—DOUGLAS MESSERLI

In *Stay*, ultimately a command to keep death at bay, Douglas Messerli realizes just how important his readings of other poets are to sustaining his own life. His poems pay homage to them.